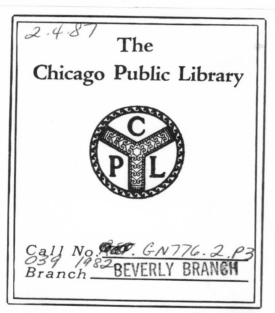

Newgrange

NEW ASPECTS OF ANTIQUITY

General Editor: COLIN RENFREW

Consulting Editor for the Americas: JEREMY A. SABLOFF

MICHAEL J. O'KELLY

"Newgrange"

Archaeology, art and legend

with 157 illustrations, 13 in color

Contributions by Claire O'Kelly and others

THAMES AND HUDSON

For Helen, Ann and Eve

'To be a restorer of ancient monuments one should be sheltered by a triple coat of brass, but even a repairer of such required a coat of mail.'

Dr E. P. Wright, Presidential Address to the Royal Society of Antiquaries of Ireland, delivered 30 January, 1900 (JRSAI 30 (1900), 7).

© 1982 Thames and Hudson Ltd, London

First published in the USA in 1983 by Thames and Hudson Inc., 500 Fifth Avenue, New York, New York 10110

Library of Congress Catalog Card Number 81-86413

Printed and bound in Hungary

Contents

General Editor's foreword

Newgrange is unhesitatingly regarded by the prehistorian as the great national monument of Ireland; in the words of the late Seán Ó Ríordáin, 'one of the most important ancient places in Europe'. Its special importance has been widely realized since the early description by Edward Lhwyd in 1699, and each generation finds in it something new and interesting. The widespread realization in recent years that the very early 'megalithic' architecture of western Europe is something notably and essentially European, owing little or nothing to the Near East, has only served to heighten our admiration for some of these great and early constructions, of which Newgrange is undoubtedly one of the very finest.

Our own generation has been particularly fortunate that, since 1962, this important site has been the subject of investigation by Professor O'Kelly, ably assisted by his wife Claire. To them we are indebted for a number of important discoveries and conclusions which are set out in full here. Indeed in the face of so much new information, it is interesting to look back to the pessimism which prevailed nearly two centuries ago, to the gloomy view that very little could ever be known about it. In his *Tour in Ireland,* published in 1807, the distinguished English antiquary, Sir Richard Colt Hoare, wrote of Newgrange:

I shall not unnecessarily trespass upon the time and patience of my readers in endeavouring to ascertain what tribes first peopled this country, nor to what nation the construction of this singular monument may reasonably be attributed for, I fear, both its authors and its original destination will ever remain unknown. Conjecture may wonder over its wild and spacious domains but will never bring home with it either truth or conviction. Alike will the histories of those stupendous temples at Avebury and Stonehenge which grace my native country, remain involved in obscurity and oblivion.

Now we know so very much more. In the first place, as reported here, the mound and its contents have been reliably dated. The 'uncorrected' radiocarbon date of around 2500 bc must be the equivalent, after the calibration of the radiocarbon time scale (using the corrections afforded by tree-ring dating), of a date in calendar years of about 3200 BC. There can be no doubt, therefore, that Newgrange is older than Stonehenge, older than Avebury, and indeed older by several centuries than the pyramids of Egypt.

This early construction highlights still further the great fascination of the carved stone decoration of the Boyne tombs, and of Newgrange itself. Mrs O'Kelly's corpus of the art from this site makes an important contribution here. The precise purpose of this decoration is still a matter for discussion, and great interest was aroused by Professor O'Kelly's discovery that some of the stones were decorated on surfaces which could never have been visible to the visitor to the tomb: their secret was revealed only in the course of excavation and restoration work. Here the case is convincingly argued that these stones were not re-used from some earlier monument. Moreover the care with which the construction was planned and executed does not support the view that these carved surfaces were obscured by accident or by the incompetence of the builders. Was this hidden carving then the consequence of some secret piety of its makers, invisible to mortal eyes, but present nonetheless for eternity?

The most remarkable discovery reported here came about unexpectedly in 1963, when the investigation of a seemingly anomalous slab led to the recognition of the 'roof-box', a carefully constructed aperture above the entrance. It is so situated that at midwinter's day the rays of the rising sun penetrate the full length of the entrance passage, and reach into the chamber itself. Whatever one's scepticism for some of the claims made on behalf of 'megalithic astronomy' or of 'astroarchaeology', it is difficult not to see this as a deliberate and successful attempt to incorporate the midwinter sunrise as a significant element in the planning and use of the monument. This arrangement constitutes one of the very earliest astronomical, or rather solar, alignments ever recorded, earlier by far than those of Stonehenge and the other British stone circles and standing stones. It still works today, despite the small changes over the millennia in the earth's position relative to the sun, and according to Professor O'Kelly will continue to do so as long as Newgrange continues to stand.

This volume constitutes the final and definitive report of these excavations and researches, with studies by a number of specialists given as appendices. But it has turned into something very much more than simply an excavation report: into a review of the history of research at Newgrange, a survey of its place in prehistory, and a corpus of the remarkable carvings which embellish the stones of this 'cathedral of the megalithic religion'.

As discussed in chapter 12, former generations held that Newgrange, and those other great monuments of the Boyne valley, Knowth and Dowth, were the work of colonist-builders, representing the end of a line of devolution which had begun in the Mediterranean world, starting perhaps with the impressive stone tombs of Mycenae. Now we know that it is older by far than these Aegean comparisons, and that Newgrange is not the work of immigrants already greatly skilled in architecture, but instead the product of a more local evolution, from simple to complex. Some at least of the questions so pessimistically posed in 1807 by Colt Hoare can now be answered, and we can instead share the view of another early antiquary, George Petrie, and, on the basis of the careful researches reported here, with him agree 'to allow the ancient Irish the honour of erecting a work of such vast labour and grandeur'.

Colin Renfrew

Preface

When this book first came to be written it was thought of as just another excavation report, detailing the results of the investigations at Newgrange from 1962 to 1975, but gradually it became clear that the great monument could not, and indeed should not, be fitted into what was virtually a strait-jacket. It has so many aspects which have nothing to do with the excavations and which often seemed to us to dwarf our own puny efforts, that we felt the whole tale as we know it up to the present should be told, with the excavation results forming but one section. Apart from this, there was the necessity to give a rounded picture of the whole in view of the hundreds of thousands of visitors who have come to the site in the past and will continue to do so in the future. Their interests are seldom solely confined to the purely archaeological aspects of the site but range over its history, its place in literature, its Romano-British associations, its layout and structure and in the conservation and restoration work carried out so successfully in the post-excavation period by the Office of Public Works. It is hoped that the present volume will go at least part of the way towards doing justice to one of the finest megalithic monuments extant in western Europe.

The secondary Late Neolithic/Beaker-period occupation which took place around the perimeter of the mound after it had begun to collapse is not dealt with here and has been reserved for a future publication. The three smaller passage-graves adjacent to the main monument have already been published elsewhere, as have the finds of Romano-British type consisting of gold coins and other objects of first-to-fourth-century AD date, and consequently these are referred to only in passing (see bibliography).

Part I of the present volume contains a summary of the main features of the monument and is chiefly intended as a source of reference when details are being discussed in later sections. Part I also discusses the previous history of the site as known from antiquarian accounts and from small trial excavations of more recent date. Apart from their intrinsic interest, it was felt that gathering these earlier descriptions and accounts into one section would obviate the necessity for lengthy explanations at a later stage when various features connected with the excavation came up for examination and exposition. The important role of the monument in early Irish literature is also discussed. Part II deals with the excavation itself; Part III with conservation and restoration; Part IV is devoted to discussion and endeavours to interpret some of the findings, to place the monument in the Irish passage-grave series as a whole and to offer a personal view of the building sequence which might have been employed by the men of Newgrange in the fourth millennium BC. The final part presents a corpus of the Newgrange art.

My own involvement and that of my wife came about almost by accident, since Newgrange was far removed from the 'territory' of Munster to which my archaeological activities had previously been confined. Had I known it would occupy me for the best part of two decades perhaps this book would not have had occasion to be written. The Newgrange excavations of 1962–1975 may be said to have been instigated by the late P. J. Hartnett, Archaeological Officer of Bord Fáilte Éireann, the State Tourist Board. During and immediately after the last war the monument was sadly neglected and the toll taken by time, nature and unsupervised visitors became a matter for concern. During the 1950s the number of tourists began rapidly to increase and it became more and more obvious that Newgrange could not be left to deteriorate further, no less from a scientific than from a purely materialistic viewpoint. The inward-leaning orthostats (uprights) of the passage were being rubbed smooth by visitors' clothing and the mound was being pulled about by animals and people clambering over it. The trees planted on and around the mound in the previous century had grown to a considerable size and were posing a threat to the structure. Scrub and coarse vegetation plate 17 flourished and it was scarcely possible to make out even the outline of the kerb. Furthermore, the public had no right of access to the monument though successive landowners had cooperated willingly in allowing passage.

It was clear that something more than another tidying up operation, of which there had been all too many in the past, was needed and in the winter of 1961 Mr Hartnett caused a meeting to be held at Newgrange of all those with a professional interest in the monument. Those present were: Mr P. J. Hartnett and Mr G. Bagnall of Bord Fáilte Éireann; Mr W. P. le Clerc, Inspector of National Monuments; Dr A. T. Lucas, Director of the National Museum of Ireland; Professor G. F. Mitchell of Trinity College Dublin; Professors R. de Valera, M. J. O'Kelly and M. V. Duignan of the University Colleges of Dublin, Cork and Galway respectively; and Dr S. Ó Nualláin, Archaeological Officer of the Ordnance Survey.

The state of the monument was inspected and carefully considered and it was recommended that an area of land surrounding it be acquired forthwith and be vested in the Office of Public Works which would be responsible for its future maintenance. In the event, about 3 hectares of land were purchased by Bord Fáilte from the landowner, Mr P. Delaney, and presented to the State through the Commissioners for Public Works. This ensured access for the public at all reasonable times.

Before any restoration or conservation work could be done it was necessary to find out what form this should take, and accordingly it was recommended that exploratory excavations be carried out in an area extending from kerbstone 92 (K 92) on the east side of the tomb entrance as far as K 96 just short of it, and from the kerb outward to a line outside the great circle of standing stones. This was approximately a 30° sector. The objectives of the excavation were defined as locating original ground levels, establishing the relationship between the cairn and the great circle and defining in respect of the bank of material outside the kerb what was slip from the mound and what, if any, was an original archaeological feature. If sockets of the missing orthostats of the great circle were found it was recommended that they be marked at the surface when the grass had been reinstated. It was unanimously agreed that the present writer be asked to undertake the excavation, starting in the summer of 1962.

The excavation was carried out by workmen paid from grants administered until the end of 1965 by the Special Employment Schemes Office and thereafter by the Office of Public Works (OPW). Volunteers from Irish, British, European and American universities worked on the site each summer and enabled surveying, drawing, cataloguing and the other multifarious duties of a large excavation to be carried out. They are far too numerous to be thanked individually but our gratitude is none the less for that. The National Parks and Monuments Branch of OPW gave considerable help with equipment, as did University College Cork with surveying gear, photographic materials and excavation equipment and tools. In the early years Bord Fáilte contributed towards the expenses of overseas students.

I should like to make special mention of the contribution of Miss Frances Lynch, MA, of the University College of North Wales, Bangor, during the early years of the excavations. She undertook the comprehensive survey of the passage and chamber of the tomb, and the plans and sections illustrated below in figs 4 and 17 are based on her meticulous draughtsmanship. She also annotated the decoration encountered during the survey of the tomb and these notes provided a very useful check on the full-size tracings which were made of the stones at a later stage.

I have been greatly helped by the many colleagues who visited the excavations and gave of their knowledge and advice and particularly by those who took part in the work itself, often for many seasons at a time. I must confine myself to listing but a few: the late Professor T. G. E. Powell of Liverpool University; Dr Elizabeth Twohig and Mr J. Fogarty, BE, both of University College Cork; Mr Ingmar Jansson of the University of Uppsala; and Dr Jon Patrick, now of Prahran College of Advanced Education, Victoria, Australia. Invaluable help has been given by the A. E. van Giffen Instituut voor Prae- en Proto-historie of the University of Amsterdam in the persons of Dr Willi Groenman-van Waateringe and Dr Louise van Wijngaarden-Bakker, and by the Laboratorium voor Algemene Natuurkunde of the University of Groningen in the persons of Professors H. T. Waterbolk, J. C. Vogel and Dr W. G. Mook. Professor J. P. Fraher and Dr V. R. O'Sullivan of the Department of Anatomy of University College Cork undertook the examination of the human remains.

Most sincere thanks must be given to those who have contributed the specialist reports included in the appendices, and not least, to the officers and staff of OPW with whom the closest collaboration was maintained throughout the excavation period.

Note on the radiocarbon dates

In Appendix H, and throughout the book, radiocarbon dates are given as they came from the laboratories – that is, they are radiocarbon years and are followed by a lower-case 'bc' or 'ad' to show that they have not been calibrated to calendar years. Where calendar years are involved, they are marked with upper-case 'BC' or 'AD'.

The radiocarbon method of dating is based on the fact that living matter absorbs radioactive carbon from the atmosphere. When Professor Willard Libby of the Chicago Institute for Nuclear Research invented the technique, it was assumed that the level of radioactive carbon (C14) in the atmosphere was constant through time around the world until it was affected by the large-scale burning of the fossil fuel, coal, during the Industrial Revolution and later by the burning of oil. Burning of these substances releases carbon into the atmosphere and upsets the supposed balance.

Research, however, has shown that even in the distant past, the level of radiocarbon in the atmosphere did not remain constant. Some very long-lived trees such as the American bristlecone pine (*Pinus Aristata*) can be calendar-dated exactly by counting the annual growth-rings of the timber. When samples were subjected to the radiocarbon dating method, the results obtained did not correspond with the calendar dates. It was also found that the amount of difference between the radiocarbon dates and the calendar ones varied for different parts of the time-scale.

A number of calibration graphs have now been published which enable radiocarbon years to be converted to calendar years, and while the graphs are still somewhat tentative and require further refinement, they give a useful indication of what radiocarbon dates mean in terms of our calendar. Thus, if the Newgrange radiocarbon dates are calibrated using the graph of R. M. Clark (*Antiquity,* XLIX [1975], 256), the construction date for the tomb goes back from 2500 bc to 3200 BC and the central date for the post-Newgrange Late Neolithic/Beaker-period settlement from 2000 bc to 2500 BC.

Nomenclature

figs 3, 4

In the text and illustrations K denotes kerbstone; the numbering is clockwise, beginning with the entrance stone which is K 1. L and R denote the orthostats on the left (west) and right sides of the passage, numbered from the entry. C denotes chamber orthostat, numbered from the left as one enters. Co. denotes corbels (horizontally-laid slabs) and they bear the same number as the orthostat or orthostats beneath them, e.g., Co.1/C2 is the first corbel over C2 and Co.4/C8 is the fourth one over C8. RS denotes passage roof-slab and, with the exception of RS17 which can be viewed from the chamber, the ornamented surfaces can only be seen by special arrangement.

Part I INTRODUCTION TO NEWGRANGE

Claire O'Kelly

1 Brief description

Newgrange is situated on the highest point of a long low ridge, 61 m above sea level (OD), about 1 km north of the River Boyne and 14 km from its mouth near Drogheda, a town 50 km north of Dublin. The village of Slane lies 8 km upriver from Newgrange, and for visitors coming by road from Dublin this is the best line of approach. As the Boyne meanders across Co. Meath on this final stretch of its course it loops markedly to the south after passing Slane, and the area thus enclosed on three sides by the river contains the Boyne passage-grave cemetery, of which Newgrange is the focal point. This area is approximately 4.3 km east-west and 3.7 km north-south, if one includes the outlying sites to the north.

    The ridge on which Newgrange stands runs east-west and is one of a series of low glacial hillocks and terraces which descend towards the flood-plain of the river. There are three smaller passage-graves on the Newgrange ridge (sites K and L to the west and site Z to the east) and other remains – tumuli, standing stones, enclosures, and so on – in the immediate vicinity of Newgrange, most of them between the main monument and the Boyne.

    The mound of Knowth, equal in size to Newgrange and containing two passage-graves, lies upstream on another ridge about 1 km to the northwest. Clustered round this mound are seventeen smaller passage-graves. The mound of Dowth, again comparable in size, lies on high ground to the east of Newgrange and also contains two passage-graves. From any one of the three great mounds the other two are visible. If one includes the sites north of the River Mattock, a tributary of the Boyne, over forty prehistoric sites can be seen in the 'loop of the Boyne', more than half of them passage-graves. Many other sites are undoubtedly present of which no trace can now be seen above ground.

    The Newgrange tomb consists of a passage and chamber the walls and roof of which are built of large slabs without mortar, hence its name of megalithic passage-grave. A large circular mound or cairn of loose stones covers the tomb. A circle of standing stones surrounds the cairn but the two are not concentric; at its nearest the circle is 7 m from the edge of the cairn and at its farthest 17 m. Only 12 stones survive out of a possible 35 to 38. They are irregularly spaced except for 3 opposite the tomb entrance, which are among the largest, standing on average 2.5 m above ground level. Some of the remainder have been broken off close to the ground; none are decorated. The average diameter of the circle is 103.6 m and it encloses an area of about 1 hectare.

plates I, 1, 2
fig. 1

fig. 2

fig. 23
plate 16

fig. 3

plates II, 34

1 *Map of Ireland, showing the location of Newgrange.*

2 *Map of Boyne passage-grave cemetery.*
Key: passage-graves I, J, K, L, T, Z; *tumuli* A, B, E, S;
enclosures M, N, P, Q, R, V, W; *standing stones* C, D;
destroyed sites F, G, H, U.

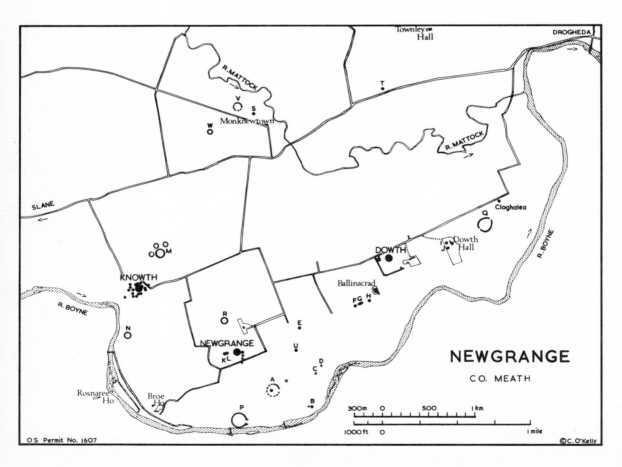

NEWGRANGE

CO. MEATH

OS Permit No. 1607

©C. O'Kelly

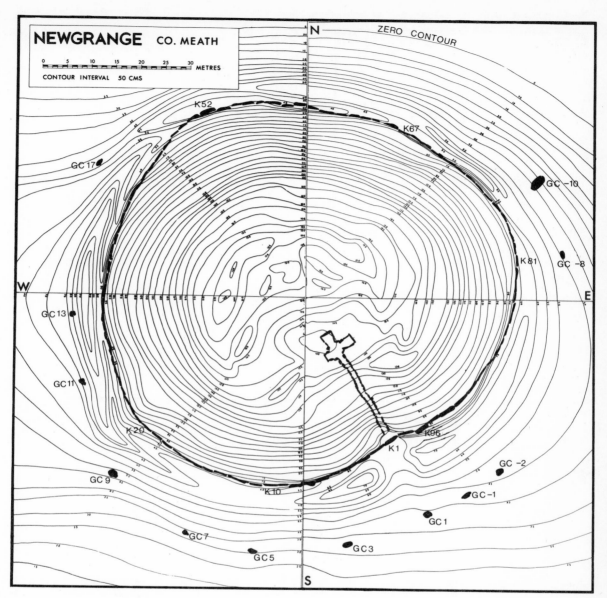

3 General plan of Newgrange.

The cairn is made up of medium-sized water-rolled stones, 15–22 cm in average diameter, interspersed with layers of turves. A kerb of massive contiguous slabs laid on their long edges surrounds the base of the mound. There are 97 in all and none is missing. Motifs and designs characteristic of Irish passage-grave art are picked on many of the kerbstones, the best known being the entrance stone and K52 diametrically opposite it on the north side of the kerb. The stones vary in length from 1.7 m to 4.5 m and average 1.2 m in height above ground level. White quartz stones and round

plates IV–VI

Colour plates

IV

V

VI

VII

granite boulders were used to build a revetment above the kerb all along the front or south side but elsewhere ordinary boulders were used. The revetment wall is estimated to have stood to *c.* 3 m above the kerb. The diameter of the cairn NW–SE is 78.6 m and NE–SW 85.3 m, so it is not completely circular. The top is flat and 32 m in diameter. Before excavation the height of the cairn, measured from just outside the entrance stone on the south side, was 10.9 m and outside K53 on the north side it was 13.4 m. The capstone of the chamber was covered by a layer of cairn material 1 m thick. Since the floor of the passage and chamber of the tomb follows the rise of ground of the hill on which the monument is built there is a difference of almost 2 m in floor-level between the entrance and the interior of the chamber.

plate 11

The tomb passage opens in the southeast of the mound and runs SE–NW.* It is 18.95 m long, lined on each side with orthostats, 22 on the west (left) and 21 on the east. They average 1.5 m in height above ground level though there is considerable variation. Those nearest the chamber are the tallest – 2 m and more above ground level. The passage is roofed by means of massive slabs laid transversely and resting either on the tops of the orthostats at each side or on corbels supported by the orthostats. The roof rises as it approaches the chamber and at its entrance is 3.6 m high. The passage entrance was blocked by a closing slab which now stands to the right of the passage mouth.

fig. 4

plates 74–79

plates IV, 3, 4

A so-far unique structure, the roof-box, was discovered in 1963. It rests partly on the first roof-slab (RS1) of the passage and partly on RS2. It is open at the front and its roof-stone or lintel is expertly ornamented on the forward-facing edge. It was found that at the time of the winter solstice (21 December) the rays of the rising sun shine directly into the chamber through a narrow gap between RS1 and RS2. The roof-box is 90 cm in height, 1 m wide and 1.2 m from front to back.

plates 40–43

plates VIII, 8

The chamber is cruciform, containing three recesses or side-chambers. It measures 5.25 m from its entrance to the back of the north or end recess and 6.55 m from the back of the west recess to the back of the east recess. The latter is the largest of the three and is the most profusely ornamented. Two basin stones lie in this recess, one inside the other, and there is a single basin in each of the other recesses. The chamber is roofed with a corbelled vault which rises and narrows gradually until it is closed by a single capstone, 6 m above the floor.

plates XII, XIII, 12

plate IX

The bank of material which lay outside the kerb when excavations commenced (and which is still present in the unexcavated areas) was found to consist of the collapsed original revetment together with the part of the cairn which lay behind and above it. After being excavated this material was replaced on the mound and a new revetment built, utilizing the quartz and granite boulders found during the excavation.

plate VII

The incomplete circle of standing stones surrounding the mound, the great circle, was investigated to determine its relationship to the rest of the monument. The results, though fairly inconclusive, did at least show that it was earlier than the

---

* Although the tomb is aligned SE–NW, for convenience it has become customary to refer to it as running S–N, and for the three side-chambers or recesses to be referred to as the west, north and east recesses, respectively, though correctly speaking, they are in the SW, NW and NE. It is proposed to retain here the simpler nomenclature.

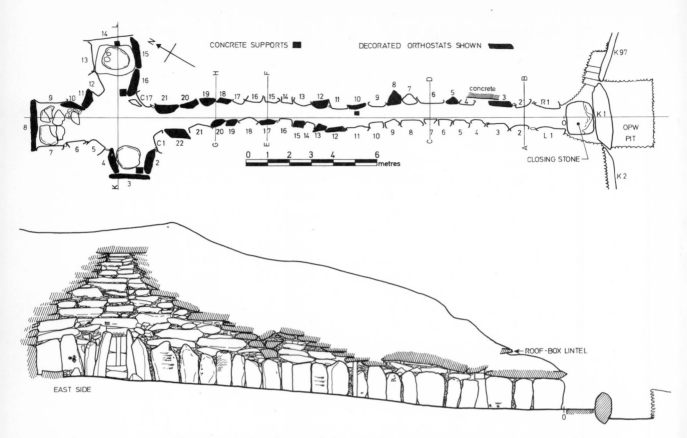

4 *Plan of the tomb and sectional elevation of the east side of the passage and chamber before excavation.*

Beaker-period settlement, dated to *c.* 2000 bc, and that therefore it may either be contemporary with the monument or earlier.

The tomb was found to be sophisticated in structure, the front part of the passage having been built as a free-standing entity independent of the main cairn mass. The inner part of the passage was integrated with the chamber and was similarly free-standing when built. The chamber was surrounded by its own supportive mini-cairn. When the cairn material was removed from over the passage roof to enable conservation to be carried out, hitherto unknown ornament was found on many of the roof-slabs and on their supporting corbels. It was also discovered that a series of grooves had been cut on the slabs to enable the rain-water percolating through the cairn to be led off outside the confines of the passage beneath. The interstices of the roof were caulked with a mixture of burnt soil and sea sand to render them waterproof and from this mixture two radiocarbon dates centring on 2500 bc were obtained for the structure of the tomb (see Appendix H).

Bone fragments representing a small number of people, as well as grave-goods typical of Irish passage-graves, were found when the floor of the tomb was excavated. plate X Apart from these no further finds were made, other than chance ones attributable to visitors from AD 1699 onwards (when the tomb was discovered). Outside it, however, in the cairn slip and beyond, there were extensive finds associated with a later settlement of the Late Neolithic/Beaker period. There were also many finds of Roman coins and objects of glass and metal of Romano-British type.

East of the tomb entrance two features were discovered and excavated: a multiple fig. 5 arc of great pits and a destroyed satellite passage-grave, site Z. Two other satellites, sites K and L, immediately west of the great mound, were also excavated, as was a standing stone, site C, ESE of Newgrange near the River Boyne. (The three satellites and site C have been published – see bibliography.)

In all, something over one-third of the perimeter of the monument was excavated, fully exposing 37 kerbstones at the front of the mound and 7 at the back or north side. As already mentioned, the revetment wall has been reconstructed along the front of the mound and the surface of the mound has been regraded as nearly as possible to its original contours. The flat top has been made good by the filling in of the numerous holes made there in the past. These and other conservation measures were undertaken and supervised by the National Parks and Monuments Branch of the Office of Public Works. The entrance area had to be modified from what we envisaged its original appearance to have been in order to accommodate the great numbers of visitors. Aside from this, the restored part of the monument is now as close as possible to what it was when built c. 2500 bc.

Concurrently with the excavations, research was undertaken into earlier accounts and descriptions of the monument and into the various investigations carried out previously. The early accounts of antiquarians such as Lhwyd, Pownall, Wilde and others were especially valuable as they often helped to elucidate puzzling features encountered in the course of the excavations. The fact that the file relating to work carried out by the Office of Public Works from the 1880s onward could not be found during the course of our work rendered the research detailed below particularly vital.

2 Previous history of the site

Antiquarian accounts

The discovery of the 'cave' at Newgrange came about through the need for stones on the part of the then landowner, Charles Campbell. Realizing that such were to be found in plenty under the green sod of a prominent mound on his farm, he instructed his labourers to carry some away and in so doing the entrance to the tomb was discovered. This was in the year AD 1699. It was fortunate that at that time the Welsh scholar and antiquary, Edward Lhwyd, was making a tour of Ireland and on being told of the discovery he came to Newgrange and took careful note of all that was to be seen and heard. He wrote to his friends about it and four of his letters are preserved, all giving substantially the same information.

The first letter is dated 15 December 1699 and it is to be inferred that the 'cave', as it was called, had been opened not too long before and that Lhwyd was able to obtain first-hand accounts of its discovery. He described what he saw in the same precise terms he was accustomed to use in his botanical and other studies. He said that 'a very broad flat stone, rudely carved' (the entrance stone) was placed edgewise before the entrance and that he had first to creep along the passage but that it gradually became higher until he reached the cave which was 20 ft high. He described the 'pillars' on either side of the passage and also the chamber with its three cells or 'apartments'. He mentioned the basin stones and the 'barbarous sculpture' of the orthostats and clearly took careful note of every item which seemed of interest (Lhwyd 1709, 694). The finds seem to have consisted of 'bones of beasts' of which there appear to have been many and which Lhwyd variously described as part of either a stag's or an elk's head, or else as pieces of deers' or stags' or elks' horns. In one of the letters he refers to 'a great quantity of bones – stags horns and, as they said, a piece of an elkshorn, pieces of glass and some kinde of beads'. His uncertainty about the various objects would lead one to suppose that in this instance he was speaking from hearsay, even without his addition of the words 'as they said'. The pieces of glass and the beads are difficult to account for unless they refer to the polished 'marbles' and pottery beads that are now known to be a normal feature of Irish passage-graves and examples of which were found in the tomb in 1967 during the excavations.

We know that after the cairn had started to collapse there was a Beaker-period occupation of around 2000 bc outside the southern part of the mound but no trace of this was found in the tomb so the entrance must by then have been hidden. Nor was there any sign inside the tomb of the gold coins and ornaments of Romano-British type deposited around the edge of the collapsed mound and on the mound itself during the early centuries of the Christian era. When the tomb was entered in 1699 it is probable that the deposits of cremated bone and the grave-goods which had originally been placed in the basins were brushed aside or ignored in the quest for the more prestigious type of find with which 'caves' were associated in the popular imagination. As already mentioned, a certain amount of the original deposit was found in the floor near the basins during the 1967 excavation.

The mouth of the passage had originally been closed by a stone which exactly fitted the aperture, but this was no longer in place in 1699. It lay tilted away from the entry with its top surface against the back of the entrance stone, and was so covered by stones and debris that the visitors of 1699 and later were not aware of its existence. It was first noted only in 1845. The question arises as to when and by whom the closing stone was levered back. It has been generally assumed that Newgrange was one of the tombs plundered by the Norsemen in the ninth century, but the evidence is dubious, resting on two annalistic entries, one in the *Annals of Ulster* under AD 862 and the other in the *Annals of the Four Masters* under AD 861. To quote from the former, which is the earlier of the two annals and is a very reliable compendium of early material, 'The cave of Achadh Aldai, and the cave of Cnodhba and of Fert Boadan over Dubadh... were searched by the foreigners...'. Dowth and Knowth are readily identifiable in the annals since the Irish names used are very close to the present anglicized forms, but the other cave which was 'searched', that of *Achadh Aldai*, cannot be reconciled with Newgrange which was originally known variously in the early Irish literature as *Brug Oengusa, Brug maic ind Óc, Síd in Broga,** and so on, all names designating it the Brú or mansion of Oengus, son of the Dagda, the chief god of the pre-Celtic pantheon. *Achadh Aldai* means the field of Alda, who was a member of the same race of supernatural beings as the Dagda and Oengus. If a reference to Newgrange was intended, it is unlikely that Oengus would have been set aside in favour of the much less prominent Alda. An earlier entry in the *Annals of Ulster,* for example, records that a man named Cellach died at *Brug mic an Óg* in AD 656 and there is no ambiguity in identification in this instance. As regards the later entry therefore, the one of AD 862, it is doubtful if Newgrange was the monument, or rather 'cave', alluded to.

The Norse were in the area throughout this period. It is recorded in the *Annals of Ulster* that they had a fleet on the Boyne in AD 836 and again in 841, so there was ample opportunity for them to raid Newgrange; but the nature of the monument, allied to the probability that the position of the entrance was not known, would seem to militate against any motivation. Knowth and Dowth were much more tempting targets. The Norse and their Irish allies did not go on raiding expeditions for the sake of the exercise or for the purpose of destruction, but mainly because of the booty to be obtained. We have been somewhat conditioned in the past to think of this as consist-

---

* *Brug Oengusa,* the house or mansion of Oengus; *Brug maic ind Óc,* the house of the Youthful Hero (another name for Oengus); *Síd in Broga,* a síd is an Otherworld or underground location.

ing in the main of articles of gold and precious metals, chiefly because it is plunder of this type which survives to bear witness. In fact, however, as Dr A. T. Lucas has pointed out, the raiders were probably more interested in supplies of food and these were available in the larder, that is, in the *uam* (the 'cave' or souterrain), an underground structure ideally suited for the preservation of essential commodities in normal times, and for the temporary preservation of life and limb in abnormal ones (Lucas 1971, 180).

Excavation has shown that there were at least ten of these *uama* or souterrains at Knowth, seven of them in the mound itself, and at least one is known in the mound of Dowth. None are present at Newgrange nor is there any evidence for reuse of the mound for habitation purposes as is the case at the two former sites. It may be that the closing stone was already tilted back when the first collapse of the perimeter took place and that the latter effectively rendered the tomb entrance indistinguishable from the rest of the perimeter. This theory would at least account for the indisputable fact that no finds which could be linked either to the Late Neolithic/Beaker-period occupation of about 2000 bc, or to the Romano-British-type finds of the first to the fourth centuries AD, were found in the tomb itself, unlike at Knowth and Dowth, where finds relating both to the Early Christian period and to the Norse one were discovered in the tombs.

plate 19   On a plan of Newgrange made by Edward Lhwyd's draughtsman, Will Jones, an interesting stone object is shown. An original annotation on the plan describes it as 'a stone wrought in the form of a cone half a yard long and about 20 inches in the girth having a small hole at ye big end. This I mett with in ye right hand cistern under ye bason above mentioned.' This object must have been discovered by Jones in the course of taking measurements and Lhwyd probably did not know about it at the time of his visit. Herity (1967, 130) has suggested that it was an axe similar in type to the polished greenstone ones found in large numbers in the tumuli of the Morbihan in Brittany. These axes have a link with passage-graves in that several lifelike examples are carved in relief on one of the orthostats of Gavrinis, Larmor Baden, at least one of them showing a perforation, but it is at the butt rather than at the broad cutting edge. The artefacts themselves are sometimes perforated also, and always at the butt-end. These are usually the smaller examples and P.–R. Giot (1960, 111) thinks they may have been used as pendants, a not unlikely theory considering the decorative nature of the jadeite from which they were made. The hole in the Newgrange object, however, was said to have been at the 'big end', that is, the opposite end to the butt. The illustration in Herity (1967), taken from one of the two originals preserved in Trinity College Dublin, is misleading because it shows what looks like a small hole towards the butt; this is due to a block imperfection and does not appear in either of the two original illustrations. While Jones mentioned the hole he did not depict it in his sketch nor is there any guarantee that it was in fact a through-perforation. Can the object have been a small baetyl or pillar-stone that had become dislodged at some stage?

Another enigmatic item from this period is a pillar-stone which Lhwyd maintained was standing 'pitched on end' on top of the mound. None of the later observers mentioned having seen it and yet Lhwyd was such a careful witness that it is difficult to discount his evidence. Since the top of the mound was a flat surface 32 m in diameter, it would have had to be a very tall stone to be seen without ascending the mound and there is no evidence that he did this; yet he specifically said that the stone was a lesser one than those of the great circle. There is little doubt that Lhwyd saw a stone on top of the cairn, but it must be questioned if it was a pillar-stone and even if it was, whether it was an original feature of the monument or not. A sketch of the tumulus made at this time survives in the Stowe collection of manuscripts in the British Museum (BM Stowe MS 1024) and is reproduced in the Ó Ríordáin and Daniel book on Newgrange (1964, 37). It depicts the mound as a steep-sided truncated cone, rather like an upturned flower pot, with a pillar-stone protruding from the top.

After Lhwyd the next visitor to record his impressions was Sir Thomas Molyneux, 'Professor of Physick in the University of Dublin', who came there some time later, though his account was not published until 1726. What is one to make of his statement (1726, 204) that 'when first the cave was opened, the bones of two dead bodies entire, not burnt, were found upon the floor, in likelyhood the reliques of a husband and his wife, whose conjugal affection had joyn'd them in their grave, as in their bed'? The origin of this account may perhaps be traced to an undated copy of a memorandum among the Molyneux papers in Trinity College Dublin (Herity 1967, 131) that runs as follows:

Mr Charles Campbell told me since (who was the Second man that went into the Cave upon its first Discovery) that he found the skull and bones of a man in one of those Cisterns and the bones of another humane Body Lying on the Ground in another part of the Cave somewhat remote from the Cistern, from which I gather it must certainly have been the Sepulchre or burying of some person of note that had his wife Interred with him and not a place for Sacrifice... The Staggs horns and Elk or rather Mose horn that were found here seem to Import that the person here buryed had been in his lifetime a great lover of the Chase...

While it is strange that the presence of human bones had not come to the attention of Lhwyd, one must nevertheless conclude that such had been found when the tomb was opened, for unburnt human bones, representing at least two individuals, and also part of a human skull, were found in 1967 when the floor of the chamber was excavated. If, as Molyneux asserted, 'the bones of two dead bodies entire' were discerned, it would imply that two skeletons, or the greater part of them, were then present. This raises interesting questions regarding the burial practices of the Newgrange people (to be dealt with in the Discussion in Part IV). Molyneux's assertion elsewhere that the bodies were those of a husband and wife must surely be discounted as one of the flights of fancy to which he was somewhat inclined, as may perhaps also be his statement that 'along the middle of the cave, a slender quarreystone, five or six foot long, lies on the floor, shaped like a pyramid, that once, as I imagine, stood upright, perhaps a central stone to those placed round the outside of the mound, but now 'tis fallen down' (1726, 204). Have we here some confusion with the cone-shaped stone described by Will Jones? It is to be noted that Molyneux did not mention the presence of a pillar-stone on top of the cairn.

While giving remarkably accurate measurements for the monument in general, Molyneux fell into the same error as Lhwyd and all the later observers until the time of

Colour plates

VIII At dawn on midwinter's day the sun shines through the slit in the roof-box, its rays illuminating the passage and chamber. The thin line of the River Boyne is visible beyond orthostat GC1, outside the entrance.

IX The corbelled vault of the chamber, closed by a single capstone 6 m above the floor.

X Grave goods found in the tomb during excavation in 1967: marbles, pendants and beads.

XI The 'Conyngham find' of 1842, now in the British Museum, consisting of gold torques, a gold chain and two rings, all of Romano-British style.

XII The chamber and passage seen from the end recess. The beam of light at midwinter sunrise reaches across the chamber floor as far as the front edge of the basin in this recess. Note the three-spiral stone C10 on the left (cf. plate 14).

XIII View of the tomb taken with a fish-eye lens, the camera being placed on the centre of the chamber floor, looking up. In the middle of the picture one sees the corbelled vault, the end recess is at the top, the east recess at the left and the west recess at the right. The light at the bottom of the picture represents the sun seen through the slit in the roof-box at the winter solstice.

VIII

IX

X   XI

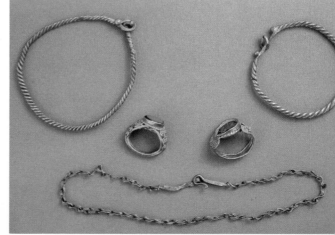

XII

Sir William Wilde in believing that the collapsed mound, the base of which coincided roughly with the great circle, was an original feature. Consequently, their estimates of its height had no bearing on the true state of affairs, Molyneux making it 150 ft and Sir Thomas Pownall, the next antiquarian of note to visit the site (in 1769), 70 ft. The latter's surveyor, Samuel Bouie, seems to have been the first observer to distinguish between the collapsed mound and the original one, because he took his measurement from just outside the tomb entrance and gave it as 42 ft – very close to the 1962 survey figure of 10.9 m. Pownall would have none of this, however, and adhered to his own measurement of 70 ft. He declared that the mound was originally pyramid-shaped and that the entrance 'under the perfect state of the monument, lay concealed or shut up near 40 feet within the body of the Pile'. He believed that a triangular segment of this pyramid, 40 ft at the base and 70 ft high, had been removed from in front of the entrance 'as from a stone quarry' and he asserted that Newgrange was 'but a ruin of what it was'. This statement of Pownall's gave rise to the belief frequently expressed even in modern times, that vast quantities of material had been removed. Undoubtedly some amount of stone had been taken but the triangular segment envisaged by Pownall had never existed in the first place. During the recent excavations no evidence was found that wholesale removal of cairn material had taken place, such as happened at Dowth, for example. The measurements given by Molyneux and by Pownall for the base of the collapsed mound and for the circumference of the flat top were practically the same as those obtaining at the present day and as we have seen from Bouie's figure, the height was also more or less the same. There is no evidence to warrant such statements as 'the later surveys measured a mound considerably altered by quarrying' (Herity 1967, 133).

The notion that Newgrange was originally much higher has been something of an *idée fixe* up to the present. It should be clear from the foregoing that the height of the mound has remained more or less unaltered and that whatever amount of stone was removed came mainly from the edge in the entrance area. It may be mentioned in passing that in 1844 it was reported to the Royal Irish Academy that the removal of a portion, if not the whole, of the mound of Newgrange was contemplated, to be broken up for the repair of the roads. Newgrange escaped this fate, but Dowth was not so lucky. In 1879 it was reported to the Royal Society of Antiquaries (Graves 1879, 13) that 'the great tumulus of Dowth, one of the wonders of the island ... has, after two thousand years, been in our day used as a convenient quarry by more than one person'.

Bouie's plan and section of the tomb (Pownall 1773, 254) are remarkably accurate considering the difficulties of measuring the dark interior and the fact that the stones forming the sides of the passage were, in the outermost part at least, leaning inwards and rendering access difficult. Furthermore, a great wedge of cairn material had entered the passage reaching almost to the roof at the entrance and tailing off gradually towards the centre of the passage. Pownall describes his entry as follows:

This gallery at the mouth is three feet wide, and two feet high. At thirteen feet from the mouth it is only two feet two inches wide at the bottom, and of an indeterminate width and height. Four of the side stones, beginning from the fifth on the right hand, or eastern side, stand now leaning over to the opposite side; so that here the passage is scarce permeable. We made our way by creeping on our hands and knees till we came to this part. Here we were forced to turn upon our sides, and edge ourselves on with one elbow and one foot. After we had passed this strait, we were enabled to stand; and by degrees, as we advanced farther, we could walk upright, as the height above us increased from six to nine feet.

This description brings graphically to mind the manner in which the newly discovered tomb in the eastern part of the mound of Knowth had to be negotiated at the time of its discovery in 1968. The same crab-like progress had to be made along the 35 m-long passage, though with the important difference that electric torches were available, whereas Pownall and the other early visitors to Newgrange had no such aid, rendering all the more remarkable the accurate delineations, plans and descriptions they provided. An interesting feature shown in Bouie's section-drawing of the right-hand side of the passage is a gap between the third and fourth orthostats which appears to have been filled by dry masonry. Why this space, about 60 cm wide and sufficient to accommodate another orthostat, was left is not known. Excavation showed that no stone had previously stood there and one must assume that the dry walling shown by Bouie was original. It brings to mind a similar gap on the right-hand side of the passage of Dowth North between orthostats 7 and 8, though of course in that case there has been no modern excavation to determine whether or not an orthostat was at one time present.

A point raised by Pownall which has been responsible for a good deal of subsequent speculation was his conjecture that some of the decorated stones of the interior 'had formerly belonged to some other monument of a much more ancient date, and that they were brought from the sea coast indiscriminately with the rest of the materials, and without knowledge of their contents, as well as without reference to the place they were here fixed in, being placed just as the shape of the stone suited the place assigned it'. This theory was to be repeated again and again, and in recent times most notably by R. A. S. Macalister. Indeed, it is one of the questions frequently raised today by visitors. All the Newgrange decoration is in fact homogeneous and there is no evidence to substantiate the theory first enunciated by Pownall.

In the years succeeding Pownall's visit many eminent antiquarians and travellers came to Newgrange and wrote about it, among them Thomas Wright (1748), Gabriel Beranger (1775), General Sir Charles Vallancey (1786), De Latocnaye (1797), Edward Ledwich (1804), Sir Richard Colt Hoare (1807), L. C. Beaufort (1828), George Petrie (1833), John O'Donovan (1836), G. Wilkinson (1845), Sir William Wilde (1847 and 1849), William Wakeman (1848), J. Lefroy (1865), James Fergusson (1872) and, greatest of them all, George Coffey (1892–6 and 1912). With the notable exception of Coffey and possibly of Wilde, a good deal of what they wrote was based on Lhwyd, Molyneux and Pownall and, all too often, personal inspection of the monument was cursory. Molyneux's account became more widely known than Lhwyd's and his statements about the finding of 'two dead bodies entire' and about the fallen pillar-stone in the chamber were to be brought forward time and again, often with embellishments. For instance, Beaufort (1828, 132) said that the two dead bodies lay one on either side of the fallen pillar-stone and that two gold coins were found beneath it. Fergusson claimed that a gold coin was found in the chamber. No warranty for any of these statements can be traced.

The writers indulged also in a good deal of speculation as to who had erected such a remarkable monument and it is interesting to note that up to the time of George Petrie none of the early visitors, with the sole exception of Lhwyd, attributed it to the natives. It is to Lhwyd's credit that he deduced that Newgrange was 'some place of sacrifice of the ancient Irish', even though his deduction was made, not on the basis of any known past achievements of the Irish, or because of the association of the mound with the mythological ancestors of the Gael, but because it seemed to him that the finding of a Roman coin in the cairn showed that the monument was 'ancienter than any invasion of the Ostmans or Danes and the carving and rude sculpture, barbarous'. Most of the other writers attributed Newgrange to the Danes and influences were also invoked from Egypt, India, Ethiopia, Phoenicia, Celtic Gaul, and so on; in fact, almost any race under the sun was considered eligible save for the natives themselves.

George Petrie was one of the first to place Newgrange in its proper perspective and he castigated Molyneux, Pownall and others for their unwillingness to 'allow the ancient Irish the honour of erecting a work of such vast labour and grandeur'. He also re-established the link between Newgrange and the store of myth and saga enshrined in the references to Brú na Bóinne in the early Irish literature. No matter that he wrongly attributed the mounds on the Boyne to the Tuatha Dé Danann, the mythical semi-divine ancestors of the Gael; the significant thing was that he initiated a new approach to this ancient monument. The renaissance in Irish studies, of which Irish archaeology was an important part, had begun. In fairness, it must be said that almost all the early accounts, certainly those given at first hand, despite their lack of understanding of the native background, contributed something to our understanding of the monument and have frequently thrown invaluable light on problems that arose in the course of the recent excavation and conservation.

A case in point is Wilkinson's description of the closing stone (1845, 53). While studying the geology and architecture of the monument he noted that 'a large flat stone appears, from the peculiarity of its position, to have closed the entrance'. A useful sketch (by du Noyer) shows the stone tilted back towards the entrance stone, exactly the position it would have occupied if it had been levered back from the mouth of the passage. The stone was later removed from this position, turned through 90° and laid flat in the space between the back of the entrance stone and the mouth of the passage   plate 37
where it acted as a paving slab. This may have been done during OPW conservation in 1890, for Coffey showed it in its prone position in 1892. Wilkinson also noted that 'the ornamented stone in front of the entrance appears to have been one of a series which encircled the base of the mound, and probably extends around the mound, but is now covered by the masses of oversliding stones and earth'. He was thus one of the first to envisage Newgrange as it originally was. Many subsequent writers, including Wilde, continued to believe that the original mound extended as far as the great circle, the stones of which marked its edge.

Although the entrance stone had been uncovered in 1699 it later became buried again. Beranger noted on a sketch he made of Newgrange in 1775 (RIA MS 3C 30, f4):

'the place of the entrance, which is not seen from the base, being hid by a heap of stones'. He describes the entrance as being 3 ft wide and 2 ft high, but he makes no mention of the entrance stone nor does he depict it. Wilde (1847, 733) says that in the 1840s 'a gentleman, then residing in the neighbourhood, cleared away the stones and rubbish which obscured the mouth of the cave, and brought to light a very remarkably-carved stone, which now slopes outwards from the entrance'. Thus was the entrance stone once more uncovered and perhaps it was also then that the closing stone was noticed.

plate 40

At about the same time another feature was revealed which was in due course to lead to one of the most important discoveries of the modern excavations. According to Wilde: 'The edge of another very curious, and most exquisitely-carved stone, was found projecting from the mound, a short distance above, and within the line of the present entrance.' He surmised that it might 'decorate the entrance into some other chamber, which further examination may yet disclose'. In fact, it proved to be the roof-slab of the structure now known as the roof-box. The stone was then called the false lintel because of Wilde's theory and several attempts were subsequently made to penetrate the mound at this point. One Richard Burchett reported unashamedly to the Society of Antiquaries of London in 1874: 'I uncovered its [the lintel's] whole surface and found two men with crow bars incapable of moving it without greater risk to its safety than I was willing to incur.' In 1928 Macalister carried out some digging beneath the lintel, also in pursuance of a chamber, but fortunately he backfilled the hole before any structural damage was done. It says much for the skill of the original builders that the monument so successfully resisted these and other vandalistic acts.

plate XI

At about the time the entrance stone and false lintel were uncovered, Wilde reported that 'a labourer, digging a little to the west of the entrance, discovered two ancient gold torques and a golden chain and two rings', apparently at a depth of 2 ft and not protected in any way. A little later, further coins were found near the same place and D'Alton (1844, 440) alleges that still more coins came to light, though this statement is of doubtful validity. All the coins were Roman and the ornaments were Romano-British in style. Previously Lhwyd had recorded the finding of a gold coin of Valentinian 'near the top of the mount' and Molyneux had similarly stated that 'about ten or twelve years since' – at about the time of Lhwyd's visit – when removing 'some of the heap of stones on the outside of the mount, two Roman golden coins were found by accident, near the surface, buried among the stones'. He described and illustrated the two coins, one of Valentinian and the other of Theodosius. Presumably the Valentinian is the same as the one mentioned by Lhwyd. It may be that these two gold coins should be bracketed with the find of 1842, above-mentioned (called the Conyngham find, since it was Lord Conyngham who brought the objects to the notice of the Society of Antiquaries of London [Conyngham 1844, 137]). It is not known where any of the coins now are but the gold ornaments found their way to the British Museum, something which aroused Wilde's indignation:

Where are these? Are they in the great national collection of the Royal Irish Academy? Have they been recorded in the proceedings or transactions of that, or any other learned body in the kingdom? No, we regret to say they were carried out of this country by an Irish nobleman, to exhibit at a learned society on the other side of the channel, in the transactions of which they will be found figured, together with a letter from their present owner, which, as he is our countryman, we will not quote!

Some twenty years later, in 1863, Wilde presented to the Royal Irish Academy on behalf of Richard Maguire, the then Newgrange landowner, a small gold band which had been found 'in the field adjoining the tumulus of Newgrange when a large portion of rubbish was being cleared away from the opening'. The statement is unclear but it cannot be ruled out that this object belongs together with the Conyngham ornaments. The band is about 3.5 cm in length and is ornamented (Armstrong 1933, 46). All these finds have been discussed elsewhere (Carson and O'Kelly 1977).

During Wilde's examination of the chamber in the 1840s he noted that one of the orthostats (C10) forming part of the right-hand side of the north recess had fallen forward and that a large flag or corbel, ornamented on the underside, had become exposed to view. He remarked that 'the colour of the cutting and the track of the tool is just as fresh as if done but yesterday', an observation which exactly describes the appearance of several structural stones discovered in 1964 when the passage roof was being examined. James Fergusson (1872, 203) also mentions the fallen stone and shows it on a plan (though wrongly as C11) and observes that 'by creeping behind it, it is possible to see the reverse of some of the neighbouring stones, and it is found that several of these are elaborately carved with the same spiral ornaments as their fronts'. Coffey (1892, fig. 38, p. 32) also noted the decoration but by the time he published his book on Newgrange in 1912 the stone had, as he said, 'been lately built up', meaning it was no longer to be seen.

The falling forward of C10 gave rise to the notion that another chamber was present. In 1893 a Captain Keogh wrote to T. J. Westropp stating that on a visit to Newgrange he had discovered a passage between the right-hand recess and the end recess which had originally been closed by one of the orthostats of the central chamber. He apparently got his head and shoulders far enough in to see that 'the passage turned towards the middle of the mound. It is nearly filled to the top with small broken stones and the parts of the large stones forming its sides are covered with carvings and spirals.' (Westropp 1893, 213). It is best not to place too much reliance on this story as Keogh probably mistook spaces between the displaced corbel stones for a passage. On the other hand, bearing in mind the annexe that leads out of one of the recesses at Dowth North and which is entered through a very narrow opening between two stones, and remembering also the many surprises that Newgrange has provided already, it would be unwise to discount the captain's claim entirely.

At the present day a design of small triangles and chevrons can be seen on the corbel directly behind C10 but the design of double spirals, arcs and triangles illustrated by Coffey is no longer visible. Perhaps it was never intended to be seen and only came to light because of the dislodgment of C10. 'Hidden' ornament of this nature is not unusual at Newgrange and many further examples were found during the excavations. C10 was later restored to the vertical, but since it had broken off from its base just above ground level it now rests on the fractured end beside its stump which protrudes through the floor.

fig. 49

plate 82

37

The basin stones which are such a noteworthy feature of the chamber received a good deal of attention from the antiquarians though certain ambiguities and misconceptions were present even from the start. Lhwyd, for example, thought there was no basin in the end recess. In Molyneux's plan, however, all the basins are shown and Pownall gives the dimensions of the basin in the end recess (rightly calling it a floor-stone rather than a basin) as 6 ft 11 in. by 4 ft 11 in. It appears to have been whole at this time. In 1828 Beaufort noted that it was 'much broken by injudicious curiosity of visitors' and in Wilkinson's plan (1845) it is shown in four pieces, obviously incomplete. A French visitor throws light on the destruction (De Latocnaye 1797, 311) as follows:

The interior of this monument was up to a few years ago, regularly paved; but unfortunately a Connaught peasant having dreamt that there was a treasure hidden beneath it, came here expressly to search it out; he was aided by others of the area as credulous as himself and equally as persuaded of the veracity of nocturnal visions; they removed all the stones forming the *pavé,* they broke one of the basins and carried one that was in the centre to a corner and set it on one of those in the angles, and not having found anything, they left the stones all disarranged.

In the 1967 excavations, it was found that a very large hole had been dug in the end recess, the aim of which seemed to have been to get below the base of the back-stone of the recess (C8). In this the vandals were unsuccessful, but the floor-stone was badly broken in the process, perhaps by De Latocnaye's Connaughtman. It may have been at this time also that C10 was damaged. It is difficult to explain the statement that the would-be treasure hunters took one of the basins from the centre and moved it to the east recess. Until Pownall's visit in 1769 there had been no basin in the centre but there were two in the east recess (and, incidentally, C10 was then in an erect position). Wilkinson (1845), however, mentions that 'the oval-shaped granite stone formerly stood in the centre', so it may have been moved to that position shortly after Pownall's visit in 1769 only to be replaced in the east recess as detailed by De Latocnaye. It remained there until the OPW conservation work of *c.* 1890. According to Coffey (1892) 'a . . . carefully wrought basin at present stands in the centre of the chamber. It was found in the east recess, and stood within the basin still in that recess. It has been recently moved into the centre, on the supposition that, as at Dowth, it originally occupied that position.' In the plan of the tomb, published in his paper of 1892 and again in the book of 1912, Coffey shows the basin in the centre of the chamber and rightly points out that that is not its correct position. The basin was later replaced in its original position in the recess and during the operation a stone object, possibly a lamp, was found. It seems possible therefore that the granite basin was moved on two separate occasions.

plate 59

Newgrange in state care

Under the provisions of the Ancient Monuments Protection Act 1882, Newgrange, Knowth and Dowth were taken into State care, and the Board of Public Works became the authority responsible for them. In 1890 some long-overdue repairs and conservation were undertaken by the Board under the direction of the first Inspector,

Thomas Newenham Deane. Several public-spirited citizens had previously called the Board's attention to the state of the monument, detailing the deterioration taking place due to 'natural decay and the attentions of evilly-disposed visitors'. One of them wrote: 'I am sorry to say that many of the interesting carvings on the surfaces of the stones are fast becoming obliterated by the rude inscription of brutish-minded and self-   plate 20
ish men's names all over the surfaces of the various stones.' Another said that some of the inscriptions had been scaled off and recently removed, and Mr Balfour of Townley Hall was of the opinion that 'the greatest danger in these matters seems to me to be the behaviour of tourists', a prophetic utterance indeed. The placing of an iron gate at the entrance was recommended and this seems to have been done. In the absence of the   plate 21
relevant OPW files uncertainty surrounds the work carried out, apart from those oper-ations for which there is visible evidence, such as the shoring up of orthostats and lin-tels with wooden beams, concrete, and so on. Many of the measures were found to be superfluous during the recent conservation work and were removed, as for instance some of the ugly props which had been inserted in the west and east recesses. Others have had to be retained and contrast unfavourably with the Neolithic building work.

In 1890, work was undertaken on the exterior also. Coffey (1892) notes that the earth was removed from in front of the lower half of the entrance stone so as to expose the whole of the carved surface and an oblong pit was dug in front of it. He said that: 'the floor of the chamber has been recently cleared of the loose stones mentioned by Lhwyd, a number of which have been placed at the bottom of the pit dug in front of the carved stone at the entrance. They appear to be carefully chosen water-rolled stones, and are of interest as a portion of the original pavement of the chamber.' Apparently the only finds noticed were some animal bones. This pit survived until the recent excavations. Macalister (1949, 74) wrote of it: 'When the Government took this and other monuments of antiquity into public guardianship, the then Inspector of Ancient Monuments made it all tidy again, not by endeavouring to reconstitute the pavement, but by digging an oubliette in front of the entrance, and bundling all the   *fig. 4*
debris unceremoniously into it.' It is likely that in the course of the 'tidying' further archaeological material and evidence were destroyed.

The Inspector seems to have explored the kerb also. According to Coffey: 'Sir Thomas Deane's happy speculation that the spirals on the stone at the back of the west recess were intended as a plan of the mound led to the discovery of two additional carved stones in the boundary circuit.' These are K52, on the north side diametrically   plate VI
opposite the entrance stone, and K67 on the northeast. It is not clear whether he excav-   plate V
ated all the way round the kerb or not. He may have made trial diggings at the west, north and east and have considered the first two the only ones worth exposing fully. Coffey also writes that 'the sides of the mound, where it had ravelled out at the entrance, were, at the same time trimmed and faced with dry walling'.

Deane was not the first to explore the kerb. Even before his time a ditch and bank existed outside it and Coffey in his 1892 paper wondered whether or not this was an original feature, as indeed did many others subsequently, even up to the time of the recent excavations. Coffey remarked that the feature was well defined for most of the circumference but less so on the east side where it tended to peter out. The recent

plate 22

excavations have made it clear that the original purpose of the trench or ditch was to expose the kerbstones all round the mound and that the material thus removed had been piled outside to form a high bank or rampart. By Coffey's time material had again rolled into the trench, almost covering the kerbstones, except for the two exposed by Deane. Still visible from the first operation, however, was a revetment wall of dry stones that had then been built on top of the kerb so as to keep back the steep sides of the cairn mass. The dry walling curved in towards the entrance at the front and it was presumably this which had 'ravelled out' and been repaired by Deane. It is thought that he repaired the remainder of the wall also. Of this feature Coffey said (1912, 4): 'a

plate 23

retaining wall, or revetment of dry rubble, some five to six feet high, is built immediately on the base stones. This retaining wall, I have been informed, is a modern feature, and was made in the time of Mr Tiernan, a former tenant of New Grange.' An interesting unpublished manuscript of 1874 by Richard Burchett, brought to light by Dr Herity (1967, 135), shows that the kerb was visible in the early 1870s. Burchett said: 'Many of these stones are now, in part, visible, but upon them a late occupant of the land has constructed a dwarf-wall, or revetment, about 7 feet in height, and thrown up outwards the waste material, forming a rampart around the mound.' James Fergusson, whose account was published in 1872 and who must have visited Newgrange just before that date, does not mention having seen either the kerb or the dry wall and he assumed that the collapsed mound was the original one. The work must therefore have been done between the time of his visit and that of Burchett, that is, certainly before 1874. It is probable that the idea of the revetment wall was not entirely Tiernan's invention. He may have found traces of an original revetment as soon as he began to clear material from the tops of the kerbstones, as was found, for example, on the north side of the mound during excavation work in 1970. No doubt too Tiernan realized, as did the first builders, that the loose mass of water-rolled stones of which the cairn is largely composed, could only be kept in place by a built revetment.

The kerb, or part of it, was again explored in 1928 when Macalister and others (1943, 149) began digging at the left of the entrance stone, working clockwise round the mound until they had exposed 54 stones.* 'At this point', says Macalister, 'the then tenant interfered, and owing to his objections the work had to be suspended.' He gives a brief and incomplete description of the stones and remarks on 'the contrast between the remarkable poverty of New Grange and the wealth of Knowth' where he conducted a similar operation in 1940. He wrote elsewhere (1935, 65) of the Newgrange kerbstones:

As a decoration of the great burial-mound nothing more pointless or undignified could be conceived, it would have been better to have left them in their unadorned simplicity. But we suggest that each of these may have once marked a grave, and that the zigzag or spiral would have told a contemporary passer-by all that he needed to know about the dead man underneath. So far as the present writer is concerned, the results of this partial and preliminary excavation strengthened him in the view that the stones were collected by the builders on the spot from the graves of an earlier people.

A strange viewpoint surely and one which must have given added weight to the theory that the stones had originally been employed elsewhere. Oak posts were placed

---

* Macalister says that they went 'right-hand-wise' which might be taken to mean anti-clockwise as one stands looking at the monument, but from his published description of the kerbstones which he uncovered, it is clear that he worked from K2 to K54 consecutively.

against the outside of the kerbstones exposed by Macalister so as to keep them in an upright position. In the course of the recent excavations other posts were found supporting stones not exposed by Macalister. These may have been inserted in 1936, since Hartnett mentions elsewhere that the OPW were working at Newgrange in that year.

Macalister also explored the fallen orthostat of the great circle on the east side (numbered on the plans as GC-10). S. P. Ó Ríordáin (1956, 53) conducted an investigation of the same stone and says: 'Information kindly made available from the records of the Office of Public Works... indicated that the work was carried out in June, 1928, and was directed by Dr Praeger and Professor Macalister. In conjunction with their work on the kerb they dug a pit under this stone in order to examine the under-surface.' The pit was not filled back but was covered over by loose planks which were still there when Ó Ríordáin excavated it in 1954. The stone in question lay about 7 m from the *fig. 3* kerb, pointing away from it. Ó Ríordáin located the socket which was just beneath the end nearest the kerb and he also found some of the packing stones. He said it was certain that 'The stone was erected clear of the edge of the cairn and that it fell before any collapse took place because none of the cairn material lay underneath it.' The orthostat and circle, therefore, must either be contemporary with the mound or earlier.

Ó Ríordáin's observations on the stratification of the cairn collapse in the vicinity of the fallen stone are interesting and correspond closely with what was observed elsewhere at the site by O'Kelly, although Ó Ríordáin's section, unlike the O'Kelly ones, did not run as far as the kerb and was in an area where the quartz facing of the mound had tailed off. Ó Ríordáin found a bottom layer of stones mixed with soil, indicating a slow collapse, followed by a layer of clean stones, indicating rapid collapse, and a third layer of slow collapse–exactly the sequence found by O'Kelly in all the comparable areas. Ó Ríordáin wondered whether or not the rapid collapse of stones which formed the second layer was merely a local phenomenon but as the later excavations showed, this feature was constant throughout. In point of fact, there were two phases of rapid collapse but the second one was only readily detectable close to the kerb where Ó Ríordáin's excavation did not penetrate.

In conclusion he made a percipient statement regarding the stratification. He said of the two bottom layers that the stones of which they were composed were similar, being large and round, while those of the top layer were smaller and more angular. He deduced from this that the bottom layers had come 'from the cairn surface where such large stones would have suitably served as a facing, while the smaller material could have come from the body of the cairn'. In the excavation of the north side of the tumulus in 1965, rounded stones were found at the bottom of the stratification and were clearly a substitute for the quartz stones used as a facing in the front of the tumulus. The fallen orthostat was re-erected in 1973 and it was noted that the cupmarks mentioned in the Ó Ríordáin report were natural features, not manmade.

In the early 1950s electric light was installed in the tomb, which made it necessary to dig a cable-trench. This was done under the archaeological supervision of Mr P. J. Hartnett (1954, 181). As it approached the site from the west the trench ran parallel to, but outside, the southernmost part of the great circle and turned towards the tomb midway between GC1 and GC3. At this point Hartnett found what he thought might have been the socket of a missing orthostat, GC2. On the edge of the supposed socket he found a group of flints which appeared to him to have been deliberately deposited. In the course of Ó Ríordáin's 1954 excavations he examined this same area and found some large stones on the old ground surface. He considered that if an orthostat was originally present it had had no socket but was balanced on a flat base in a slight hollow, its balance helped by the large stones. He also dug a cutting which sectioned through the next existing orthostat on the west, GC3, and found it had a deep socket-hole wedged by large packing slabs. Having thus examined the sockets of two existing stones of the circle, GC3 and CG-10, and the possible socket of another, GC2, Ó Ríordáin observed: 'Should it be possible at a future date to continue the investigation of the sites of the missing uprights at Newgrange, the trial excavation will serve as a warning that one must expect the most varied evidence of their former position.' The truth of this was amply borne out during the recent excavations.

fig. 11g

For almost a decade Newgrange was left alone, apart from occasional conservation and repair by OPW, though damage to the ornamented stones and the carrying away of quartz fragments continued. In effect, very little was known about the monument in spite of all that had been written and said about it in the past 250 years. Officially, it was regarded as a Bronze Age monument of perhaps 1500 BC or later. A good deal of what was promulgated concerning its date, its builders and its original appearance was incorrect due to faulty interpretation both of the early accounts and of what was actually visible on the ground. One of the most prevalent misconceptions concerned the height and original shape of the mound. A threepenny guidebook by R. A. S. Macalister, published in 1939, referred to it as a Bronze Age monument about 42 ft in height above ground level at the entrance, and added that 'to judge from the accumulation of debris at the bottom, fallen from the top and sides, it must have been originally about ten feet higher'. The process by which material could fall from a flat top, 32 m in diameter, was not explained. Macalister envisaged that the cairn when new must have been 'a shapely hemispherical mound of stones, the entire surface of which was covered with a layer of broken fragments of quartz'. These statements have unfortunately gained as much currency as Molyneux's concerning the husband and wife supposedly interred in the chamber and are proving almost as difficult to eradicate. The tendency to compare Newgrange with Dowth and Knowth merely reinforces the misconception. Since the two latter sites approximate fairly closely to Macalister's 'hemispherical mound', the assumption is made that the steep sides and flat top of Newgrange must have been caused by slip and other disturbance. As is now known, the contrary is the case; it is the other two sites which have been modified. In the case of Dowth, a souterrain was inserted inside the kerb, a deep crater was dug in the centre of the mound and there was wholesale removal of cairn material. Numerous souterrains were constructed in the Knowth mound, structures were erected on the mound and a deep ditch was dug all around its perimeter inside the kerb. In both cases the top of the mound was interfered with. None of this happened at Newgrange and its steep sides and flat top, even before any restoration took place, must have been much closer to the original appearance of all three monuments than the bell-barrow-like shape assumed by Knowth and Dowth as a result of later interference.

plate 18

3 Newgrange in early Irish literature

Traditional associations

No less interesting than the accounts of antiquarians is Newgrange's place in early Irish literature and tradition. There are few early books, compilations or annals in which some mention cannot be found of Brú na Bóinne, the house or mansion of the Boyne. It plays a significant role in the mythology and heroic life of early Ireland and the corpus of tales, poems, *dindshenchas* (place lore) accounts, and so on, in which it is mentioned has been common currency among scholars ever since the revival of interest in native learning began at the close of the seventeenth century. The locale referred to, however, was not pinpointed until George Petrie (1845, 101) demonstrated the similarity between *dingnai in Broga* (monuments of the Brú) and those of the Boyne passage-grave cemetery.

The antiquarian writers, learned as some of them were, had no knowledge of this rich body of tradition because almost without exception they were of alien rather than Gaelic culture and stock. While the poets, chroniclers and scholars of the old Gaelic Ireland were clear in their minds that *Brug na Bóinne* and *dingnai in Broga* referred to the Boyne monuments and to Newgrange, by the time the entrance to the tomb was discovered in 1699 this learned class had largely ceased to exist and their books, when not destroyed, were reposing undeciphered in various libraries and private collections in Ireland and abroad. Those who filled their place had inherited a different culture, and the language and traditions of Gaelic Ireland were either unknown to them or went unheeded. None of the eminent visitors who came to see Newgrange after its discovery and who wrote about it knew that it was the mound in which, according to ancient tradition, 'three times fifty sons of kings abode for three days with their three nights' (O'Grady 1892, 101). Nor did they know that it was the mansion to which *Oengus an Broga* brought the body of Diarmaid, one of the great Irish folk-heroes, after his death on Ben Bulben so that he could 'put an aeriel life into him so that he will talk to me every day' (Ní Sheaghdha 1967, 101). It is probable that the labourers who were instrumental in uncovering the entrance were more attuned to this aspect of Newgrange than the scholars who came to marvel at it or the landowner Charles Campbell, whose Newgrange holding was part of the confiscated lordship of Mellifont (Claire O'Kelly 1978, 86–9).

The reasons for the neglect and ignorance of what must once have been a vivid tradition are largely historical and have particular relevance to the area in which the monuments are situated. This was part of what became known as the 'English Pale', the region where British rule was most effective. In the course of the hundred years that had elapsed since the battle of Kinsale in 1601, which marked the final stage in the conquest of Ireland by the Tudors, a great part of the land had changed hands owing to large-scale confiscation and settlement by English and Scottish soldiers of fortune. Charles Campbell, the owner of Newgrange in 1699, was one such. Since the Boyne valley contains some of the richest land in the country it would have been strange indeed if many elements of the old Gaelic world had survived in the area. After Kinsale the ancient Gaelic learned and literary caste effectively ceased to exist and although a few lingered on, it was in remote parts far from the 'fat lands' of the Pale.

The last of the Irish annals, chronological records of Irish history from earliest times, was compiled between 1632 and 1636 by some of these survivors, the Four Masters, as they are commonly known. In a convent of the Franciscans in Donegal, grateful no doubt for the daily allowance of food which made their work possible and conscious, as one of them put it, of 'the cloud which at present hangs over our ancient Milesian race', these men collected the past history of Ireland from the old manuscripts available to them so that 'posterity might be informed how their forefathers employed their time, how they continued in power and how they finished their days' (O'Donovan 1851, ix).

Between scholars such as these and men such as Sir Thomas Molyneux, Sir Thomas Pownall and others of their class, there was no common ground. Much could have been achieved if the march of events had allowed the old traditional Gaelic scholarship to merge naturally with the scientific knowledge and more outward-looking philosophy of those who were in political ascendancy, but there were too few opportunities and perhaps too few attempts, with the exception of a small minority, such as Sir James Ware and Archbishop Ussher.

For the most part, either the 'Danes' or the Normans were credited with every past achievement of the native Irish. Sir Thomas Molyneux, 'Professor of Physick in the University of Dublin, Physician to the State and Physician General to the Army in Ireland', was much given to the Danish theory. In 'A Discourse concerning the Danish Mounts, Forts and Towers in Ireland' (in Boate 1726), he demonstrated to his own satisfaction and that of most of his fellow scholars for many years to come that almost every ancient monument above ground in Ireland, including Newgrange, was the work of the Danes. Yet a few years before the publication of his 'Discourse', a work had appeared entitled *A History of Ireland from the earliest times to the Anglo-Norman Invasion* (O'Connor 1723). This was an English translation of Geoffrey Keating's *Foras Feasa ar Éirinn* which had been written 'among the caves and woods of Tipperary when the author was proscribed and hunted' (O'Curry 1861, 442). Since the gulf between the old and the new worlds in Ireland was almost total by this time, Keating's work, even in translation, was unlikely to come to the notice of those who would have most profited by it.

This was the background against which Newgrange, in the earliest years of its discovery, was evaluated; but on the credit side it must be added that it was these same scholars and antiquarians, however misguided their views on Ireland and the Irish, who kept alive the knowledge of, and interest in, the 'mounts, forts and towers in Ireland', until in the next century a new generation of scholars of the calibre of George Petrie, John O'Donovan and Eugene O'Curry was able to lay the foundations of modern archaeology, to unlock the stone of native learning and forge a connection between the old scholarship and the new.

This is not the place to enter into the chronological relationships of the various sources in which the Brú is mentioned in early Irish literature. In the form in which they are now preserved, the earliest is as late as the eleventh century but it is generally agreed that most derive from much older written sources and that, preceding this again, there was a long oral tradition. Some of the tales, poems, *dindshenchas* (place lore) accounts, and so on, are undoubtedly based on very old material. Tales which are told and re-told, whether in oral or written form, must constantly undergo change but a basic and ancient theme or themes can often be detected regardless of the date of the versions.

With regard to the Brú, or Brú na Bóinne, there seem to be two main concepts: the Brú as the abode of the mythological or supernatural beings known as the Tuatha Dé Danann (peoples of the goddess Danu) and the Brú as the burial place of the pagan kings of Tara. It is upon these foundations that the corpus of references mainly rests, in so far, that is, as the prehistoric character of the monument is concerned. Another body of references, mainly annalistic, refers to its role in later times. Some of these have already been mentioned.

The word Brú (Old Irish *Brug*) means 'abode, hall, mansion or castle' and is used 'particularly of early monumental sites' (Royal Irish Academy Dictionary 1975, 212). In mythological or supernatural contexts the Brú was associated with the Dagda, the Good God*; his wife, Boann; and his son Oengus; all belonging to the Tuatha Dé, a people said to have inhabited Ireland before the coming of the Gael or Celts and who thereafter retreated into the fairy mounds and forts of Ireland. They were not gods in the sense of deities to be revered, but were regarded as supernatural beings who could and did perform deeds beyond the power of mortals. They were unequivocally pagan and were mainly portrayed as belonging to a remote past; nevertheless, in some unexplained way, they were able to live on from age to age so that they seemed always present and could intervene at will in the affairs of men. They were fairly strictly localized. Some, such as the Dagda and his family, were associated with Brú na Bóinne; mounds elsewhere had other deities, such as Midir in Brí Léith, Bodb in Síd ar Femen in Co. Tipperary, and so on.

There are various versions of how the ownership of the Brú came about. According to the tale entitled *Tochmarc Etaíne* (Bergin and Best 1938) the Brú formerly belonged to Elcmar who was married to Bóand, or Boann, the divinized River Boyne. The Dagda stole both her and the Brú from Elcmar by a trick and some see in this the symbolic marriage of god and river deity. Others regard the ousting of Elcmar as the victory

---

* The Good God. This name for the Dagda is not to be taken as implying that he was good in a moral sense, but rather that he was 'good for everything' (Dillon and Chadwick 1967, 145). Dr T. F. O'Rahilly makes the point that the Dagda and his son, Oengus (the Youthful Hero), were ultimately one and the same person (1946, 516).

of the Goidels, or Gael or Celts, over the former inhabitants. In another version of the story, from the eleventh-century *Book of Lecan,* the Dagda built a great mound for himself and his three sons, 'Aengus, Aed and Cermaid; it was upon these four that the men of Erin made the *síd* (mansion) of the Brugh' (O'Donovan 1851, 22). A story in the *Book of Leinster* (an early-twelfth-century compilation) narrates how Oengus took the Brú from his father, the Dagda, who allowed himself to be persuaded to let his son have the dwelling for a day and a night, and when the Dagda asked for the return of his abode, the son explained that day and night meant forever and so Oengus remained in possession. Oengus's ownership of the Brú is implied in the great romantic tale known in translation as *The Pursuit of Diarmaid and Gráinne,* which gives the moving account of the death of Diarmaid on Ben Bulben in Co. Sligo. When Gráinne came there she found Oengus of the Brú with three hundred of his household gathered about the body of her lover, Diarmaid, and Oengus said: 'I have never been for one night since I took you with me to the Brugh over the Boyne, when you had completed nine months, until tonight that I was not watching you and guarding you against your enemies, Diarmaid, and alas for the treachery that Fionn has done to you.' He continued: 'Horsemen of the fairy-mound without defilement / let Diarmaid of the fine shape be lifted by you / to the Brugh, sweet, full of hosts, everlasting' (Ní Sheaghdha 1967, 99).

The Brú was obviously regarded by the various storytellers not merely as a burial place or mausoleum, but as an abode of some sort into which people could enter and out of which they could emerge at will. It is usually made clear, however, that they are of a supernatural order and that the abode or house is not a conventional one, as an extract from *Bruidhean Chaorthainn* illustrates. A *bruidhean* is another name for a dwelling or mansion and there are a number of bruidhean-tales in the early literature. They are thought to have derived primarily from oral tradition and to exist only secondarily in the manuscripts so that their origins are ancient.

The extract is in the form of a riddle which was posed to Fionn in verse and answered by him in prose: 'I saw a house in the country / out of which no hostages are given to a king, / fire burns it not, harrying spoils it not; / good the prosperity with which was conceived that kingly house.' Fionn answered: 'I understand that verse for that is the Brugh of the Boyne that you have seen, namely, the house of Oengus Óg of the Brugh, and it cannot be burned or harried as long as Oengus shall live...'

Not all stories about the Brú concern mythological personages, some have a supposedly historical context. The Brú was said to have been the burial place of the pagan kings of Tara before the advent of Christianity in the fifth century. Previously they had been buried in the royal cemetery at Cruachain in the west of Ireland, but because the wife of one of the kings was of the Tuatha Dé Danann he asked to be buried at the Brú and it continued to be used by his descendants. This is an obvious rewriting of an old tradition by 'historians' in Christian times and is probably an attempt to aggrandize the dynasty then ruling at Tara, the Uí Néill, by associating their ancestors with the famous Brú. The fact that the chroniclers adverted to the link between the Brú and the Tuatha Dé shows the strength of what must have been even then an old tradition. This invention had a very long life, and even up to the start of the present century the

Boyne tombs were considered to be of first-to-fifth-century AD date, roughly the era to which the pagan kings of Tara would have belonged. Indeed, a story told about the most famous of these pagan kings, Cormac mac Airt, who reputedly lived in the fourth century AD, is still very much alive today. Many myths and legends surround this ancestor–figure of the Uí Néill and there is even a strong probability that he actually existed. The story runs that on his death, his followers tried to take his body across the Boyne to bury him in the Brú with his pagan forbears even though he had declared that he did not wish to be buried in 'a cemetery of idolators'. The River Boyne, however, 'swelled up thrice, so as that they could not come; so that they observed that it was violating the judgement of a prince to break through this testament of the king, and they afterwards dug his grave at Ros na Righ, as he himself had ordered' (Petrie 1845, 98). The traditional site of Cormac's grave on the south side of the river, opposite Newgrange, is pointed out even to the present day.

The archaeological evidence

It has already been shown that many of the findings of the antiquarians and travellers of the eighteenth and nineteenth centuries were later confirmed during the excavations. To what extent can the traditions surrounding Brú na Bóinne, of which only a meagre number have been mentioned above, be validated? The pseudo-historical material which sought to associate the ruling dynasty of the Uí Néill with the older stratum of society represented by the supposed descendants of the Tuatha Dé Danann can be regarded as little more than a clever propaganda exercise. But it was a very sucessful one because even today Newgrange is popularly regarded as the burial place of the kings of Tara rather than as the abode of the all-powerful Dagda and his son, Oengus. The chroniclers of the eighth and ninth century were well aware of the older tradition, but whereas the latter sprang from an oral source the accounts of the 'historians' were written down and had a more widespread dissemination in the long run.

If a connection is to be sought, therefore, between the archaeological evidence and the early literature it is to the older and more genuine tradition we must turn. The concept of Newgrange as a house of the dead and as an abode of spirits at one and the same time, was in no way contradicted by the findings of the excavation. There were the efforts to keep the tomb dry, there was the roof-box through which the sun's rays penetrate at midwinter. Was this to enable a once-yearly visitation by the sun to the gods who dwelt in the Brú, and does it tie in with one of the traditional roles of the Dagda which was that of sun-god? There are the carved symbols on the stones which surely must have had a meaning for those who executed them. The three great Boyne tombs must have been sources of awe, wonder and superstition from very early times, perhaps even from their very beginning; indeed the arousal of these emotions may have played no small part in the minds of their builders in the first place. Perhaps the tombs were built as much to commemorate and arouse respect for the gods or spirits as to provide resting places for the newly-dead. Newgrange, unlike Knowth and Dowth, was not tampered with throughout the thousands of years of its life. Was this because of its particular association with the chief of all the gods, the Dagda and his son, Oengus? Were these the spirits to whom offerings of Roman coins and objects of jewelry were made in the early centuries of the Christian era? It may be of interest to mention that, although far more extensive excavations have taken place at and around the mound of Knowth, no Roman coin has so far been found.

By any standard, Newgrange is a remarkable monument and its architects, artists and artisans must have been of a high cultural level. Can we grant them achievements in these fields and deny them achievements in another – in the possession of an oral literature? Is it fanciful to suggest that the people who built the Boyne tombs had a mythology of their own and a repertoire of poems and stories? To what extent was the design and structure of their monuments governed by their myths and beliefs, perhaps inherited from far-off ancestors in far-off places? The Boyne passage-graves are only one component of a widespread cult of megalith-building and it could be argued that the gods or spirits to whom the people of Newgrange gave allegiance were part of a wide-ranging pantheon or mythology, one which is no longer regarded as being wholly confined to the Celtic realms. Indeed, evidence of a primitive stream in Irish mythology is being propounded by scholars more and more nowadays, following the pioneering work of Myles Dillon, Gerard Murphy and others. As a general rule, however, the most that scholars will allow in regard to the ancient Irish myths and traditions is that they may go back in oral form to the centuries immediately preceding the introduction of Christianity in or about the fifth century, that is, to so-called Celtic times, and that the actual events and persons of these times provide the basis for the material.

In the past three decades archaeologists, as a result of scientific dating techniques, have become accustomed to drastic revisions of chronologies which were previously held to be almost immutable. Radiocarbon dating has shown Newgrange to be a thousand years older than the date popularly assigned it in pre-excavation days and, from having been regarded as an echo of the civilization that had produced Mycenae and Stonehenge, it has come to be recognized in its own right as one of the finest manifestations of Neolithic culture, pre-dating these latter sites by almost a millennium. Perhaps a similar lengthening of perspective is overdue in respect of Irish mythology and heroic saga. One cannot help feeling that the richly accoutred warriors of the Irish Bronze Age are far more convincing prototypes for the *dramatis personae* of the Irish heroic cycle than the shadowy figures revealed by archaeology for the centuries immediately before and after the start of the Christian era. If this were the case it would not only free a great deal of early Irish tradition from the Celtic strait-jacket in which it has hitherto been confined, but it would also bring it nearer in time to the people who built the Boyne tombs. Can it have been they who planted the first seeds of Irish oral literature and should one begin to think of this not as a window on the Iron Age but as one on the Late Neolithic?

Newgrange from afar

1 Air view of Newgrange (between sites z and l) and surrounding area, with the River Boyne at the top of the picture. Note figure-of-eight-shaped pond near site P.

2 Newgrange from the east, after the restoration of the mound.

3,4 The entrance today *(right)*: to the right of the passage mouth stands the closing stone and above it the roof-box. The entrance stone (K1), in the foreground, has a vertical groove *(above)* dividing the decorated face. The relief-bands of K1, each about 4 cm wide, stop at a line corresponding to the ancient ground level.

The restored monument

5,6 The northern side of the mound *(left)* after conservation, showing the richly ornamented kerbstone, K52. In the detail of K52 *(above)*, the vertical groove, about 9 cm wide, divides the ornament into two sharply contrasting panels, a division continued on the top of the stone by a picked line.

Newgrange at midwinter

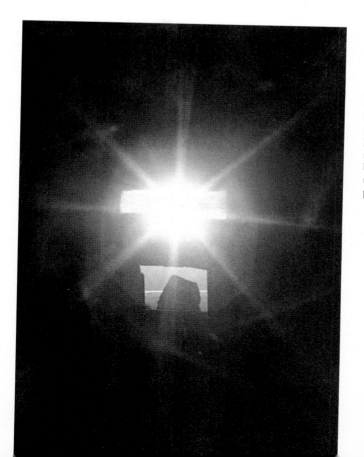

7 The valley in early morning fog, as seen from the tomb entrance. Orthostat GC1 is in the foreground.

8 Midwinter sunrise: at dawn on the shortest day of the year the sun's rays shine through a slit in the floor of the roof-box, illuminating the passage and end recess of the chamber. Since the closing stone is no longer in place, the back of the entrance stone and GC1 (with the River Boyne beyond) are visible through the passage mouth. (Horizontal bar is a modern safety precaution.)

The passage

9–11 *(Left)* Orthostats lining the passage near the entrance. *(Below left)* The chamber and end recess seen from the passage (orthostats L22 on the left and R21 on the right). *(Below right)* The passage viewed from the chamber (R21 on the left and L22 on the right).

The chamber

12–14 *(Above)* The end recess (left) and east recess (right) seen from the chamber. Cf. pls. 57–8. *(Left)* The west recess, with the basin stone in the foreground. Cf. pls. 54–5. *(Below)* The three-spiral (30 cm in width) on orthostat C10 in the chamber. All three spirals are double spirals.

Newgrange and Dowth

15–18 *(Above)* The Newgrange mound from the northeast. *(Below)* Tumulus B on the floodplain of the Boyne. *(Opposite above)* Newgrange before excavations began in 1962. *(Opposite below)* Dowth: note the gradual slope of the mound towards the kerb and the absence of a bank of cairn slip outside it.

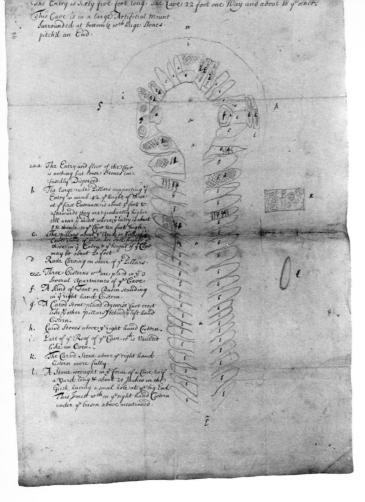

Before excavation

19 Plan of the passage and chamber made for Edward Lhwyd in 1699 or 1700.

20 Apart from its striking ornament, this corbel (Co.1/C15–16) beneath the roof-stone of the east recess is noteworthy for its inscriptions of 'brutish-minded and selfish men's names'.

21 The entrance to Newgrange as it appeared in the romantic days of candlelight and cattle.

22 The kerb in the southern part of the mound showing the partly filled-up trench outside the kerb and the stone revetment (not ancient) above it.

23 The revetment (not ancient) as it appeared while excavation of the cairn slip outside the kerb on the south side was in progress (fallen kerbstone at left is K96; last kerbstone at right is K92).

24 The cairn slip outside K92. The highest part of the bank is formed of material dug from the trench outside the kerb.

The cairn slip

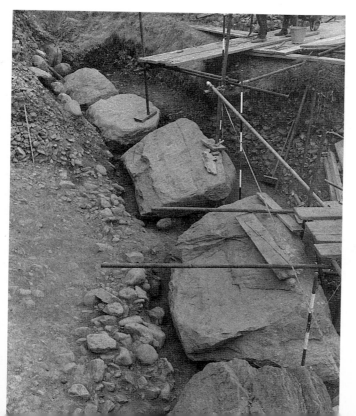

25 The cairn slip outside K53 on the north side of the mound. K52 to the right has not yet been raised to the vertical.

26 Kerbstones 49–53 on the north side of the mound before being raised to the vertical. Cairn at left, bank of slip at right.

27 Two disc or plate brooches of Romano-British type found just below the turf outside the kerb, on the south side.

Oval setting

28–30 Stages in the excavation of the stone setting, east of the tomb entrance, *c*. 2.5 m outside K97. Mixed through the low mound of water-rolled quartz pebbles were fragments of quarried quartz and rounded granite boulders. A setting of small thin slabs *(below)* formed an oval, 3 × 2 m, and served as a border to a pavement, partly cobbled and partly flagged.

Hut foundation

31 Situated west of the tomb entrance, 4 m south of K3, the hut foundation was delineated by a trench enclosing an area approximately 2.8 × 3.8 m (the trench is absent on the northern side – bottom of picture). Although there was insufficient charcoal for a C14 date to be obtained, the hut must be contemporary with, or only slightly later than, the tomb itself.

The great circle

32 The first season's excavation (1962). Seen from the east, the orthostats of the great circle visible here are (reading top to bottom): GC3, GC1, GC-1 and GC-2.

33 Another view of the great circle (nearest orthostat is GC-2), showing in the foreground a large pit, 2 m in diameter, which may have been the socket of GC-3 (now missing).

34 View from the west of the three great circle orthostats opposite the tomb entrance: left to right, GC-2, GC-1 and GC1.

35 GC-1 during excavation. Note the comparatively unweathered area at the bottom, formerly covered by the cairn slip.

The embrasure cutting

36,37 *(Above)* View of the cutting from above the entrance. Note the layers of redeposited turves to the west of the passage. The closing stone, lying prone in the foreground (and *right,* viewed from another angle), was placed in this position in modern times to act as a paving slab for the tomb entry.

4 Methods

Excavation commenced in 1962 and continued every summer for an approximate four-month season up to and including 1975. The first priority was to examine the nature of the bank of cairn slip outside the kerb, particularly along the south or entrance area as it was here that repair and conservation were most urgent. As a preliminary to the excavation, the considerable growth of trees and scrub had to be cleared   plate 17
from the relevant areas so that work could begin; later the whole monument was similarly cleared. A contour plan of the tumulus was made and accurate dimensions for the separate parts of the monument were obtained. The survey was later extended to in-   figs 3, 23
clude the whole ridge on which Newgrange and its three satellite passage-graves stand.

On the south side of the mound, an area extending from K80/81 on the east to K20/21 on the west and comprising a total of 37 kerbstones was excavated. It had a circumferential length of *c.* 110 m and extended from the kerb for an average radial   fig. 5
distance of 22 m, though in the extreme eastern part this was greatly exceeded due to the discovery of a satellite passage-grave, site Z, just where we had expected our southern boundary line to be drawn. As the excavations proceeded, season by season, plans of each section were made and detailed sectional profiles were recorded, each running from the kerb as far as the southern limit of the excavation. In all, 25 profiles were drawn, 12 east of the entrance and 13 west of it.

The slip was excavated on the north side of the mound also, in a cutting centring on K52, the kerbstone diametrically opposite the entrance stone. The cutting was set out in front of K51, 52 and 53 and extended for a radial distance of 27 m. A small lateral extension was made to the cutting so as to include the adjacent kerbstones, K48, 49 and 50. Apart from the need to obtain a profile of the cairn slip on this side of the mound for comparative purposes, another aim was to re-erect K52 which was lying on its face, the ornamented surface of which rivals that of the entrance stone. There was also the necessity to test the oft-repeated theory that the entrance to another passage lay behind K52. In the event, this was not the case.

In the first season we began excavations at the eastern edge of the sector which had originally been designated by the 1961 Committee, the aim being to work westwards to a point just short of the entrance, i.e., from K92 to K96, a distance of 16 m. The sec-   plate 23
tor ran southward from the kerb for a distance of up to 18 m and included orthostat GC-2 of the great circle. At a later stage this area had to be extended still further

southwards in order to follow up medieval ditches and other features. The area was set out in 4 m squares which included dividing baulks, 1 m wide. After the first season we abandoned the system of 4 m squares and when we moved westward in front of and beyond the tomb entrance as far as K6, we made a series of cuttings 3 m wide separated by 1 m-wide baulks. The cuttings extended southwards for an uninterrupted distance of 23-24 m. From K6 westward to K21 – the limit of our excavation in this area – we felt we had sufficient experience of the nature of the terrain to be able to open sectors up to 11 m wide at the kerb and radiating outward from it for a distance of up to 22 m, separated by 1 m-wide baulks. When we began to excavate to the east of where we had commenced in 1962, i.e., from K92 to K80, we adopted yet another system. A grid of 5 m squares undivided by standing baulks was set out and excavated as a single unit; this in many ways proved to be the most satisfactory system of all. At the same time it must be remembered that by then we were able to read the ground both horizontally and vertically with a good deal of confidence and so the small-scale approach of the earlier seasons was no longer called for.

Throughout the excavation of the area outside the kerb, efforts were made to locate the sockets or the previous positions of the presumed missing stones of the great circle. The sockets of existing stones were excavated in each case. The structure of the cairn itself was examined also in a number of cuttings made into the mound behind the

plate 35

5 Plan of the area excavated between 1962 and 1975.

kerb, including one on the north side. The tomb, its design and structure, was surveyed and examined and the floors of passage and chamber excavated. Besides the excavation of these separate parts of the monument, considerable conservation, repair and restoration work (to be described in Part III) was undertaken by the National Parks and Monuments Branch of the OPW, which acted at all times in the closest cooperation with the archaeologists. By 1975 the objectives originally outlined had been achieved and we felt it desirable that the remainder of the site should be left for future generations of archaeologists who, presumably, would have newer and better techniques and fuller knowledge at their disposal.

As it would be needlessly confusing to describe the excavations season by season it is proposed to deal with them under four separate heads: the cairn slip, the great circle, the cairn and the tomb, though it will be appreciated that this order is not a chronological one, since several different operations were usually taking place concurrently.

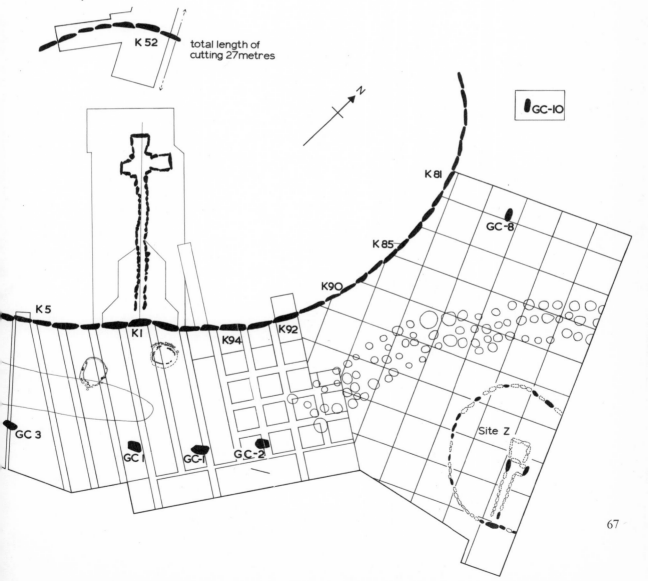

5 The cairn slip

While it was essential to proceed slowly and with the greatest caution in the early stages, it was also necessary to obtain reasonably quickly a series of sectional profiles which would reveal the stratification of the material outside the kerb and indicate its

plate 24

true relationship to the cairn. From immediately below the modern turf the bank of material was found to consist very largely of stones, a material very difficult to read horizontally, but the story became clear when seen in sectional profile. We recorded seven profiles in the first (1962) season, each running from the kerb southward for a distance of up to 18 m. One of them ran from K94 through orthostat GC-2 of the great circle and enabled the way in which this stone had been set up, etc., to be investigated. All the profiles showed the trench which had been cut in the past immediately outside the kerb, so as to expose the kerbstones and which had been many times reopened. Some of the upcast had been thrown back on the cairn and some on the collapse itself where it formed a bank all round the mound, giving rise to the mistaken impression that a bank-and-ditch feature of archaeological origin was present. The profiles showed minor variations from place to place, as was to be expected, but basi-

fig. 6B

cally they were the same throughout, and a profile which commenced at K95 serves as a good exemplar.

The bottom line outside the kerb represents, not an old turf but a subsoil surface from which the turf and humus had been cut off. This was clear, not only from direct observation but also from soil analyses (Gardiner and Walsh 1966). Lying directly in contact with the subsoil surface and spreading for a distance of 6-7 m outward from the kerb is a layer composed entirely of angular pieces of white quartz and water-or glacially-rolled grey granite boulders, the quartz being very much the predominant material. The layer is wedge-shaped in section, thickest at the kerb and tails off to nothing farther out. The layer would originally have been thicker at the kerb face than is shown in the section but the previous trench diggings had removed much of it and it lay scattered on and through the upcast. It was noted that where kerbstones had fallen over fully no quartz or granite lay underneath. Kerbstone 96 is a good example and shows that the quartz was not on the ground outside the kerb before it fell over.

fig. 37

This stone has a series of ornamental scratches on its outer face which are very fine and difficult to see and are in effect little better than 'doodles'. The stone is a rather soft coarsely laminated slate, easily weathered, and had it been exposed to weathering for any considerable period of time the lines would not have survived. It seems therefore

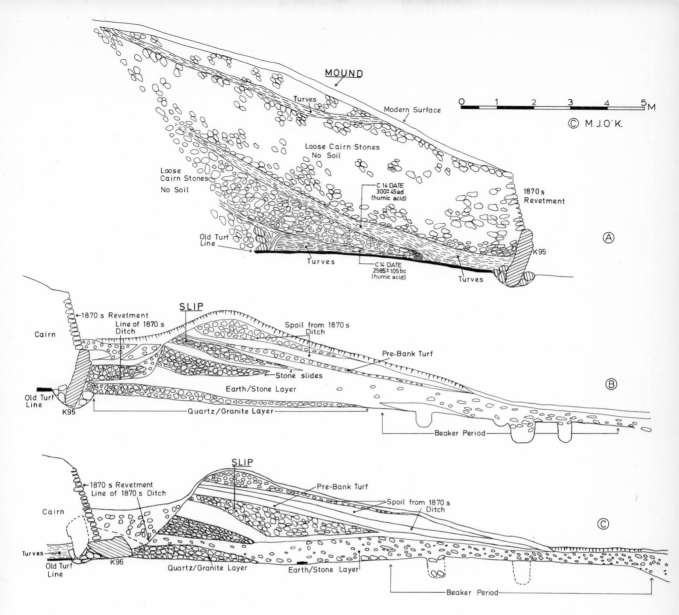

6 A, profile showing the structure of the mound behind K95; B, profile of the cairn slip in front of K95; C, profile of the cairn slip in front of K96.

that it must have fallen over at an early stage and when the quartz revetment gave way it covered the stone.

Above the quartz the profile shows a fairly thick layer of ordinary cairn stones in a matrix of soil, a noteworthy feature of which was the presence in it of innumerable snail shells (Appendix F). During the excavation this was referred to as the earth/stone layer and the term is retained here for convenience. It continued outward beyond the tail of the quartz/granite and petered out at a distance of up to 14 m from the kerb.

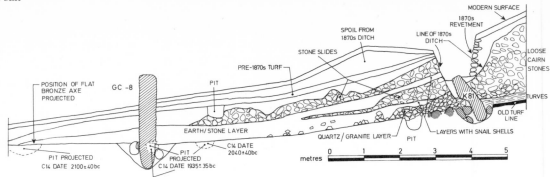

7 Profile through K81 and GC-8, showing positions of radiocarbon (C14) samples and the bronze axe.

This layer was, from an archaeological point of view, the most rewarding one as it contained flint artefacts, pottery, animal bones and a number of bone objects denoting the presence of squatters in Late-Neolithic/Beaker times.

Above the earth/stone layer was a considerable one of loose clean stones with no earth, followed by an earthy stratum representing a stadium in the collapse of the cairn edge when vegetation grew over the spill. Above this was a further wedge-shaped layer of loose clean stones and on top of it the turf layer which developed and persisted until the digging of the trench covered it with upcast.

When the slip had been removed from in front of the kerbstones it was found that, while most of them were set in boulder-packed sockets, e.g. K94, others had been set up on boulders, e.g. K92 and K96. This arrangement seems to have been adopted so that the finished kerb should have as even a top line as possible having regard to the varying sizes and shapes of the slabs and it was later found that the arrangement was a consistent one. All the stones showed an outward cant and some had fallen forward completely, particularly those not packed in deep sockets. Sections through the sockets showed that when originally set up the stones were vertical or even had a slight inward cant, e.g. K96; their subsequent outward tilt is to be explained by the settlement pressures which developed in the great cairn, composed as it was of layers of turves and loose stones.

fig. 6C

The next area to be excavated (from K96 to K6) lay in front of, and at each side of, the tomb entrance and also included three orthostats of the great circle. Twelve further profiles were recorded. As already mentioned, from this area westwards to the limit of the excavation at K21, instead of narrow cuttings, large sectors radial to the kerb were opened up as by this time the interpretation of the slip itself was no longer a problem and our attention was mainly focused on the Late-Neolithic/Beaker settlement which lay on and beyond the slip. Five further profiles, however, were recorded in this western area and when we moved operations to the eastern part of the site yet another was recorded.

fig. 7

The stratification of the slip revealed in all these areas proved consistent with the previous interpretation. We found that the quartz/granite layer was thickest and most extensive in the area outside the tomb entrance and at each side of it and that it de-creased gradually in amount and extent until it had virtually disappeared at K21 in the west and K80 in the east. The earth/stone layer which lay on top of it again contained snail shells and also Beaker-period material, and as before, the layer continued outward beyond the tail of the quartz/granite. Living floors with central stone-set hearths, flint artefacts, flint debitage and much pottery and animal bones were asso-ciated with this layer throughout. (For a report on the animal bones recovered between 1962 and 1965 see Van Wijngaarden-Bakker 1974.)

The north cutting

The upper part of the slip as shown in the profile was in general similar to that found elsewhere. The two major slides of stones were present as was the slow-forming earth/stone layer with snail shells. The latter layer contained few artefacts compared with the south side. Those found were consistent with the Late Neolithic/Beaker-period con-text. There were two striking differences however. When the earth/stone layer was removed there was no quartz beneath it but instead, a layer of carefully selected boulders lay on the ground outside the kerb in the same position as that occupied else-where by the quartz/granite. Another difference was that the boulders were not rest-ing on a subsoil surface but on the sloping surface of a layer of redeposited turves. The edge of the turves lay at 4.5 m outside the base of the kerb and the layer became thicker as it approached the kerb where it was 65 cm in thickness. The old turf and humus layer, much compressed and blue-black in colour, was clearly visible under the redeposited turves and an old turf line was visible also in the part of the cutting not covered by them. The kerbstones were set in sockets dug in the turves and were packed with

fig. 8

plate 25

8 Profile through K53 in the north cutting showing turf mound, positions of snail shells and of C14 and pollen samples.

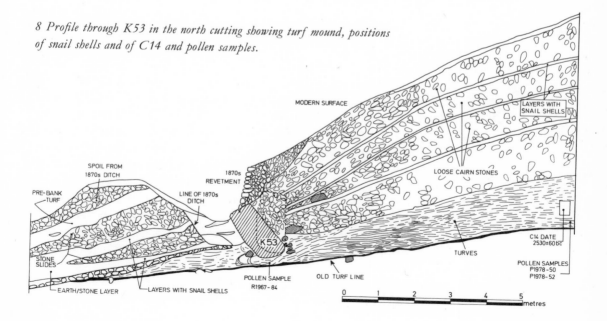

boulders as elsewhere. The slabs in question are all heavy ones, estimated to weigh from 2 to 5 tonnes apiece, and it seems inconceivable that such could have been set into a freshly laid loose and soft layer of sods, because any attempt to do this would have so disturbed the individual sods of turf that they would no longer be recognizable in plan or profile. In fact, they showed no such disturbance, which must mean that the stones were set up when the turves were already consolidated, that is to say, into an existing turf mound. As will be shown later, evidence for the existence of this was obtained when a cutting was made into the cairn behind these kerbstones.

On plan the kerb shows a marked outward bulge in this area, K52 being at the apex of the bulge. That this was deliberate and not due to movement downhill of the kerb-stones, as was thought possible at first, was demonstrated when the sockets were in-

plate 26   vestigated. Kerbstones 49, 50, 51 and 52 were almost in a horizontal position while K48 and 53 were nearly vertical. In all cases, however, the base of the stone was in contact with the socket. When the survey shown in fig. 3 was made the kerbstones were still in the tilted position, and though this exaggerated the bulge somewhat it only amounted to *c.* 1.3 m at its maximum. The peak or bulge is therefore an original feature. Can it have been that the kerb was set out in this way so as to do as little damage as possible to a pre-existing mound? Another question which came to mind at

plate VI   the time concerned the vertical groove which is picked on the front surface of K52 and which continues up over the top edge. Was this designed to indicate that the stone had some particular significance, in this instance that it marked the site of a small pas-sage-grave or other structure under the pre-existing turf mound? There is a similar

plates IV, 3   groove on the front surface of the Newgrange entrance stone (K1); there is one on K47 at Knowth which is directly outside the entrance to the western passage-grave within the main mound; and there is one on the kerbstone outside the eastern tomb (Eogan 1978, pls XVI-XVII).

Interpretation

How were the various layers in the cairn slip to be interpreted? Since the quartz/granite layer was at the bottom all along the southern or front part of the monument it was the first material to fall and it had come down in a fairly rapid and clean collapse. It must therefore have been the material of which the outside of the mound above the kerb was composed and its fall would have been due to the outward movement of the kerbstones as settlement pressures developed behind them and as they themselves shifted from their original positions. Long before we had completed investigation of the slip it had become clear that the simplistic approach of the 1961 Committee – in which we ourselves had shared at the time – could no longer be sustained. The Com-mittee had recommended that 'the original natural sloping face of the mound be re-stored', but the layers identified in the collapse could not have derived from such a sur-face and must have come from a near-vertical one. It had become obvious that the quartz/granite made up this surface at the front of the mound and that elsewhere selected boulders of the normal cairn material had been used, that it had been built on top of the kerb as a revetment and that when it fell there was nothing to hold the cairn behind it in place. A slow roll-down of the upper part of its edge began – the part containing the uppermost layer of turves and whatever humus had developed on top of the finished cairn. This material covered the quartz layer, and vegetation grew on the subsequent mixture of turf and stones, persisting despite the continual slow deterioration of the edge of the cairn.

Next came a sudden great slide of stones, the cause of which is unknown. It could have been due to a sudden thaw after an especially severe frost or, for all one knows, it may have been caused by an earth tremor, such as that experienced in 1979 in southwest Scotland and felt also in northeast Ireland. Vegetation became established on top of the stones of the collapse, marking a period of rest in the deterioration of the mound. There was then another sudden slide of stones and this brought the now sloping edge of the cairn to its angle of repose. The collapse had by this time run outwards as far as the great circle in the area opposite the tomb entrance and well beyond the circle at the east and west where the latter is nearer to the kerb. The kerb and the tomb entrance would have been completely hidden from view. Vegetation grew over the slope and united the true mound with the collapse so that the great circle appeared to mark the perimeter. This was the appearance of the site in the early centuries of the Christian era when Roman coins and objects of Early Iron Age and Romano-British type were deposited along and inside the line of the great circle.

As a check on the interpretation, a new cutting, 2 m wide, was made through the slip at a point which seemed least disturbed by previous investigators. The quartz and granite boulders collected from this cutting were then built as a revetment upon the 2 m length of kerb and the space behind was filled in with the remainder of the excavated material. The revetment finished at 2 m in height – the difference between this and the calculated height of 3 m postulated for the original revetment can be accounted for by several factors. A good quantity of the quartz found in the trial excavation was shattered and could not be used, also a good deal had been removed in the trench diggings of previous years, but the most important reason was that at the point selected for our trial trench the quartz facing was tending to peter out, although we did not realize this until several seasons later. We caused the newly-built revetment to collapse so as to compare the new stratification with the original. In the lower layers the results were well-nigh identical, such slight differences as existed being due to the fact that turves had not been incorporated into the upper part of the rebuilt cairn.

The succession of events deduced from excavation of the collapse and tested by experiment demolished the old notion that an ancient 'bank-and-ditch' feature existed outside the kerb. Demolished also was the 'shapely hemispherical mound of stones, the entire surface of which was covered with a layer of broken fragments of quartz', as it was described in the guidebook to the monument current before the excavations. It has been understandably difficult for those who knew Newgrange in the romantic days plates VII, 21 of candlelight to accept the fact that, when originally built, the mound was drum-like rather than dome-shaped. Those who accept the 'new archaeology' of Newgrange, however, can observe for themselves how much more impressive it now is than if it had been restored to a bogus hemispherical shape in accordance with the misconceptions of earlier days.

Archaeological content

Almost 1000 flint artefacts and 65 kg of flint debitage (comprising an estimated 10,000 waste flakes) were recovered from the area excavated outside the kerb, both on the south side and in the north cutting; this included the cairn slip and the area beyond it as far as the limit of the excavation. In addition, 274 finds of pottery were registered, most of which represented multiple numbers of sherds. Objects of stone, bone, glass and metal were recovered and there were important finds of Roman coins. There was a vast quantity of animal bones, some of which have already been reported upon and a further report is ready. None of this impressive list of finds, however, can be associated with the actual builders of the monument.

Forty to forty-five per cent of the flint and about seventy-five per cent of the pottery was found in an area between 4 m and 10 m from the kerb in the lowest levels of the slip, i.e. in the earth/stone layer, or more exceptionally, in the quartz immediately beneath it. These finds, together with some of the bone and stone objects, form part of a Late Neolithic/Beaker complex and will be dealt with in a future publication. A number of other finds came from the topmost layer, i.e. just under the sod and date in the main from the first to the fourth centuries AD. We recovered 19 Roman coins of that period, consisting of 6 gold, 2 gold uniface pendants, 4 silver coins and 7 copper coins. Together with those found in 1842 and in 1699 the coins amount in all to 25 specimens. Ornaments of comparable date to the coins were also found: the hook-end of a gold torc on which Roman letters (the significance and meaning of which are so far unknown) are inscribed, 2 disc brooches of fairly common Romano-British type, finger rings, bracelets, a melon bead, a bronze strap loop and a 'packet' consisting of a piece of tightly folded gold foil. More than a score of glass 'pinheads', similar to beads but without a through-perforation, were also found just beneath the surface cover. Together with the 'Conyngham find' of 1842, these objects form an impressive collection and a case has been made (Carson and O'Kelly 1977) that many of them, including the coins, represent votive deposits made during the early centuries of the Christian era. A small amount of medieval pottery was found also, mainly recovered from two parallel ditches which ran east-west outside the line of the great circle.

A few artefacts were found beneath the quartz/granite layer, i.e. in the area within 6 m of the kerb, but by and large this part was devoid of finds. Since this was a subsoil surface one must presume that whatever objects had been dropped during the construction of the monument were removed with the turf when it was stripped. It must be mentioned that an old turf surface was clearly detectable inside the kerb and it was clear too that the sockets for the kerbstones had been dug through it, therefore the stripping outside the kerb was done after the kerb was set up. When the quartz fell from the cairn it fell on to a subsoil surface; this was to be observed in all the profiles recorded along the southern part of the mound and one must conclude either that it fell before turf had had time to re-establish itself after the first stripping or else that the stripping took place more than once. This turf stripping was not found outside the kerb on the north side. It is not known how long a period elapsed between the finishing of the cairn and the collapse of its edge. Between the radiocarbon dates obtained

plate 27

plate XI

74

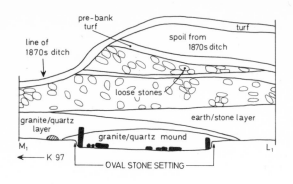

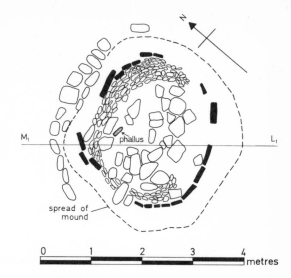

9 Plan and section of the oval stone setting.

for the tomb structure and those obtained for pottery-associated material in the far eastern part of the excavation there is an interval of 500 radiocarbon years. During this period the layer of quartz/granite was formed and also the slow-forming earth/stone one which overlay it and extended beyond it. The various concentrations of flint, pottery and animal bones in the latter layer, together with hearths, living floors, and so on, point to a fairly intensive occupation by Late Neolithic/Beaker-period squatters. There is reason to believe that similar squatting took place in at least part of the unexcavated area, for when S. P. Ó Ríordáin excavated the then fallen orthostat of the great circle (GC–10) on the northeast of the mound, he found evidence of what he judged to be a 'temporary occupation of the area' in the form of postholes, flint and a layer of charcoal which stopped at the socket of GC–10 and was not found in its fill (Ó Ríordáin and Ó hEochaidhe 1956,56).

fig. 7

Two features – an oval setting and a hut foundation – were found on the subsoil surface outside the kerb, the first of which may reasonably be related to the early use of the monument, while the second appears to pre-date the squatting at the latest.

Oval setting

This feature was found east of the tomb entrance about 2.5 m outside K97, the kerbstone immediately to the right of the entrance stone. It was covered by the quartz boulders of the collapse and when these were removed a low oval mound of waterrolled quartz pebbles, each about the size of a medium potato, was found and mixed through it were fragments of quarried quartz and rounded boulders of grey granite. There were 607 water-rolled quartz pebbles, 103 granite boulders and 612 fragments of quarried angular quartz. The total spread of the mound measured approximately 4 × 3.4 m and it was about 50 cm in height. Protruding through it were the tops of a setting of small thin slabs forming an oval, 3 × 2 m. The largest of the slabs, which

figs 5, 9

plate 28

stood in the northern arc of the oval, was roughly triangular in shape, having a basal length of 65 cm and a height of 46 cm, set with the apex upwards. It was 8 cm in maximum thickness and was of soft friable mica-schist. Its western sloping edge had a horizontal slot 1 cm wide and 12 cm deep at a height of 18.5 cm above the base.

When the covering of quartz and granite pebbles was removed these standing slabs were found to form a border to a pavement partly cobbled and partly flagged. Lying as a cobble in the northwest quadrant was a highly polished piece of sandstone, 24 cm in length, oval in cross-section, 7.4 cm × 4.5 cm, and displaying a fractured surface at one end and a blunt polished point at the other – a phallus? It lay east-west, pointed end to the east. Two flint artefacts were found, a blade and what may be a fragment of a flint knife; the former was in the heap of pebbles and the other came from the pavement beneath. The function of the feature remains unknown but a similar one is known to exist near the entrance to Cairn T at Loughcrew and Eogan has found somewhat similar ones at Knowth (Eogan 1974, 15). All are marked by the presence of quartz pebbles within a stone setting. It must be taken as certain that the settings are associated with the primary use of the monuments.

plates 29, 30

fig. 56

Hut foundation

figs 5, 10
plate 31

The second feature, clearly a hut foundation, was situated west of the tomb entrance, 4 m south of K3. When the overlying slip was being excavated a considerable amount of habitation refuse, consisting of flint, animal bones and a good deal of pottery, was found in the earth/stone layer. It extended over the area of the hut and southwards beyond it but at this stage the presence of the hut foundation was not suspected. Most of the pottery was decorated and there were many sherds of typical beaker. When the underlying quartz layer was excavated, further finds of flint and animal bone were present but no pottery. When this layer was removed a hollow was perceptible in the ground filled with dark earth and flecks of charcoal and it was only when this material in turn was excavated and removed that the outline of a hut was revealed.

The western half of the hut was marked by a foundation trench, *c*. 40 cm wide and 15–20 cm deep, in which were 6 irregularly spaced postholes averaging 12–13 cm in diameter and 22–25 cm in depth. There were a number of quartz boulders in the side of the trench. At the south the hut was defined by a row of small stones set upright and 3 postholes were present while at the east there was a suggestion of a trench and 2 or possibly 3 further postholes. The floor of the hut was lower than the surrounding old ground surface, particularly at the east where it was as much as 15–20 cm lower. On the north the outline of the floor overran the centre of a circular area, 1 m in diameter, which consisted of burnt earth and charcoal which clearly pre-dated the hut as part of it had been cut away for the hut floor. Because of the absence of postholes or slot trench the hut may have been open towards the north. The external dimensions of the hut were: N-S 4.2 m; E-W 3.2 m. Only a few finds were recovered. A portion of a flint axe was found outside the row of stones on the south and a microlithic point and a hollow scraper came from the same general area. In the fill of the foundation trench there was a fragment of a stone bowl.

figs 56, 57

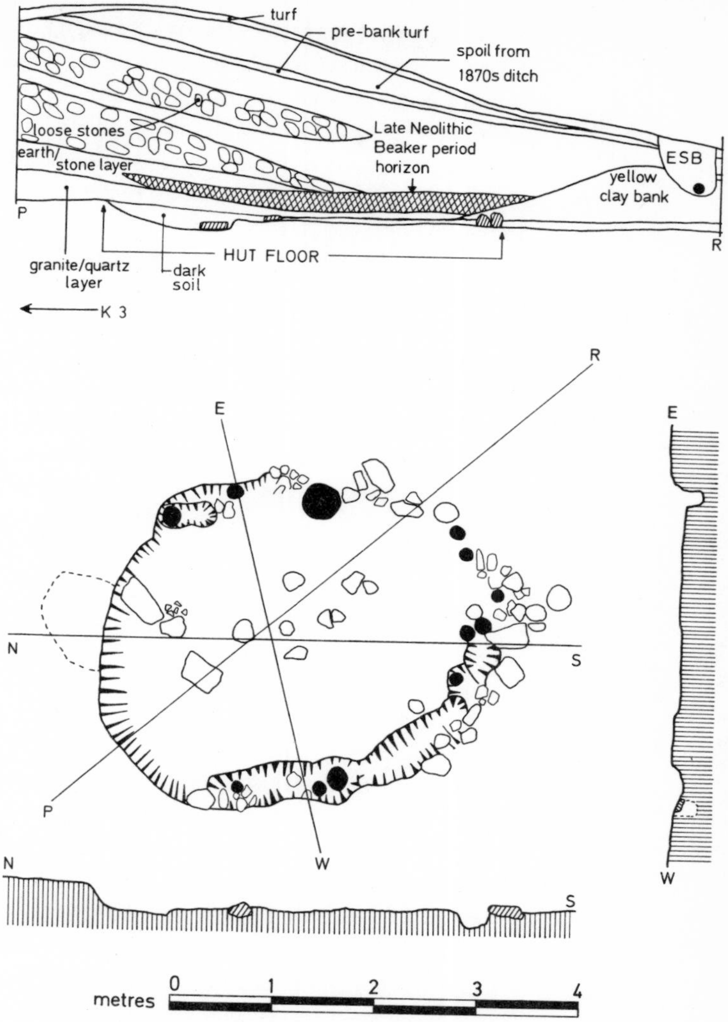
turf
pre-bank turf
spoil from
1870s ditch
loose stones
earth/
stone layer
Late Neolithic
Beaker period
horizon
ESB
yellow
clay bank
P
R
HUT FLOOR
granite/quartz
layer
dark
soil
K 3
R
E
E
N
S
P
W
W
N
S
metres
0
1
2
3
4

*10 Plan and sections of the hut foundation (*ESB *= modern electricity cable).*

The hut pre-dated both the earth/stone layer and the quartz one, though since at its nearest point the hut was 4 m from the kerb, the quartz was already tailing off. At its farthest point, *c.* 8 m from the kerb, there would have been little or no trace of it as a layer though random boulders of both quartz and granite were consistently found at a considerable distance from the kerb. The quartz boulders in the foundation trench were at the southern limit of the hut and could thus have rolled there from the mound after it had begun to decay but it may also be that they were placed there deliberately. It was unfortunate that sufficient charcoal for radiocarbon dating could not be obtained but at any rate the hut must be regarded as early, being either contemporary with the monument or somewhat, though not much, later. If the hut were contemporary with the primary use of the tomb could it have been a mortuary house of the kind found at Tustrup and elsewhere in Denmark (Becker 1973, 75)?

Bank of boulder clay

fig. 5   Another feature which emerged for the first time in the same area and which has a bearing on the Beaker-period occupation level may be mentioned briefly, detailed discussion being reserved for a future publication. This was a low bank of almost stoneless yellow boulder clay which paralleled the kerb from about K2 westward to the limit of the excavation at K21. Outside K2 it was *c*. 8 m from the kerb, at K6 it was 6.5 m and thereafter it was between 5.5 m and 4.5 m from it. It averaged 5.5 m in width and about 60 cm in maximum height, tailing off to nothing at its north and south edges. It is to be assumed that the bank as we found it was collapsed and that it would have been higher and narrower in its original state. The earth/stone occupation layer ran underneath the bank and also ran up along the northern shoulder so it must have been erected while this layer was being formed and while the Beaker-period squatters were in occupation. Its northern edge just overlay the southern edge of the hollow beneath which was the hut foundation. We were unable to explain the function of the bank and are likewise in the dark as to where the material for its construction was obtained.

6 The great circle

Twelve orthostats of the great circle are present today, exactly as in 1699 when the monument was first brought to public notice. For convenience during the excavations it was necessary to number them, as was done with the other structural stones, but since the spacing was irregular it had to be decided whether to number the existing stones consecutively or to allow for the possibility that other orthostats or their sockets would be discovered. The latter course was the one adopted. There are three consecutive orthostats opposite the tomb entrance with a spacing of 8.5 m and 9 m respectively between each pair, measured centre to centre, and this was taken as an indication of the spacing which might be expected if a regular circle had been erected in the first instance. The most westerly of the three orthostats stands almost directly opposite the tomb entrance, and since the best north-south axis for a reconstructed circle runs through it, the stone was numbered great circle 1 (GC1). Proceeding clockwise, i.e., westwards, the other existing orthostats were numbered GC3, 5, 7, 9, 11, 13 and 17, because it was apparent that in theory there was space for a single stone between each pair from GC1 to GC13 and space for three between GC13 and GC17. Since there were no orthostats visible north of GC17, we recommenced the numbering from the starting point and proceeded anticlockwise from GC1, prefixing the minus sign; thus, in the eastern arc there are GC–1, –2, –8 and –10. We calculated that had the circle been complete and fairly regularly spaced, with a distance varying from 7 m to 9 m between each pair of stones, it would have contained from 35 to 38 orthostats. It must be stressed, however, that very little evidence was forthcoming in the excavated areas for the original presence of these 'missing' stones and the system of numbering must not be taken as anything more than a convenience for excavation purposes. One must be prepared to accept the thesis that the circle may never have been complete. It is also possible to argue that the wide or double spacing shown from GC1 westwards is original and that this spacing was originally mirrored in the eastern arc from GC–2 eastwards, though the only present survivors are GC–8 and GC–10. If GC15 or its socket is ever found, this would lend weight to the argument. The matter is of course highly speculative and it has been gone into in some detail only because of the present interest in the mathematical and astronomical possibilities which are alleged to be inherent in these structures.

plate II

fig. 3

Excavation

plate 33

fig. 11c

fig. 5

One of the aims of the excavations, as outlined by the 1961 Committee, was to investigate the circle and to establish if the gaps in its circumference had originally contained orthostats, and further, to endeavour to establish the chronological relationship between circle and cairn. In the first season a pit, 2 m in diameter and 1 m in depth, was found opposite K91/92 in line with the circumference of the circle and approximately 9 m east of the existing GC–2. Near the latter a number of sharply broken boulders of diorite were found, one of them weighing about 100 kg. Nearby and just under the turf was an iron wedge and we felt at the time that we had found fragments of the missing GC–3 and also the implement used in splitting it. On the other hand, when a multiple arc of up to 70 great pits was found several seasons later, extending from the eastern limit of the excavation towards the area now under discussion, we wondered whether the supposed socket may not more convincingly have belonged to this feature.

East of the supposed GC–3 we found no further evidence until we came opposite K85 although, if a regular spacing had been maintained there should have been two further sockets, those of GC–4 and –5. Opposite K85, however, an oval boulder-packed pit was found at old ground level, 2.3 m in diameter at its mouth and narrowing to 70 × 50 cm at the bottom and 50 cm deep. Since neither the butt nor any fragment of a broken stone was present one cannot say that the pit had contained orthostat GC–6 and again it must be queried whether it was not part of the multiple arc. One must also allow for the possibility that orthostats may originally have been present both here and in the pit already mentioned but were later removed to facilitate the construction of the multiple arc. The space between the supposed GC–6 and the next extant stone, GC–8, is 15 m and therefore another socket might have been expected but none was found. It will be appreciated that we were constantly on the alert for such traces. The space between GC–8 and the next existing stone, GC–10, is approximately 16 m, again sufficient for another upright, but this area has not been excavated. GC–10, which at the time of our excavation was lying prone, had been investigated twice previously (p. 41). We relocated its socket and re-erected it in 1973 although it was outside the excavation area. There are no further orthostats between this point and GC17 in the northwest, or at least, none that are detectable since the area has not been excavated except for the cutting on the north side which failed to produce any pit or trace of a socket. If the single spacing of between 7 m and 9 m was maintained, an orthostat or its socket should have been found in this cutting, but if the spacing was the double one averaging from 14 m to 16 m this would not necessarily have been the case.

As far as the western arc of the circle is concerned the evidence was not a great deal more conclusive. The area midway between GC1 and GC3, where a stone was presumed to have stood, was investigated separately both by Hartnett and by Ó Ríordáin but no socket was found. Ó Ríordáin concluded that if a stone had been present it must have been balanced on a flat base in a slight hollow in the ground, a hypothesis which is in keeping with methods adopted by the circle builders because our excava-

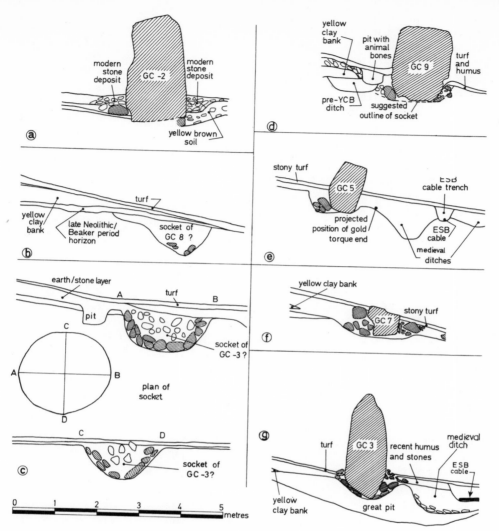

11 *Profiles through the sockets (or presumed sockets) of the orthostats of the great circle.*

tion showed that GC–2 was balanced in such a way. It had no socket but boulders had been used under one side of the base to ensure that the stone stood vertically. Ó Ríordáin also made a cutting which sectioned the next extant orthostat on the west, GC3. He found that it stood in a deep socket-hole and was wedged by large packing stones. Since this upright was leaning towards the east and since one of our profiles ran from K6 southwards through and beyond it, we resolved to undertake a thorough re-examination and eventually to restore it to the vertical.

fig. 11a

fig. 11g

The orthostat was found to be a large and very heavy slab and before long the answer to its inclined condition was forthcoming. Before it had been erected a great bowl-shaped hollow, oval in plan, about 10.5 × 7.5 m, had been dug in the boulder clay. A few scraps of animal bones lay in the bottom of the hollow and it was found that three pits, each approximately 1 m in diameter, had been dug. These also contained animal bones (some of which were in anatomical articulation) and there were a few fragments of antler. It has been suggested that the pits could have been used as storage places for meat and for the raw materials for making bone objects (van Wijngaarden-Bakker 1974, 366). The great pit or hollow appears to have been quickly filled in again and the base of GC3 stood partly on the undisturbed boulder clay at the west edge and partly on the fill, a little more than half of the slab being on the soft fill. Hence, soon after it was set up it began to lean to the east, becoming stabilized before it fell over. After excavation the slab was moved back to the vertical and its eastern base was supported by a concrete podium, concealed by the back-fill of soil. The time-relationship between the pit and the building of the mound is not known, but clearly it was earlier than the circle. Furthermore, the great hollow is earlier than the Beaker-period settlement as a hearth was constructed on the fill of the pit and just north of this the Beaker-period bank of boulder clay overlay part of it.

Approximately midway between GC3 and GC5 we found a pit, 70 cm deep and 1.5 m in diameter, which could have been a socket, but a few metres to the east there was a similar pit and this takes somewhat from the force of the argument. There were several such pits throughout this whole area. A similar one lay midway between GC5 and GC7 and in this case a circle of boulders which could have served as packing surrounded it. West of GC7 there was another possible socket consisting of a pit in the boulder clay, 2 m in diameter and 83 cm deep, which had been filled with loose soil and some small boulders. Beaker-period habitation material extended over the fill and the boulder-clay bank overlay its inner edge. If this pit had in fact contained an orthostat (GC8), it must already have been removed prior to the advent of the Beaker-period settlers. Our excavation ended at the next orthostat, GC9.

fig. 11b
fig. 11d

The relationship of circle and cairn

Two facts are certain: the first is that the circle was erected before the cairn had collapsed – this is clear from the way in which the cairn slip had mounded up against the existing stones. It was also noted by Ó Ríordáin in his investigation of GC–10; he said that 'the stone was erected clear of the edge of the cairn and . . . it fell before any collapse took place because none of the cairn material lay beneath it' (Ó Ríordáin and Ó hEochaidhe 1956, 56). The second fact is that the circle is earlier than the Late Neolithic/Beaker-period settlement. Everywhere in the excavations along the southern perimeter it was found that the existing orthostats were in position before the habitation began, and indeed GC–2 had been incorporated into the wall of a rectangular structure of that period, the foundation trenches of which ended just east and west of the stone. Similar evidence regarding GC–10 has already been mentioned. The circle, therefore, is not later than the Beaker-period horizon, dated at Newgrange to 2000 bc, and it may be contemporary with or earlier than the cairn. If earlier, could it be that some of the stones were removed for use in the kerb? Three of the twelve extant stones (GC3, –8 and –10) are large and heavy slabs of greywacke, the material of the vast majority of the structural stones of the passage-grave, but are too large to have been used in its construction. Two others (GC11 and 17) are also of greywacke, but they are boulders rather than slabs. GC5 is limestone and the six others are of various kinds of igneous rocks and none is slab-like; they are rather shapeless elongated boulders and quite unsuitable for building purposes. Presumably they are glacial erratics and were collected from the neighbourhood rather than from the vicinity of the parent outcrops.

The 1961 Committee had recommended that when the sockets of missing orthostats were found they should be marked at the surface, but we decided that there was too much uncertainty in relation even to the putative ones for this course to be followed. Had we done so, it would have been only a matter of time before the markers became accepted as definite, despite any number of written doubts and reservations on our part. We leave it to future excavators to pursue the matter further.

The relative shapes of circle and mound

Two contour surveys of the entire monument were made, comprising both mound and great circle, one by us in 1962 and another by Dr Jon Patrick in 1970 when he was lecturer in Surveying at the Bolton Street College of Technology in Dublin. Using the Patrick survey as a basis and acting in consultation with him and with Mr John Barber, MA, then in the Department of Archeology, University College Cork, whose field of study was the stone circles of Cork and Kerry, we investigated the various theories which had been propounded, notably by Professor Alexander Thom and by Dr Euan MacKie, concerning a possible geometrical layout for the monument.

Neither the kerb nor the circle are truly circular, nor is the circle equidistant from the kerb. In the south, the circle is 17 m from the kerb, in the west it approaches to within 7 m of the kerb, and in the northwest 9 m. Both, however, are ovoid, with the blunt or broad part at the south and the pointed part at the north (though this is less clear-cut as far as the northern part of the circle is concerned, since no stones are present). The cairn has been alleged to come within the category of egg-shaped monuments, the broad part of the cairn being shown as half an ellipse and the pointed part formed of arcs of circles centred on the corners of two opposed right-angled triangles (MacKie 1977, 72). The axis of symmetry is represented as running from the east end of the entrance stone northwards to the east end of K51. While there is a quite good correspondence between the two portions thus divided, we have found that equally good axes run from the centre of the entrance stone to the centre of K52 or to K51/52. In no case, however, is the symmetry exact, not even in the small-scale plans depicted in the several publications which in recent years have dealt with this matter. (In the illustration in MacKie, *loc. cit.*, for example, the scale is approximately 1:790.) In our investigations we used the largest plan which could conveniently be handled, i.e., to a scale of 1:50, and it was evident that what had appeared as a minute deviation from the geometrical layout in the smaller plans, was quite considerable in the larger one. How much greater still must that deviation be on the ground? We concluded that if the builders of Newgrange had wished to set out the kerb on the lines proposed by

MacKie and others, it would scarcely have been beyond their powers to do so in a more accurate manner than is the case.

An even greater lack of conformity to a geometrical layout is evident in the great circle, nor do any of the axes of symmetry which work fairly well for the cairn fit the circle. The best axis which we could find for a hypothetically reconstructed circle was one running from the centre of GC1 northwards through the eastern end of K52 (there is no circle orthostat *in situ* in the northern arc), but even this was far from satisfactory. Too few stones are present on which to base a geometrical layout even were we confident that such had been employed.

fig. 2   Whether or not the people of Newgrange used some as yet unknown system in the setting out of the kerb and great circle, several interesting points have emerged with regard to the siting of several of the monuments in the Newgrange and Dowth areas. They were brought to light by Dr Patrick during a survey of the whole area with sophisticated equipment and appear in an unpublished thesis.* It was noted that Newgrange and sites E, F and H lie in a straight line, as do the Dowth tumulus and sites F, D and C. Sites U and C are equidistant from site A; similarly, C and D are equidistant from U. Lines connecting sites A and B, sites B and D, and sites D and E are almost identical in length (471 m, 475 m and 479 m respectively) – Patrick considers a discrepancy of up to 5 m in that distance admissable. Lines connecting Newgrange to site A, and site U to C are parallel (bearings 138° 32′ and 137° 50′ respectively), as are lines connecting sites B and C and sites U and E (bearings 6° 34′ and 7° 34′). Patrick concluded that 'the evidence suggests but does not prove that a geometrical/astronomical design was used to fix the position of the monuments'. He also indicated that Newgrange appeared to be the focal point of the group.

There are so many imponderables involved in these correspondences that one is tempted to dismiss them as mere coincidence, but in conjunction with the fact that Newgrange itself was deliberately orientated in the direction of the midwinter sunrise, one must be wary of dismissing these indications of alignment and positioning as mere chance. The question deserves to be left open for the present.

* 'Investigation into the astronomical and geometrical characteristics of the passage-grave cemeteries at the Boyne valley, Carrowkeel and Loughcrew' by J. Patrick, PhD, ARMIT, Dip. L. Surv. (1972).

7 The cairn

In the early years of the excavation (1962 and 1963) we made two cuttings into the cairn, one behind kerbstone 92 and the other, a deeper one, behind K95 so as to examine the cairn structure and also to endeavour to relate it to the slip outside the kerb. In order to enable the orthostats of the front part of the passage to be straightened up, another and more extensive cutting had to be made above and on each side of the passage. A number of further smaller sections were excavated behind some of the kerbstones west of the entrance, so that in all we were able to form a good idea of the way in which this southern part of the mound perimeter was constructed. The cutting made into the cairn on the north side presented somewhat different features and will be described separately.

fig. 5

 The cuttings on the south side showed that the mound had a layered structure consisting of stones interspersed with layers of turves. At the bottom, running inward under the mound from the back of the kerb was a very marked old turf and humus layer, compressed by the weight of the superincumbent mound to a thickness of 5–10 cm. It was blue-black in colour and this rendered it very visible, particularly against the yellow of the boulder clay below and it could be seen that the kerbstone sockets had been cut through it. Its surface was marked by a thin pan layer of iron oxide, bright red in colour, leached out from the higher levels of the mound. In several sections it could be seen that the old turf was overlain by a layer of redeposited turves, running from the back of the kerb into the cairn structure. In a deep cutting such as that behind K95, three such layers could be seen, two of them low down in the body of the cairn and one much higher up. In the lower layers the individual turves were clearly identifiable, both horizontally as well as in section, though of course they were very much compressed. That they were so visible means that there cannot have been much movement in the mound except by way of downward compression. The uppermost layer of turves where it survived did not show the individual turves so clearly because its structure had been upset by lateral movement of the stones above and below it. Where the turf layers occurred they were separated by thick layers of loose stones with no soil in the interstices.

fig. 6A

 The turves varied in colour from place to place, probably owing to the differences in the soil and vegetation of the areas from where they were cut. The vegetational surfaces were seen in section as dark-grey to black streaks of varying thicknesses depending on the amount and nature of the vegetation growing on them at the time they were cut and on the amount of compression that had subsequently taken place. The clods of topsoil making up the bodies of individual turves varied in colour from a light blue-grey to almost white, and in certain cases where the content of organic matter was very high, there were marked bright blue streaks of vivianite resulting from chemical changes which took place long after the turves had been deposited. The soil chemistry of these colour changes has been dealt with elsewhere (M. J. O'Kelly 1951). It could be seen also that most of the turves were laid with the vegetational surfaces upward. They were mainly small in area, approximately 30×40 cm, but there were many long turves, 60 to 70 cm in length, and there were also lengths of 2 to 2.5 m. These latter must have been rolled up when cut and unrolled when brought into position. In every case the bottom course of the layer of cairn stones resting on a turf layer had become cemented on to it by a bright red deposit of iron oxide leached out from higher up in the mound.

We experimented with cutting turves in the area. On a good grass-growing field surface the thinnest turf which could be cut with a steel spade and which would hold together during transport averaged 10 cm in thickness, and with a less efficient implement, such as the wooden spades which may have been used by the Newgrange builders, the turves could scarcely have been cut so thinly. Using the 10 cm thickness which we were able to achieve, it was possible to gain some idea of the original thickness of a deposit of turves.

Cairn profile K95

fig. 6 A   In the cutting behind K95 the innermost point reached at the base was at a distance of 7 m from the back of the kerb and at the top of the cutting it was 12 m. It will be appreciated that it was both difficult and dangerous to make cuttings such as this into a cairn of loose stones; one false move and the whole profile fell down very suddenly. The sides of the cutting were cliff-like, being up to 5.5 m high. It would have been of great interest to continue the cutting farther into the cairn to see if the turf layers were a constant feature as one approached the centre, but this could not have been done without risk and it would also have entailed the removal of a vast amount of the cairn, something which did not seem archaeologically justifiable. One may presume, however, that there are other turf layers farther in.

fig. 6 A   The figure shows, at the innermost point of the cutting, a layer of cairn stones at the bottom, held at its outer edge by a roughly built line of boulders, three courses high. Because at this stage we were operating at a distance of approximately 7 m from the kerb, we could not pursue the bottom layer of cairn stones any further but we were satisfied that the courses of large boulders were intended to retain or revet the edge. A layer of turves was laid on the old ground surface running from the retaining boulders towards the kerb. In front of the boulders it was from twelve to fourteen turves thick and it tailed off to nothing at a distance of *c.* 2.7 m from the back of K95. It also ran as a thin layer over the course of boulders and over the cairn stones behind them at the inner end of the cutting. Shrinkage and movement of the turves took place just in front of the retaining boulders and turves from above slipped into the space

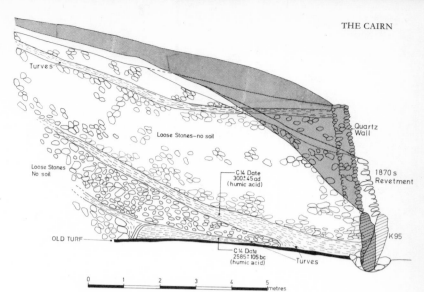

12 Suggested original appearance of the periphery of the mound above K95.

created by the shrinkage. The divisions between the turves here were very clearly marked by lines of rust-red iron oxide leached out from above and deposited in the interstices into which the leaching water was easily able to run. The next layer of cairn stones was then put on, finishing at a point *c*. 2.3 m from the kerb and its toe was again roughly retained by boulders. K95 must have been in position and its socket packed with large stones when the second layer of turves was put in place. This layer ran from the back of the kerbstone upward over the second layer of cairn stones and where it rested on the old ground surface we were able to determine that it was eight turves thick. A great layer of cairn stones lay on top of the second turf layer, 3 m in maximum height as found during the excavation. Another layer of turves was put over these cairn stones and the profile shows that its outer end stopped approximately 3.5 m (measured horizontally) from the back of the kerb. Originally it, and the thick layer of cairn stones beneath, would have run as far as a point almost vertically over the kerb where it would have been held by a revetment wall on top of the kerb. Above this third turf layer a further layer of cairn stones was laid and this was 75 cm at its maximum thickness as found. If it were continued outward to the line of the kerb at approximately that thickness the original revetment wall on the kerb would have had to be at least 3 m high if the various layers were to remain in place. That a revetment *fig. 12* originally existed was a conclusion forced on us only after several seasons of excavation and prolonged and thorough study of the various profiles. It became clear that the demonstrably missing portions at the outer edge of the mound, together with the revetment wall, must have constituted the material then lying as slip on and outside the kerb.

Embrasure cutting

When it was decided that the orthostats at the outer end of the passage should be *figs 13, 14* straightened up it proved necessary to cut deeply into the cairn above and at each side

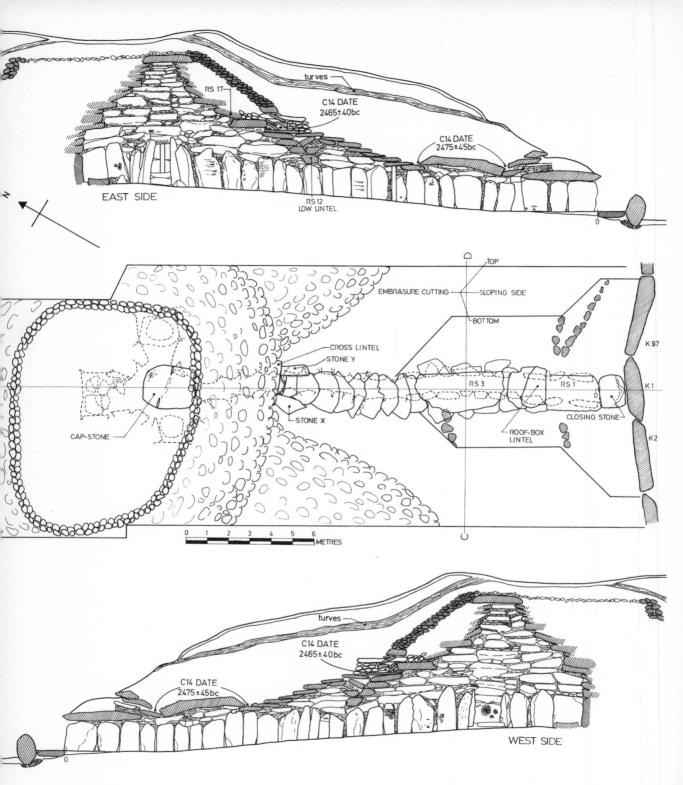

EAST SIDE

turves

RS 17

C14 DATE 2465±40bc

C14 DATE 2475±45bc

RS 12 LOW LINTEL

N

0

TOP

EMBRASURE CUTTING — SLOPING SIDE

BOTTOM

K 97

CROSS LINTEL

STONE Y

RS 3

RS 1

K 1

STONE X

ROOF-BOX LINTEL

CLOSING STONE

CAP-STONE

K 2

0 1 2 3 4 5 6
METRES

turves

C14 DATE 2465±40bc

C14 DATE 2475±45bc

WEST SIDE

0

13 Plan of the embrasure cutting; also elevations of the east and west sides of the passage and chamber before restoration of the front part of the passage.

of the passage structure. This gave a further opportunity to study the composition of the cairn. The material was first taken off roof-slab 1 (RS1) of the passage, the cutting being gradually widened and extended inward over the remainder of the passage roof. This exposed the hitherto unknown roof-box of which only the lintel could previously be seen. The cairn material was particularly loose here on account of disturbances in the past. Because of this looseness the cutting took the form of a great embrasure, *c.* 6.5 m from east to west and 10 m north to south at ground level, with the passage more or less centrally placed. The cutting sloped back on all sides so that a much wider area was exposed in the upper part than at ground level – a width of *c.* 13 m east-west. At the innermost point reached, the cutting was 6.5 m in height. As the sides were cleaned down it was surprising to find that a very similar embrasure must have been present originally, the sloping sides of which were covered by a layer of redeposited turves that began about a metre behind the passage orthostats and came about halfway up the slope of the embrasure. The bottom line of the turves swung *fig. 14* towards the kerb on each side of the passage so as to connect into the back of K 96 on the east and K 3 on the west. It would seem that a space had been left by the builders in which the outer part of the passage could be erected, the layers of turves acting to prevent the cairn material from sliding in on them and when the passage and the roof-box above it had been completed, they filled in the embrasure just as we did when conservation work was finished.

Other features which were revealed on the old turf surface in the embrasure cutting *plate 36* were two lines of boulders on the east side and two on the west, but only short lengths of them could be seen without removing additional material. Two similar lines of boulders had already been noted in the cutting behind K95. Later we were to establish that similar lines existed in cuttings west of the embrasure. These lines of boulders

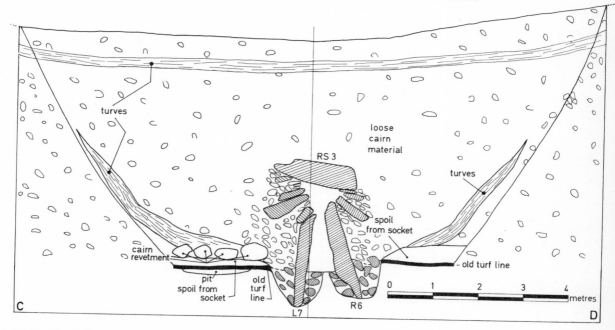

14 *Profile C-D through the embrasure cutting (see fig. 13).*

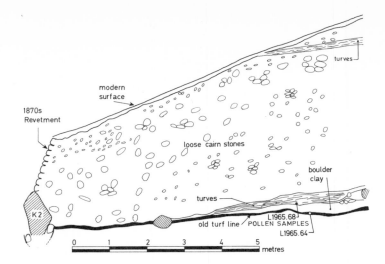

15 Profile of the west side of the embrasure cutting showing the position of pollen samples.

were structural to the extent that they seemed to have been laid in order to retain the toes of individual layers of cairn material and thus not to be compared with the arcs of stones found under or in the mounds of other passage-graves, notably sites K, L and Z at Newgrange and at Townleyhall II (Eogan 1963). It was also found that the inner-most turf layer in cutting K95 could be linked with the innermost one found in the embrasure. Pollen samples were taken from the basal layer of transported turves in the embrasure (Appendix D).

fig. 15

Other cuttings

A number of short sections were excavated behind K3, 4, 6, 10, 13 and 18, all west of the embrasure. This was necessary in the case of K4, 13 and 18 because it was found that their back surfaces were covered with ornament and space had to be made to enable this to be recorded. In the end, K13 and 18 had to be taken right out as it was impossible to make casts or take effective photographs otherwise. These stones were later restored to their original sockets and the decorated surfaces have disappeared from view once more. K3, 6 and 10 had to be straightened up into their original sockets.

It has been mentioned above that the bottom of the layer of turves on the west slope of the embrasure swung outward to the back of K3. The turf layer was now estab-lished specifically behind K6, 10, 13, 18 and 19 also and it is reasonable to assume that it occurs behind all the kerbstones, in this area at least. Knowing that the turves would compress, could the builders have thought of using them just inside the kerb to absorb some of the stresses which they knew would be set up as settlement took place in the body of the great cairn of stones? In all these cuttings it was observed that below the turves the old turf and humus layer, compressed and blue-black in colour, was present and that the kerb sockets had been cut through it. In the upper part of the cairn body the very thin earthy lines (not turves) which contained snail shells were present also.

fig. 5

North cutting

Since many of the kerbstones in this area needed to be restored to the vertical, a cutting was made into the cairn behind kerbstones 51, 52 and 53. Another objective was to follow up the turf mound already discovered outside the kerb. In its final stages the base of the cutting extended 8 m inside the kerb. The back of the cutting had to be sloped so that at the top it extended for 14 m from the kerb. The profile behind K53 shows that the layers of turves already detected outside the kerb continued inwards to the limit of our excavation, increasing in thickness from 80 cm immediately behind the kerb to 1.5 m at the farthest inward point reached. Forty-two separate layers of turves could be counted at this point, representing, if our experiments at cutting turves were reasonably accurate, an original minimum thickness of *c.* 4.2 m for the turf mound at this point. When blocks of the turves were cut out they could be easily separated into individual turves along the vegetation streaks and it was surprising to find these were still almost as green as when the turves were cut. Left exposed to the air, however, the vegetation quickly changed colour from green to dark brown. Mosses, grasses and leaves were clearly visible, though pressed flat (Appendix E). A C14 date of 2530 ± 60 bc has been obtained from this vegetation.

plate 38, *fig. 16*

fig. 8

plate III

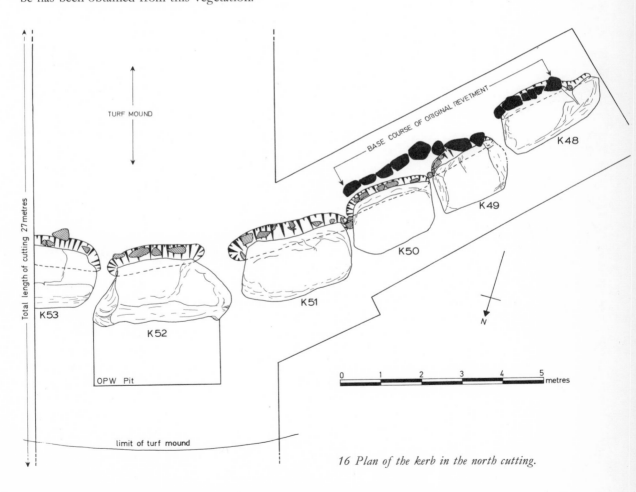

16 Plan of the kerb in the north cutting.

In the layers of loose stones above the turf mound there were at least three very thin earthy horizons (not turves) separated in each case by a thickness of between 50 and 100 cm of loose stones. These thin horizons contained innumerable snail shells, again very largely unbroken, as was found elsewhere on the site.

Interpretation

Investigation of the structure of the Newgrange mound made it clear that it was far from being the simply-constructed rounded mound of water-rolled pebbles that superficial examination had suggested. Even in the relatively limited areas which were excavated it was found that turves had been employed for the specific purpose of retaining the cairn stones at appropriate places and perhaps also at appropriate stadia in the operation – the building of the cairn may have been a seasonal rather than a continuous process. The basal layers of cairn stones were retained by lines of boulders and it was clear that, in the neighbourhood of the passage at least, a definite plan had been followed. It can safely be inferred that the same forethought was observed in the remainder of the cairn. It was clear also that the outer edge of the part of the cairn above the kerb had been retained by means of a built wall. During the 1970 season we

fig. 16
plate 39

were fortunate to find in the north cutting the bottom course of what must have been the original revetment wall, still *in situ* in a position which would have corresponded to the top line of kerbstones 48, 49 and 50 before they had tilted outwards. The course of stones consisted of the same type of boulder as those found lying outside the kerb. Interference with the cairn edge in this area had been inconsiderable and it is no doubt due to this that the bottom course of the revetment had survived in place. The increasing thickness of the turf mound running inward under the cairn in this area suggests the presence of an already consolidated turf mound and it is possible that had it been feasible to pursue it farther, a passage-grave or other structure pre-dating the great cairn might have been encountered within it.

Finds

figs 57, 58

Very few finds were recovered from the cairn itself. A number of flint objects were found behind the kerb in, and under, the redeposited turves and there were a few in the cairn itself. Three large cairn stones had some amount of picked ornament.

8 The tomb exterior

The passage

One of the most urgent matters discussed by the 1961 Committee concerned the state
of the tomb passage and the desirability of removing as many as possible of the struts
and supports, which not only caused obstruction but in many cases presented a
hazard. Also there was the difficulty of negotiating the passage owing to the way in   *fig. 4*
which many of the orthostats were leaning forward, and damage was being done to
their surfaces by the clothing of visitors rubbing against them. Many solutions were
proposed and it was eventually decided that the cairn material and the roofing slabs
should be removed from over the outer part of the passage, and the orthostats beneath
be restored to the vertical. The cairn had suffered a good deal of interference in this
area in the past so that repair and restoration would have been needed in any case.
This outer part of the passage is roofed by three trabeate slabs and it was clear that
their removal would not disturb the remainder of the passage roofing system which is
of a more complex nature. Accordingly, the remainder of the passage has had to
remain as before in spite of the fact that some of the orthostats are severely tilted. The   *fig. 17*
great cutting (embrasure cutting) which had to be made in the cairn to enable this
work to be carried out has already been described, together with the information
obtained about the structure of the cairn. One of the most surprising results, however,
was obtained when the passage roof was uncovered.

THE ROOF-BOX

Some little distance above the passage entrance and set back about 2.5 m from it, a
horizontal stone, decorated on its forward edge with a sophisticated pattern in relief,   plate 41
had for long been observed protruding through the grass and scrub which covered
the mound. Various antiquarians and scholars had commented on it from the 1830s
onwards, calling it the false lintel, and indeed attempts had even been made to shift it
(p. 36). Excavation showed that the decorated stone was the lintel or roof-stone of a
box-like structure, open at the front, to which we gave the name 'roof-box' during   *fig. 13*
excavation and by which it has been known ever since. The structure is so far unique.
It rested partly on RS1 (roof-slab 1) of the passage and partly on RS2. Its construction
was interesting. The two sides to left and right (west and east) of the open front were
made up of low dry-built stone walls standing on RS1, and a slab, something over 1 m

93

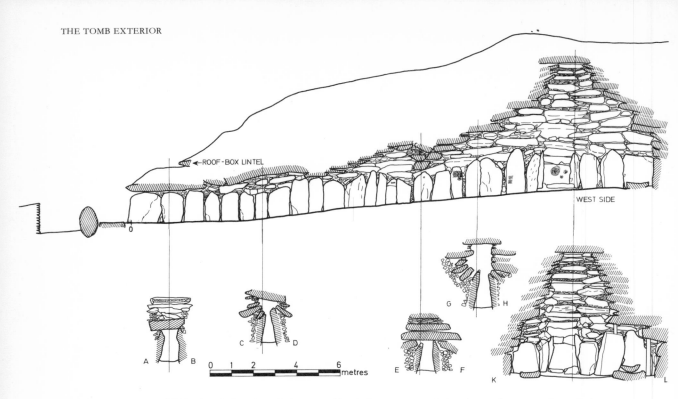

ROOF-BOX LINTEL

WEST SIDE

metres

17 Sectional elevation of the west side of the passage and chamber and cross-sections of the passage and chamber before excavation.

in length, lay along the top of each wall. The walls decreased in height from front to back (i.e. from 55 cm to 40 cm) and the slabs laid on them had a corresponding downward slope. These walls and slabs formed the lateral supports for a large slab, *fig. 52* which we named the back corbel. This is 2 m long, east to west, and has a concave undersurface. The downward-sloping lateral walls supported the front part of the corbel and allowed its back part to curve downward so as almost to touch the passage roof, thereby closing the back of the 'box'.

fig. 18a Numerous motifs – dot-in-circle, rayed dots and circles, and so on – are carved on the upper surface of the back slope of this slab. The front portion of its upper surface has a natural shallow basin-like hollow which in wet weather, accompanied by a southeast or south wind, would fill with water and occasionally spill over and enter the passage. To prevent this, a water-groove had been cut from the west edge of the 'basin' to drain the water off and allow it to dissipate into the cairn outside the side of the passage. Lying in this 'basin', in a position into which it must have been put by the *fig. 56* builders, was a natural but very curiously-shaped calcareous sandstone concretion (see Appendix A). The lintel of the roof-box rested on the forward part of the back corbel, covering the 'basin' and projecting 30 cm forward of the front edge of the back corbel. In essence, therefore, the roof-box consisted of two low side-walls which supported *plate 42* the back corbel, which in turn supported the roof-stone (the decorated lintel), the

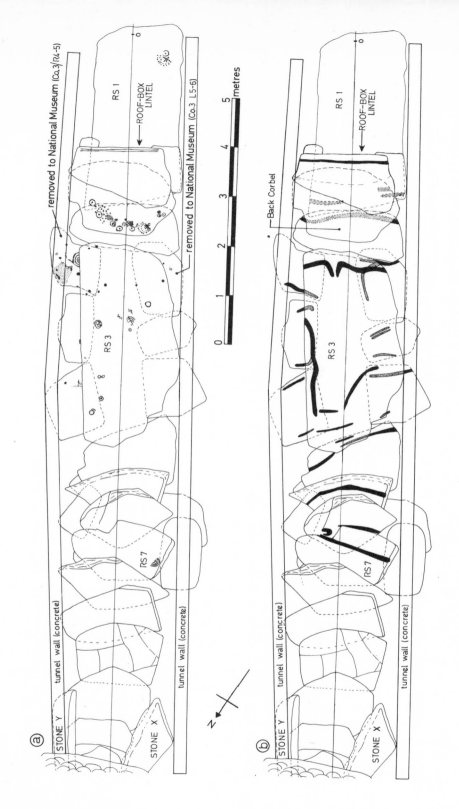

18 The passage roof from above; (a) ornament (b) water-grooves (grooves covered by other slabs are shown stippled).

whole forming a roof over a deliberately contrived slit between the back edge of RS1 and the front edge of RS2. The gap, or slit, is the full width of the passage, i.e. one metre. It may or may not be a coincidence that its eastern end is directly over the space between passage orthostats R3 and R4 which had been filled with dry-walling as already mentioned. The slit had been lightly closed by two blocks of quartz, one of which was *in situ*. There was evidence in the form of scratch marks on the surface of RS1 in front of the slit that the quartz blocks had been pulled out and pushed back a number of times and the arrises of the surviving block were rubbed smooth from this movement. The back edge of RS1 and the front edge of RS2 were provided

fig. 18b
fig. 52

with channels to prevent rain-water from running into the passage through the slit, and one on the upper surface of the lintel, parallel with the front edge, had a similar purpose.

When the roof-box was being dismantled to enable the passage orthostats to be restored to the vertical, it was found that two of the corbels directly behind the roof-box

fig. 18a
fig. 53

were profusely decorated. They helped support the front end of RS3, one on the west side (Co.3/L5–6) and the other on the east (Co.3/R4–5). The former was the third corbel (counting from below upwards) of three which rested on the fifth and sixth of the orthostats on the west or left side of the passage, and the latter the third corbel resting on the fourth and fifth orthostats of the eastern side of the passage. It can scarcely be coincidence that stones occupying such significant positions were decorated, and they call to mind stones X and Y at the junction of the passage and chamber roofs, which were also decorated, though in nothing like such an elaborate manner. The decorated surfaces were completely hidden as the corbels formed part of the roof structure; the western corbel was decorated on the underside and the eastern one on the upturned surface. Owing to their completely protected position, the ornament was strikingly fresh and unweathered and demonstrated in an unforgettable way what passage-grave art must have looked like in its pristine state. Because of this, and because when the passage was restored and the cairn replaced they would be totally hidden from view once more, they were replaced by substitute corbels and the originals preserved and displayed in the National Museum, Dublin.

THE PASSAGE ORTHOSTATS

Before these could be straightened up, the roof-box and four roof-slabs, together with their supporting corbels, had to be removed (see Conservation and restoration, pp. 111–12). The first roof-slab of the passage, RS1, was a large slab, 3.5 m N-S, 1.7 m E-W and 45 cm in thickness, and it rested directly on the first three orthostats on either side

fig. 17

of the passage. Very little movement if any had taken place here, but from this inwards the roof-slabs had been supported on one, two or three courses of corbel stones as required, which had themselves originally rested on the tops of the orthostats. As can be imagined, when the orthostats tilted inwards the corbels also became displaced and tended to slide in behind the uprights. This process can still be seen in the remainder of the passage and also in the chamber. In fact, it was the altered positions of corbels such as these which gave rise to the often expressed but erroneous belief that the tomb orthostats were non-structural and merely stood in front of dry-built walling. This

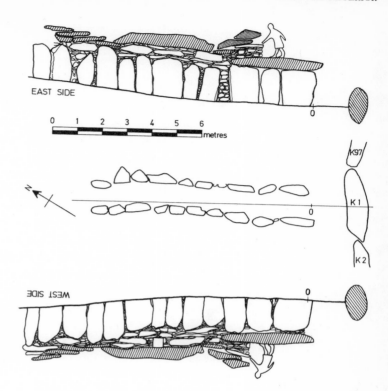

EAST SIDE

0 1 2 3 4 5 6
metres

K97

K1

K2

WEST SIDE

19 Plan and sectional elevations of the restored part of the passage showing the roof-box.

movement of corbels led to displacement of RS2, 3, 4 and 5, indeed RS5 was shattered and had for many years been supported by a concrete pillar standing on the passage floor. Another slab was substituted for it and the pillar was dispensed with.　*fig. 4*

When the four roof-slabs and the corbels had been removed and the cairn material behind the passage orthostats excavated down to the old turf surface (as already detailed in the section on the embrasure cutting, pp. 87–90) the bases of the orthostats were examined. It was found they had been set in two more or less parallel rows about 1 m apart in sockets dug in the old ground surface. The sockets varied in depth from 50 to 80 cm and the butts of the orthostats were well packed with stones and earth. This material was removed in order to straighten the orthostats to the vertical but no finds were made. Ten stones on the west and nine on the east were restored to the vertical – the discrepancy in numbers being due to the gap between R3 and R4.　*plate 47* *fig. 14* *plate 48* *fig. 19*

The straightening up of the orthostats had a beneficial effect not only on the passage but on the roof structure also, because when the courses of corbels were replaced they were once more horizontal instead of tilted, and the roof-slabs involved, RS2, 3 and 4, were once more in proper relationship to one another, both in horizontal and in vertical profile. In particular, the structure of the roof-box took on new meaning as it could now be seen that the slit or gap in the floor between RS1 and RS2 was not adventitious but had been carefully and accurately contrived. RS2 had been set at a higher level than RS1, leaving a regularly spaced gap, 20–25 cm in vertical height, between them. A few years later we were to discover that the rays of the rising sun enter directly through this slit at the winter solstice. From observation of the way in which the front part of the passage had been constructed it was clear that it had been erected as a free-standing structure independent of the main cairn mass and of the remainder of the tomb.

CLOSING STONE

fig. 13
plate 37

The space between the mouth of the passage and the back of the entrance stone was occupied by a single large horizontal stone which acted as a paving slab for the tomb entry. It was necessary to raise it in case useful evidence lay underneath and also to enable the back of the socket of the entrance stone to be examined. It was found, however, that the area beneath the slab had previously been dug out in order that the slab could be bedded with its upper surface level with the passage floor between the entrance jambs. Likewise the back of the socket of the entrance stone had been interfered with so no useful information was forthcoming. The upper surface of the slab had been worn smooth by the feet of visitors, but when we raised it the undersurface was found to have retained its natural surface. The stone measures 1.65 m × 1.25 m, is 25–30 cm thick and weighs about 1 tonne. The edges were dressed and picked over in the ancient manner, leaving one end square to the sides while the other had been dressed to a curved line. The measurements showed that it was an exact fit as a closing stone for the mouth of the passage.

It was already known from our researches that the position in which we had found the stone was comparatively modern, and since the measurements had indicated that it was a closing stone for the tomb entrance we experimented to determine in which position it would best achieve that purpose. We discovered that with the curved end on the ground and the straight one uppermost it fitted exactly under the overhang of RS1, closing the passage perfectly. We carried out another experiment also. Leaving the bottom edge against the jambs of the passage we tilted the slab outward at the top and found that it rested at an angle against the back of the entrance stone in a similar position to that shown in the sketch of 1845 (see p. 35).

Passage and chamber roofs

When the orthostats at the front part of the passage had been straightened up and the roof restored, it was felt that if the pressures and stresses which had caused the distortion and damage in the first instance were not to be repeated in course of time, some amount of protection was necessary. To this end it was decided to enclose the entire

fig. 18

passage in a light, reinforced concrete tunnel which would be hidden from view beneath the cairn material. The vertical walls of the tunnel would be built on the old ground surface outside the excavated part of the passage and for the remainder they would run up over the sloped-back surface of the embrasure at the inner end of the cutting. The roof of the tunnel would run from just behind the roof-box as far as the junction of passage and chamber roofs. To accomplish this it was necessary to remove the overburden of cairn from the remaining roof-slabs of the passage, though without interfering with the roof structure itself. Once again, the results were surprising and well worth the extra labour involved.

When these remaining roof-slabs were exposed, from RS5 as far as their junction with the chamber roof, the full run of slabs, when viewed from above, resembled an ascending flight of steps. Viewed from inside the passage, however, it could be seen that the roof suddenly lost height over orthostats L17/R15, and it was now possible to examine the reason for this, both from above and below. The profiles show that a low but very strong lintel (RS12) lies across the passage at this point. It supports two others laid side by side immediately above it, the one on the chamber side being the bottom corbel of the chamber roof and the other supporting a built infill of stones and a small tilted slab which together support the rising corbels of the passage roof. This point is therefore the meeting place proper of the corbels of passage and chamber, the great weight here being adequately taken by the low lintel. From here towards the chamber the roof as seen from the passage below rises until at the chamber entrance the final roof-slab is 3.6 m above the floor. This slab, RS17, is ornamented on the edge facing into the chamber. It is interesting that the same structural procedure has been noted in the passage of the eastern tomb at Knowth, a cruciform tomb with a corbelled chamber comparable to that of Newgrange (Eogan 1969, 10).

plate 44
fig. 13

fig. 50

BOULDER CAP

On the upper side of the passage roof the 'flight of steps' appearance is maintained without interruption as far as the intersection with the roof of the chamber. At this point, directly over RS15, two stones, one at each side, support a massive cross-lintel. They rest on the cairn outside the line of the passage, their long axes parallel with it. Both were found to be decorated – the western one (stone X) on its underside, and the eastern one (stone Y) on its western-facing edge. A comparison has already been drawn between these two decorated stones and the two decorated corbels found behind the roof-box because both pairs of stones occupy significant positions. Two loose slabs were found under the cross-lintel, both with deliberately scratched lines, and those on one of them (stone Z) appeared to be part of an unfinished pattern.

fig.13
plate 44
fig. 55

The discovery of stones X and Y and of the significantly placed cross-lintel led to a close examination of the area and it was found that the lintel supported the bottom course of a covering or cap of carefully selected rounded boulders which appeared to surround the outside of the chamber roof. When the cairn was cleared away from an area to left and right it could be seen that this was indeed so and that the boulders sloped upward until they reached the capstone of the chamber which they surrounded but did not cover. The boulders were all large, rounded and uniform in size, with a maximum dimension of *c.* 30 cm. They were thus easily distinguishable from the normal cairn material which was smaller and more angular, so that, as the latter was being removed the cap of boulders could be discerned without the least difficulty. The cross-lintel could now be seen as a deliberately conceived 'relieving arch' construction set up to take the weight of the boulder cap and to transfer it onto the cairn body, and thus prevent the weight from damaging the passage roof. Much of the front surface of

plate 50

the boulder cap was exposed for examination and recording, as was an area around the top edge. It was not feasible or expedient to conduct a more extensive examination but it was clear that the boulders surrounded the chamber roof, and this suggests that the latter was built as a free-standing structure which had its own mini-cairn, the outside of which was held in place by the built cap or revetment of boulders. This device provided the necessary counterweight on the tails of the roof-corbels to keep them in place at the correct outward-sloping angle and prevent them from collapsing inward into the chamber. It would have been interesting to cut through the boulder cap revetment to see the structure of the mini-cairn and the outside of the chamber corbels, but to do so might have upset the structural balance and caused the roof to collapse. We did not take the risk.

ORNAMENT

fig. 18a

fig. 54

Most of the ornamented stones found in the roof structure of the passage have already been referred to, i.e. the lintel and back corbel of the roof-box, the two corbels supporting the front part of RS3 and also stones X, Y and Z. In addition, motifs were present on RS1 and RS3, mainly random, rather inexpertly executed devices and, on RS7, a single motif of concentric arcs was found. All of this ornament, with the single exception of the forward-facing edge of the roof-box lintel, would have been hidden under the cairn when the monument was completed.

WATER-GROOVES

fig. 18b

plate 52

fig. 52

The channels or grooves cut on some of the stones forming the passage roof have already been mentioned. It was found that they were arranged so as to run the rain-water off to the sides as it percolated onto the roof through the cairn. One or more of these grooves had been cut on each of the first seven roof-slabs of the passage, and on the supporting corbels also when they were positioned so that water would flow onto them from the roof-slabs. As can be seen in fig. 18b, the grooves must have been cut on the corbels after they were positioned but before the roof-slabs were put on. The grooves or parts of grooves shown in full black are those visible when the roof-slabs are *in situ*, and the parts shown in stipple are covered by the slabs. There is a groove the full length of the lintel of the roof-box about 15 cm back from its front edge. In the past this had been taken by many to be a modern feature, cut perhaps by OPW workmen as a throating to prevent water from damaging the decorated outer edge, but a comparison with the other grooves shows it to be indubitably ancient. From RS8 onwards there are no grooves, nor is there need for them as the rain-water runs down the 'flight of steps' to the point where the grooves on the flatter part of the roof collect it and run it off to the sides. We observed this for ourselves many times while the roof surface was exposed.

The grooves vary in width and depth but the best examples are about 5 cm wide at the top and 1 cm deep. They had been picked in the same way as the ornament, i.e. by means of a pointed chisel, and in some instances the grooves were then deliberately rubbed smooth, the artificer using a pebble with sand and water. The only comparable water-groove known to us in Ireland is on the huge granite capstone of the portal dolmen at Brennanstown, Co. Dublin. This runs across the back slope of the cap and, if observed on a rainy day, can be seen to run the water off to the sides where it falls outside the chamber. It has been thought that this was a modern attempt to cut up the capstone, as is undoubtedly the case, for instance, at Capel Garmon in Wales, but it seems to us that the Irish example is ancient.

Another precaution taken to ensure protection for the monument consisted in packing the interstices of the passage roof with a mixture of burnt soil and sea sand. *fig. 13* The burnt soil had been taken from a habitation area as it contained small quantities of animal-bone fragments as well as a few fragmentary flint artefacts. The sea sand was used principally in the space under the 'relieving arch' structure where it was packed in before the burnt soil 'putty' had been put in place. So much of the latter was present that it seemed probable it had been burnt specially for the purpose. The sea sand is identical with that on the present sea-shore around the mouth of the Boyne, 20 km down river. Samples of the burnt soil provided radiocarbon dates centring on 2500 bc for the structure of the tomb (Appendix H).

9 The tomb interior

The tomb had of necessity to be closed to the public while work was going on in the entrance area and in the passage. By 1967 this was completed, but before being re-opened it was decided that the entire floor of passage and chamber should be excavated so that, if at any time in the future further conservation was necessary, the archaeolo-

fig. 20

gical horizon would no longer be at risk. A considerable amount of disturbance had taken place in the past, some of it relatively recently and some of it a good deal farther back in time. One of the worst disturbances had been caused by a deep hole which had been dug in the north recess (*c.* 1795), and the flag which acted as a basin stone was broken in the process (p. 38). Another smaller pit was found in the centre of the central chamber and this appeared to have been dug from the old floor level. It was about 15 cm deep, filled with broken stones in dark earth. The mixture had the appearance of having been deliberately buried. The pit does not seem to have been original nor even very ancient. Another pit north of it, 20 cm in depth, was filled with ash and charcoal and was also probably dug from the old floor level. There were no finds in these pits except for a waste flint flake.

The floor of the front part of the passage from the entrance inward as far as orthostat L12 had been greatly disturbed also, so that no culture layer survived. This must have been of relatively recent occurrence because until the 1830s this part of the passage floor was covered by a wedge-shaped mass of cairn debris, rising about half-way to the roof at the entrance. When this had eventually been cleared away by various land-owners and other interested parties, the expedients adopted to shore up the structural stones caused much damage. Pits were dug and the debris left over from the various attempts at conservation was buried in them. As well as this, holes were dug all along in front of the orthostats, probably in search of decoration and also to facilitate the taking of casts, an operation carried out in the passage and the chamber in 1901. It was found that similar holes had been dug in the chamber. The amount of concrete used in the former conservation work was excessive and we were able to remove much of it without loss. A deep pit had been dug behind passage orthostats R3 and 4 on the east, starting at the cairn surface and penetrating as far as the bases of the orthostats. This was done in order to build a concrete wall outside the gap between them, under the mistaken impression that a stone had been removed from there and

plate 51

had been replaced by dry-walling. As we have already shown, the gap was original, as was also the dry-walling. We removed the concrete and filled the gap once more with

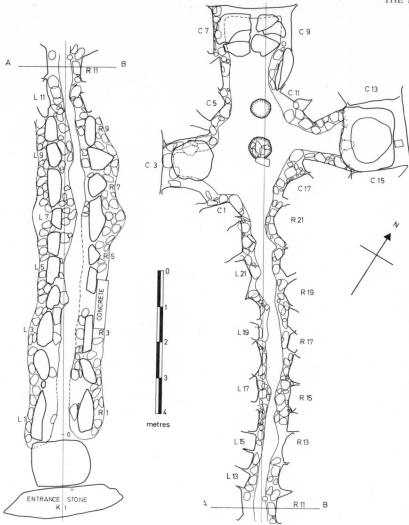

20 Plan showing the excavation of the passage and chamber.

a dry-built wall, as close as possible to that shown in Pownall's sketch (1773). An iron gate had been inserted at the passage entrance and here too an unnecessary amount of concrete had been used with consequent disturbance. The present gate was substituted for it after excavation. Concrete, stone and wooden supports in the form of pillars, struts, plinths and chocks abounded and we were able to dispense with many.

The recesses in the chamber had suffered badly as the basins had been moved or, as in the case of the end recess, broken. The basin in the west recess had been moved so that a stone plinth could be inserted as a base for timber supports which were considered necessary for one of the back stones of the recess. Old photographs of the recess

plate 55

plate 54

show this 'support' contrivance, which was clearly unnecessary since its base had rotted away by the time we examined it. A rebate had actually been cut in one of the decorated side stones of the recess (C4) in order to take one end of the horizontal support. We removed the timbers and the plinth and restored the basin stone to its original position. We excavated the hole which had been dug in the north recess and put together as many fragments of the floor-stone as possible. It is clear that the stone is incomplete and also that some of the fragments now in the recess may not belong to the original basin; they were found there when we started our excavation and we thought it best not to remove them. A good deal of concrete had been used in the east recess also. We were not able to remove all of it as it was impossible to shift the lower of the two basin stones because the orthostats had moved in upon it, making the concrete inaccessible. Two of the concrete pillars used as props for the decorated roof-slab of the recess have had to remain, even though the one on the north side totally

fig. 50

obscures an area of ornament on one of the lintels. There was a corresponding 'support' on the south side of the recess at the front (an iron one) which was intended as a prop for the south end of the roof-slab. We were able to remove this but the concrete by which the top of the iron was attached to the roof remains; to attempt to remove it might have caused damage. Another large area of concrete lay outside the base of C10 (the three-spiral stone) and we were able to remove it, but the stone itself had broken from its butt just above the base and we could not restore it to its original position. As was mentioned earlier (p. 37), C10 had fallen forward on its face and was raised to the vertical, presumably by OPW staff, at some time in the early years of this century. It is possible that the stone broke from its butt when it fell, and those who raised it merely set it up in a mass of concrete as close as possible to what they conceived its original position to have been.

One other factor which contributed to the disturbance of the culture layer was not attributable to man but to the activities of small animals (see Appendix C). We found numerous burrows made by them and also found their nests, which were lined with moss, bits of paper and various small objects collected from the floor. In this way objects had been carried some distance from their original positions.

Excavation

fig. 20

A number of sections were cut through the floor to enable profile drawings to be made. One was brought from the centre of the passage entrance through the passage and chamber as far as the back stone of the north recess. Three sections were cut across the passage at right angles to this line, at 6.1 m, 13.6 m and 16 m respectively from the entrance, and another section was cut across the chamber from west to east. When these had been recorded the whole floor was excavated layer by layer, but the stratification was too shallow for illustration here.

The top layer in the chamber consisted of hard, dark, well-trampled earth interspersed with small broken stones, together with a few larger ones which had probably been dug out from the sockets of the orthostats during previous investigations. This layer was a very thin one, only a few centimetres thick, but beneath it was a pro-

nounced scatter of the dental plaster used in the casting operation of 1901. This provided us with a useful date for the top layer, and we concluded that it had probably
been spread as a tidying-up measure when the casting was finished. This top hard
black layer was also found in the passage as far south as L12 and R11, but from this to
the entrance there was no uniformity as so much disturbance had taken place. Beneath
the top layer in the passage was the sandy, gritty material of the subsoil.

In the chamber, beneath the dental-plaster layer, was another one, 8 to 15 cm in
thickness, of looser brown earth containing small broken spalls of stone which we
presumed had fallen from the roof because there is an infilling of similar spalls   plate 53
between the corbels of the vault. This layer contained most of the bones, both burnt
and unburnt, and also the faunal remains, and it may have been what Lhwyd had in
mind in 1699 when he described the floor as consisting of 'loose stones of every size in
confusion and amongst them a great many bones of beasts'. This layer tailed off in the
passage about 2.5 m from the junction of passage and chamber. Beneath the layer of
spalls was gritty brown sand, the old soil surface, much disturbed by animal burrows.

Finds

A surprising number of finds, undoubtedly forming part of the original grave deposit,   *fig. 21*
were made during the excavation, especially when one considers the amount of interference with the stratification which had already taken place, and also the numbers of
people who had visited the tomb during the previous two-and-a-half centuries. In all,
the grave-finds amounted to 7 'marbles', 4 pendants, 2 beads, a utilized flint flake, a
bone chisel and fragments of several bone pins and points.

Only two of the finds, a marble and a pendant, were in the passage, in the part nearest the chamber entrance, and just within the chamber there was a bone disc bead in an
area much disturbed by burrows. In the centre of the main chamber, near the central
pit, was a large hammer pendant and near the west recess a serpentine marble and
some utilized flint flakes. All were in the layer of spalls. No finds were recovered from
the end recess apart from a waste flint flake, not surprising in view of the disturbance
it had suffered. A pendant and several fragments of bone points and pins, three of
them burnt, were found mingled with burnt human bone in the west recess, but the
east recess was the richest in finds, even though we could neither move the lower   plate 58
basin nor thoroughly examine behind or beneath it. A bone chisel was recovered,
however. Marbles, a bead and a pendant were found in the rest of the recess, either in
the dark layer or in the layer of spalls beneath, at depths of 5 to 15 cm. There were no
finds of pottery in the tomb.

A considerable quantity of human and faunal remains was found, the former comprising both burnt and unburnt material though the unburnt was predominant. There
were eighteen lots in all, nos 1–11 and nos 13–19. Except for lot 11 (part of an unburnt   *fig. 21*
human skull), lot 1 (part of the skeleton of a dog) and lots 7 and 15 which were faunal,
the remaining lots were a mixture of human and faunal remains.

Both burnt and unburnt human remains were found in the west recess around and   plate 54
beneath the basin, which, it will be remembered, had previously been moved. In the

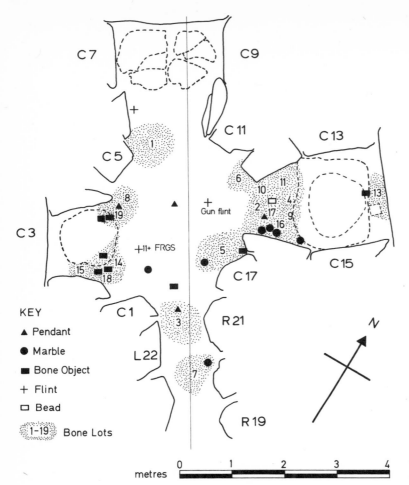

21 Plan showing the distribution of bone lots and finds in the tomb.

metres

burnt material were skull fragments and a tooth, indicating at least one individual. The bone lots from the main chamber proper, that is, the central part, were adjacent either to the east or the west recess (except for lot 1), and it must be concluded that they were associated with these recesses. The east recess was the richest in human remains, with unburnt material predominating. Lot 11, part of a skull, and lots 2, 4, 9, 10 and 17, together with lots 5 and 6 outside the recess, produced evidence of two adult skeletons. A small amount of burnt bone was present though mainly in lot 5 outside the recess. The west recess was richer in burnt material.

The human skeletal and dental remains are dealt with in full in Appendix B but summaries have been provided below by the specialists concerned.

BONES

The unburnt human material is derived from at least two adult skeletons. Comparison of the sizes and, where possible, articulations of the bones suggest that this material

106

may have been derived from a pair of skeletons, one being considerably larger and more heavily built than the other. The skeletons are very far from complete. All the bones are broken into small fragments, excepting some of those from the hand and foot regions. Large amounts of both skeletons are missing; the amount of material derived from the skull, vertebral column and the large limb bones is very small. The distribution of the material shows that the fragments had been widely scattered and intermingled with one another in the area.

Very little information can be obtained from the relatively large amounts of burnt bone. Much of this could well be comminuted fragments of an unknown number of human skulls. Among the burnt fragments were two portions of left petrous temporal bone. A number of specimens included joint surfaces. Though it is likely that several skeletons were involved, on the basis of the identified fragments it can only be stated with certainty that the burnt material included remains from three or more human skeletons, how many more it is impossible to tell.

TEETH

The dental remains consisted of thirty-two teeth, two of which had been burnt, from lots 2, 3, 4, 9, 10, 17 and 19. Lot 10 contained the greatest number (10 teeth). The specimen in lot 3 was too worn for accurate charting and the one in lot 19 was too badly damaged by fire for any useful observations other than a probable charting as 6| . The molar and premolar teeth in lots 2 and 10 very probably came from one individual whose age at death was determined by comparison of molar attrition at approximately 25–35 years. A second subject was identified on the basis of lots 16, 17, 9 and 4 whose age at death was approximately 30–40 years. It is not possible at present to state whether or not the remaining teeth come from these two subjects.

One of the points stressed by both specialists quoted above was the extent to which the human remains were scattered. The bones of one of the two skeletons identified were partly in the east recess and partly in the main chamber outside the recess. Teeth were also widely dispersed which, in the same way, were shown to have come from one individual. Some interesting observations in relation to the unburnt remains are contained in Dr Fraher's report (Appendix B).

The faunal remains are comprehensively dealt with in Appendix C and are shown to have consisted of mammals, birds, molluscs and one specimen of frog, the first-mentioned species being by far the most numerous. The specialist concludes that the remains were not of prehistoric origin.

The grave-goods are a typical Irish passage-grave assemblage, but it cannot be *fig. 59* definitely established that they were originally lying in the basins together with the burnt bone, though it is clear that both grave-goods and burnt material were concentrated around and under them, with the exception of the end recess where circumstances had made preservation of the remains impossible. In site Z the single basin stone in the chamber, though it had been moved a little from its original position, still contained some of the burial deposit, together with a number of pottery beads (M. J. O'Kelly *et al.* 1978, 291).

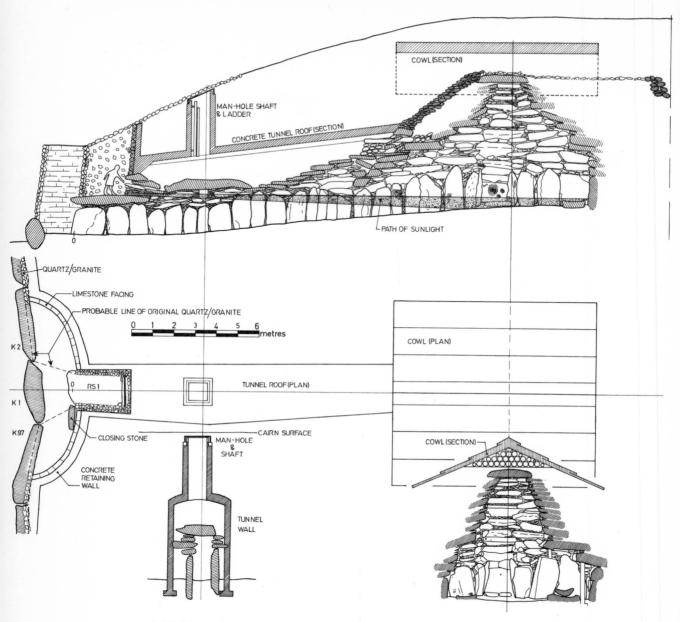

CONCRETE TUNNEL ROOF (SECTION)

MAN-HOLE SHAFT & LADDER

COWL (SECTION)

PATH OF SUNLIGHT

QUARTZ/GRANITE

LIMESTONE FACING

PROBABLE LINE OF ORIGINAL QUARTZ/GRANITE

0 1 2 3 4 5 6
metres

COWL (PLAN)

K2

K1

RS1

TUNNEL ROOF (PLAN)

K97

CLOSING STONE

CONCRETE
RETAINING
WALL

CAIRN SURFACE

MAN-HOLE
&
SHAFT

TUNNEL
WALL

COWL (SECTION)

22 Plan and sectional elevation of west side of passage and chamber, showing restoration and conservation; also path taken by sunlight at winter solstice.

10 Conservation and restoration

Conservation and restoration was carried out by the Office of Public Works and was based on the archaeological findings and interpretations. Present-day visitors to Newgrange can evaluate for themselves the high degree of architectural and engineering skills displayed by the staff, whose job it was to find solutions to the many problems involved. We cannot let the occasion pass without paying tribute also to the skill and dedication of those who supervised the day-to-day work – done at first by Mr Louis Feeley, the then Clerk of Works, and later by Mr Laurence Gaynor, now unhappily deceased – as well as those who carried it out. One has only to compare the 'before' and 'after' photographs of the monument to see the extent and effectiveness of their endeavours.

fig. 22

plates 17, 21
plates IV, VII

The kerb

Of the 37 kerbstones fully exposed along the southern arc of the kerb, all but three (K1, K2 and K97) had tilted forward and K96 had fallen over completely. The excavation had established their former positions and they were restored to these. Some, such as K12, had not been in sockets and these were readjusted back onto their built-up stone supports, while K13 and K18 had to be lifted out completely so that the ornament, which was on the back surfaces, could be fully recorded before they were replaced in their original sockets. K92 had been split by tree-roots and it was glued before being re-erected. In the case of K1, K10 and K96, it was found necessary to put low concrete chocks in front of their bases. This was needed in the case of K1 because so much disturbance of its socket had taken place in the past; K10 had no socket and K96 had had only a very shallow one, which was probably why it had fallen flat in the first instance. On the north side of the mound, kerbstones 48 to 53 were similarly reinstated. This was particularly important in respect of K52 because it rivals the entrance stone in the quality of its ornament, and when it was raised to the vertical the full extent of this was seen for the first time. The area in front of the stone was lowered somewhat and chocks inserted so that the entire front surface is now visible, including the horizontal line at which the ornament stops at the base of the stone and which must represent the old ground surface. K53 had also been split by tree roots and, like K92, was glued before being straightened up.

plate 73

plate VI

Revetment wall

It was felt that on the basis of the amount of material which had collapsed from the mound, and which thereafter lay outside the kerb, it should be possible to calculate the height of revetment originally employed to retain it in position. This was a matter for an engineer whose particular field of study involved the behaviour and movement of mounded loose materials. It was fortunate that Mr J. V. Fogarty, BE, Lecturer in Civil Engineering at University College Cork, was able to spend time on the site to study the problem and to make the necessary calculations. Having taken into account the measured amount of material and its nature – mainly cobbles and loose gravels forming a cohesionless mass with a natural angle of repose of approximately 40° – he calculated that the revetment must originally have been in the order of 3 m in height with a lay-back of about 30 cm in that height. Since the original revetment was of dry stone it had given way in time, and it was obvious that if the process was not to be repeated the edge of the mound must be stabilized in some more permanent manner. Several solutions were proposed by Mr Fogarty and by various engineers and architects of the OPW, and the one finally adopted was that of Mr W. P. le Clerc, the then Inspector of National Monuments.

plate 60 A wall of reinforced mass-concrete was built to the required height on a foundation dug behind the kerbstones, the backs of the kerbstones being covered in plastic sheeting so that no concrete could touch or adhere to them. The quartz and granite boulders found during the excavation were fixed to the outside of the wall by means of a mortar grouting, none of which shows from the front. The granite boulders are randomly distributed throughout the facing, though the possibility must be borne in mind that a pattern was achieved in the original.

In the entrance area the revetment had to be modified from what the archaeologists conceived its original form to have been. Such evidence as was available from excavation suggested that the original revetment wall extended as far as each end of the entrance stone and then turned sharply inwards to the sides of the passage mouth, over the built sides of the roof-box, and around over its decorated lintel. In no other way could the cairn material have been prevented from covering the roof-box and slipping into the entrance area itself. We also envisaged, though there is no evidence for it save that it would have been a practical measure, that the space behind the entrance stone and between it and the closing stone would have been filled with cairn stones or perhaps with a quartz/granite mixture to make it easy to climb up to the roof-box.

On account of the ever-increasing number of visitors – 70,000 in 1978 – it was evident that considerably more space would have to be provided at each side of the tomb entrance than would be available had the archaeologically correct design been adopted. Accordingly, the quartz/granite revetment wall was brought only as far as plate 63 the outer ends of K97 and K2 (the kerbstones immediately adjoining the entrance stone) where it stops at a broken line to show that it is incomplete. The quartz/granite walls coming out from the sides of the roof-box similarly terminate in a broken line since from this point onwards they do not follow the original design. Curving walls of limestone connect the two broken ends (limestone being chosen because this material is alien to the rest of the monument), the aim being to demonstrate clearly that the curving walls are not intended to represent the original form of this part of the entrance area. Wooden stairways have been provided over K97 and K2 at each end of the entrance stone so as to give access to the tomb entrance without any risk of damage to the decorated slabs.

The cairn

Since the monument stands on a ridge and the ground beneath falls away to the north and south, the rain-water quickly runs down through the loose body of the cairn and when it meets the iron-pan-indurated surfaces of the layers of turves, or the pan-coated old turf surface beneath, the natural flow is to the north and south. It seemed possible that the water might pond behind the concrete wall and to provide against this, piped drains were laid from the inside, running out under the wall foundation between each pair of kerbstones. Inside the wall the inner end of each pipe was turned upward so that its mouth was just above the surface of the old turf. Outside the wall and kerb the pipes were led off underground to a series of stone-filled sink-holes dug in the previously excavated area. The same was done on the north side. Before the cairn slip was replaced behind the wall and before the soil had been reinstated in front of the kerb, a full winter's observation of the workings of these drains was made to ensure that they were effective. It was seen that even in periods of excessive rain the pipes functioned very well and no ponding of water occurred.

When the cairn material from the excavated areas was being replaced on the mound, the bottom layer, 1.5 m thick, was made up of loose stones only and a sheet of heavy plastic was laid over it so as to prevent soil from being washed down through the layer which might in time block the drainage system. On the recommendation of the consulting engineer, the remainder of the excavated material was put on in layers one metre thick and on top of each layer a thin cement slurry was poured. This had the effect of stabilizing the narrow but high wedge of added cairn material immediately behind the revetment and of preventing any movement of the restored edge.

On the north side, behind kerbstones K48 to K53, the wall was built of concrete blocks (approx. 45 cm × 22.5 cm × 11.27 cm) laid flat. No reinforcing was necessary as the wall was brought up only to the tops of the kerbstones, the purpose here being to support a revetment of ordinary cairn stones which, because of the height of the kerb itself in this area, needed to be raised only to a height of 70 cm. The revetment wall was restored to its full original height only where complete excavation had already taken place. The surface of the cairn was regraded from the flat top down to the top of the revetment wall at the front of the mound and also at the north side. The remainder of the surface, i.e. that on the east and west, was not interfered with.

The passage

As already explained, the front part of the passage roof, including the roof-box, had had to be removed in order to restore the passage orthostats to the vertical. An eight-layer plan of the roof was drawn, on which the position of every roof-stone and corbel was plotted and as the roof was being dismantled, each stone was numbered in sequence and the same number affixed to the corresponding stone in the plan. When the work on the orthostats had been completed it was thus possible to restore the slabs to their former positions with complete accuracy.

plate 64

The largest slab which had to be removed was roof-slab 3, measuring 4 m × 1.8 m × 0.5 m and weighing approximately ten tonnes. It was enclosed in a strong wooden cradle and lifted by crane to a previously prepared position. The next heaviest, RS1, weighed about eight tonnes, and the remaining twenty-four stones were lighter. One of these, weighing about one tonne, which had been placed by crane on the ground outside K96, provided an opportunity for an experiment when the time came for it to be replaced. We decided to do this without mechanical aids – all of the remainder were replaced in their respective positions by crane. Using only a ramp, rollers, levers and chocks, all of wood, and a length of rope, three men moved it a distance of 15 m and through a height of 4 m in twelve hours. By approaching this operation in an intelligent manner, the men achieved a perfect repositioning of the slab with minimal physical effort or strain on themselves. Experience in the handling of large stones appeared to be the most important factor for the success of the operation, and the men in question had this just as the Newgrange builders must have had.

fig. 18a

Roof-slab 5 was in a completely shattered condition when found, and it was replaced by a Liscannor slab in which the quarry drill-holes were left visible so as to show future investigators that it is a modern substitute. Slabs of comparable shape and size were substituted for the two decorated corbels, Co.3/L5–6 and Co.3/R4–5, so that these could be preserved and displayed in the National Museum, Dublin. The tails of some of the larger corbels were supported on concrete-block pillars behind the passage orthostats to give added stability to the restored roof. It has already been mentioned that the corbels had slid in behind the passage orthostats and were endangering the whole roof structure.

plate 65

fig. 22

The whole of the passage and its roof was enclosed within a concrete tunnel which would resist the horizontal thrusts and weight of the restored cairn. It was agreed that the roof of the tunnel should be high enough to give space for examination of the roof structure and for inspection of the ornamented roof-slabs and the water-grooves. Access to the space was to be by means of a manhole at the restored surface of the cairn. The technical details of the tunnel were designed by Mr le Clerc and the manhole and access shaft by Mr D. N. Johnson who had succeeded Mr le Clerc as Inspector of National Monuments. An aluminium ladder gives access from the manhole and it is telescopic so that it can be slid out of sight to facilitate photography. Before the cairn material was replaced around and over the tunnel, the outside of the concrete was coated with bituminous mastic as a form of waterproofing. An electric point has been provided in the tunnel so that long-flex hand-lamps can be used to light the various features of interest to specialists.

In winter-time a small stream of water formerly entered the passage between R7 and R8 and flowed through the entrance to escape between K1 and K2. Dr H. G. Leask, a former Inspector of National Monuments, had installed a short piped drain in an endeavour to draw off the water, but this had little success. When the passage ortho-stats were being straightened up it was found that the source of the water was a spring which welled up from the socket of R8. A piped drain was laid, running from this point under the centre of the passage floor and through the space between K1 and K2, to a stone-filled sink-hole at the edge of the excavated area. This expedient proved successful.

Passage orthostats R3, L19 and L20 have appreciable areas of ornament below the level of the passage floor and, as they are of specialist interest, small inspection-pits lined with thin slabs of Liscannor stone and covered with the same material have been provided. They are not visible at the replaced floor surface but they can be opened quickly and easily. The closing stone which lay as a paving slab outside the mouth of the passage has now been set up immediately to the east of the passage entrance. The surface worn by visitors' feet in former years has been turned inward so that it should not be thought the tomb builders had deliberately produced the smooth surface.

figs 40–42

plate 3

The chamber

A number of the chamber roof-corbels had cracked, particularly the decorated roof-slab of the east recess, and there were lesser cracks in the west and end recess. In winter, water dripped through and frequently the basin stones in the east recess filled up, a circumstance obviously of long standing since in AD 1700 Lhwyd in one of his letters commented: 'We observed that water dropped into the right-hand Bason, tho' it had rained but little in many days: and suspected that the lower Bason was intended to preserve the superfluous Liquour of the upper (whether this water were sacred, or whether it was for Blood in Sacrifice), that none might come to the Ground.' It is no doubt this statement of Lhwyd's which is responsible for the persistent tradition that stains of blood can be seen on the upper basin stone!

plate 57

It has already been mentioned that the tomb builders made every effort to keep the interior dry by the caulking of joints and the provision of water-grooves, so it was clear that the leaks should not be allowed to remain. Mr Johnson devised a cowl to be erected over the whole of the chamber area, hidden under the restored cairn. A pyra-mid of concrete drain-pipes (employed for the sake of lightness) was erected over the chamber area and covered by a steeply pitched roof of thin concrete slabs laid over the pipes like slates. This was covered in due course by cairn material so that the finished surface of the cairn is now 2.8 m above the capstone of the chamber. The cowl has proved effective and the chamber remains dry at all times.

fig. 22

The infill of tabular spalls in the interstices of the chamber roof was thoroughly checked and the spalls were tightened where necessary. Obvious gaps in the infill were made good using the spalls found in the floor during the excavation, which must have fallen from the roof in the past.

The cairn slip

Two-thirds of this remain unexcavated. At four points, i.e., at the extremities of the areas excavated on the south and north sides of the cairn, the vertically cut ends of the bank of slip have been faced with a thin revetment of cairn stones, set in cement mortar to prevent slip and decay of the strata and also to mark firmly the points at which excavation ceased. As already explained, the top layer of slip immediately outside the kerb was composed of material which had been thrown up from a trench or ditch formerly dug outside the kerbstones so as to make them partly visible. This 'bank' still remains for two-thirds of the perimeter, and since there were many hollows and irregularities in its surface, they were filled in with the material which had slipped off the cairn more recently. A layer of sand was put on top to make a smooth surface for walking and to protect the stratification beneath.

All of the recently collapsed material was taken out of the ditch so that the tops of the unexcavated kerbstones should be revealed. The low revetment wall erected on top of the kerb in the 1870s and many times repaired and rebuilt by the OPW, has been refurbished, setting the stones in cement mortar as this seemed the only way of keeping them in place and of avoiding a continuous maintenance problem. Various expedients had been employed in the past to achieve this, among them being a series of oak stakes, 2 m in length, driven horizontally through the wall face into the cairn. This had proved ineffectual as there was no bond between the stakes and the stones of the wall and in any case the stakes rotted in time. We found many of them still in position, though decayed. The outer face of the ditch has been revetted by a low wall 70 cm high, of built cairn stones set in cement mortar. These measures have kept the ditch open and the tops of the kerbstones visible over the intervening period of four or five years without further maintenance being necessary except for the control of weeds.

Wooden stairways give access from the excavated areas to the sanded walkway on top of the bank so that visitors are not tempted to climb up the loose stones of the slip with consequent damage to the stratification. The outermost limits of the excavated areas (the edges farthest from the kerb) have been marked with low revetment walls, using cairn stones set in cement mortar, so that a future excavator can see the extent of the area investigated by us.

Multiple arc of pits

fig. 5 The centres of the pits in this feature on the east side of the mound have been marked with concrete posts, the tops of which protrude above the grass by about 50 cm. The pits were filled around the posts with loose stones on which plastic sheeting was laid to prevent silting-in of soil. A layer of earth was laid over all to provide a bed for newly sown grass.

Site Z

fig. 5 Some of the structural stones of this satellite passage-grave on the east side of the main monument had been buried unbroken when the site was destroyed in the past, and these were re-erected in their original sockets. The other sockets have been marked by filling them with concrete brought a little above grass level. The quartz and granite stones found outside the entrance to site Z were collected together outside the entrance stone of site Z to show that this was the area in which they were found.

11 Construction of the monument

The present appearance of Newgrange comes as a surprise to those who have not seen it since its pre-excavation days when it was overgrown with trees and scrub, loose stones everywhere, the whole exuding an air of abandonment and decay; and visitors have said to us that it is now 'too modern looking' and that they preferred it when it was 'so romantic'. This is to forget that Newgrange must have been 'modern looking'   plates 17, 21
also to the Boyne valley people of about 2500 bc when it was first built. Then the white quartz wall stood as it is now, and above its top the mound surface was one of naked stones – there were no trees, no scrub, no weeds nor grass. The weeds and grass must have grown fairly quickly if one is to judge by the rapidity with which they grow today, and scrub would also have developed in due course. But no trees; not until they were planted on and about the mound in the nineteenth century by an improving landowner.

It is difficult to imagine what a British long barrow, built on the chalk-lands, must have looked like when new, since no actual reconstruction has been attempted – a great snow-white long-mound, visible for many miles, standing in stark contrast against the greenery of its surroundings. Presumably, if a long barrow were reconstructed on the basis of the evidence from excavation (Fussell's Lodge, for instance, and one must think of Ashby's reconstruction drawing), it too would be considered too 'modern looking' and the surprise occasioned by it would be as great, if not greater, than that produced in the minds of some by present-day Newgrange.

In attempting to visualize what Newgrange looked like in the third or fourth millennium BC it must not be forgotten that it was not the only monument on the ridge.   fig. 23
Sites K and L, the mounds of which were 20 m and 23 m in diameter respectively, stood to the west of it and site Z (diameter 20 m) and probably also site Z_1 (outside the present Newgrange enclosure and unexcavated) to the east. The whole would have formed a most impressive group, particularly when viewed from a sufficient distance, as for example from the south side of the river.

One of the finest examples of reconstruction comparable to that of Newgrange is found at Barnenez South in Brittany where eleven passage-graves are contained side by side in an enormous long-mound. Excavation showed that the mound was built of small stones kept in place by a series of concentric, built revetments, two in the body of the cairn and the third forming a facing to its perimeter. The cairn stones had spilled over the outer facing but when this material was excavated, Iron Age pottery

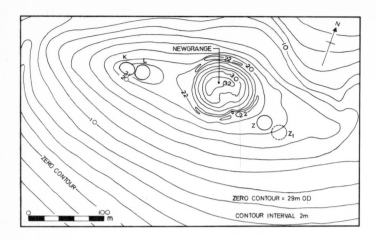

23 *Contour plan of the ridge showing Newgrange and sites K, L, Z and Z₁.*

was found at the base of the wall, showing that the collapse had not taken place until after that period. The monument has now been restored and the revetments form one of the most impressive features of the whole. The mound had been severely damaged by a contractor who had carted away quantities of the stones and as a result of court proceedings brought against him, the offender was made to pay both for the excavations and for the restoration.

When first seen by the visitor of today, Barnenez too occasions surprise. We have come to equate the monuments of the past with ruins and forget that the ruin is the corpse, not the living body. We hope that as a result of our work and that of our many and devoted collaborators and helpers over a period of almost twenty years, we have succeeded in breathing some faint spark of life into Newgrange so that it now justifies in some part its ancient claim to be the Brú or mansion of the Good God, the Dagda of early Irish tradition.

In what follows below we first endeavour to recreate the physical processes involved in the construction of the monument, such as the amassing of materials, and so on, and then we speculate on the possible processes which were involved in the alignment of the monument, the purpose for which it was built and for whom and when. The final section is devoted to the considerable body of ornamented slabs.

Building materials

What, from a purely logistical angle, was involved in the building of Newrange? We have seen that 97 slabs, none weighing less than a tonne, and some weighing considerably more, were used in the kerb. It is possible to count a further 450 slabs in the tomb structure itself – these are the orthostats of the passage and chamber and the roof-corbels. Except for a very few – two in the kerb and two others in the tomb structure that are of brown carboniferous sandstone – the rest are greywacke, a grey-green coarse slate which outcrops to the north of Newgrange. None of the structural slabs were quarried, all show geologically weathered surfaces except where slabs have been deliberately pick-dressed. Their weathered condition and the striae which can be seen on some of them suggest that they were collected from where they had been left lying about at the end of the Ice Age. Imagine the difficulty of finding so many suitable slabs, half-hidden as they must have been by scrub and forest, and of bringing them onto the site, mainly uphill since Newgrange is on the top of a ridge; and, from how far away were they brought? Were split tree-trunks laid down as roadways along which to trundle them on rollers, and was this done by manpower alone or were the older oxen used for traction? We know that some of the cattle from the Late Neolithic/Beaker settlement were ten years old when they were slaughtered, and presumably the builders of Newgrange were keeping some cattle for just as long; winter grazing must have been as good at 2500 bc as it evidently was about 2000 bc. If cattle were being used for traction were the stones carried on low pallets fitted with wooden block-wheels or were slide-carts or sleds employed? We have no evidence, of course, to support any of this speculation (but see Garfitt 1979).

We have calculated that the covering cairn contains about 200,000 tonnes of stone. From where did this come? The river terraces that lie between Newgrange and the Boyne are largely composed of gravel and stones of the kind that make up the mound. On the lowest terrace and near the bank of the river there is a figure of eight-shaped   plate 1 pond which now remains water-filled all the year around; the early Ordnance Survey maps show it as oval in shape. It is due south of Newgrange and about 750 m distant as the crow flies and it is highly probable that this was the gravel pit from which the cairn material was quarried. If this was the source, how were the stones brought to the site? Is one to envisage a line of men walking up the steep slopes of the terraces, each shouldering a leather sack containing anything up to 50 kg of stones, or again, were they delivered on site in ox-drawn sleds or carts? The site of Newgrange is 46 m (150 ft) higher than the level of the pond-quarry.

Professor Frank Mitchell (1976, 130) has speculated on the man-hours involved in the building of Newgrange and, of course, he stresses that it is speculation. He envisages the 50 sq.km land-basin surrounding Newgrange as containing 200 farms of about 25 ha. each, each farm supporting a family of 6 – a grandparent, 2 parents, and 3 children – giving a total population of 1200 people; about the same as today. He reckons that each farm could have supplied 2 able-bodied persons for duties other than farming for 2 months after the spring sowing, that is, 400 workers, each of whom would carry not more than 10 sacks of stones per day. Each day should therefore mean 4000 sacks and each working period of 2 months 240,000 sacks. He estimates that the cairn contains 1 million such sackfuls. Thus, 4 working seasons would have been spent on assembling the cairn. He adds another season for other parts of the work – assembling the structural slabs, cutting and transporting the material for the layers of turves, obtaining the quartz and granite, and carving the ornament – and in his view, therefore, Newgrange could have been built in 5 years. Professor Mitchell does not estimate the weight of a sackful but if, as I have suggested, each contained up to 50 kg, 1 million would amount to 50,000 tonnes.

We have seen, however, that the mound contains an estimated 200,000 tonnes, that is to say, 4 times more than he envisaged, and so we must quadruple his estimate for the assembly of the cairn material, i.e. 16 years, although to us even this seems too short for several reasons. If the material was quarried from the figure of eight-shaped pond, this source is almost twice the distance away postulated by Mitchell (750 m as against 400 m), and allowing for the fact that the sackfuls would have had to be carried uphill on a zigzag rather than on a direct course because of the difficulties of terrain, the round trip could not be accomplished in under an hour at the very least, and his estimate of 10 sackfuls per day would thus have to be reduced appreciably. It has already been shown that there are at least three very thin soil horizons in the mound which are not layers of transported turves but represent stadia in the progress of the work, stoppages of perhaps no more than a very few years duration, but long enough for a slight vegetation cover to develop on the stones. We have no way of estimating the duration of the stadia, but if each represents a 5-year interlude we must then add on a maximum of 15 years to the 16 or so already allowed for, making a total of 30 years or more. On the other hand, work need not necessarily have been totally suspended during these stadia, it could have been proceeding apace on some other phase of the construction.

Let no one imagine that the foregoing is any more than a guess, made in our almost total ignorance of the life-style and habits of the builders. For instance, if animals were used for transport, or if ox-drawn sleds or carts were employed, or if the working season were longer and the workers more numerous, the building time could have been shortened appreciably, if not quite to the five years proposed by Mitchell.

In this connection it is interesting to compare the man-time construction estimates made by Professor Colin Renfrew (1979, 213) for the much smaller chambered cairn at Quanterness in Orkney. The cairn is 30 m in diameter and about 3.5 m high and contains a very well-built tomb structure 7 m long, surrounded by a series of revetment walls in the body of the cairn. The stone was probably quarried from a scarp 40 m distant. He suggests that 5 able-bodied men working an 8-hour day could have built the monument in about 250 days; if there were 15 workers, the building could have been done in a single season of 90 days, while if the work were spread over a 5-year period, the 5-strong gang could have done it by working 50 days per year.

Building methods and sequence

As can well be imagined, over the seventeen or more years that have elapsed since we dug up the first trowelfuls of Newgrange soil in 1962, we have given a good deal of thought to the problem of how the building of such a vast and intricate structure was organized and carried out. As we came to know the monument better and came to discover its complexities, we had to discard one theory after another as being too simplistic, and we came to realize that we were not dealing with questions of brute force and mere strength of numbers so much as with intelligent and well-organized method, more on the lines of the organization and division of labour practised today in any comparable undertaking.

I envisage the available work-force as having been divided into groups or gangs, up to six in number. Gang 1 searched for large slabs suitable for the structure and delivered them on site, certain others of their number going as far afield as the Dublin-Wicklow mountains for the quartz blocks and the Mourne Mountains in the north for the granite. Gang 2 were the structural experts, engaged in setting up the orthostats, corbels, roof-slabs, and so on, and in due course, the kerbstones. Gang 3 collected the material for the cairn and deposited it in position as and when directed by the overseers. Gang 4 stripped turves and laid them in place as directed; they may also have been deputed to see to the sealing of joints and the caulking of roof-slabs. Gang 5 were the timber workers. They split tree-trunks, made planks, rollers, chocks, scaffolding, perhaps shear-legs and perhaps also pallets and even block-wheeled carts. Gang 6 were the artists – the carvers. Some of their work was done while the slabs were still lying about the site; they selected the most suitable surface and applied the various motifs. When the time came for the slabs to be utilized it sometimes happened that in the building the decorated surface was covered over by other stones, or if it was a kerbstone, had to be turned back-to-front as this was the way it fitted best. This fate did not befall the work of the master-carvers. They applied the ornament when the stones were *in situ* and when and where it would show to best advantage, e.g. the entrance stone, the lintel stone of the roof-box, K52 on the north side of the mound, and so on. The apprentices were at work also, as witness a good deal of inferior ornament, that is, inferior in relation to the very best work. We suspect that quite a few freelancers were present too, carving their own graffiti – the various doodles and criss-cross scratchings which occur on many surfaces – perhaps while the overseer's back was turned.

plate 61

plate 67

plate 62

Who was the overall man responsible for this vast undertaking? Was he king, king-god, priest or merely the then version of our modern tycoon? Did the entire community take part? Did the women and children lend a hand with the lighter jobs? How many more questions of this sort can be posed without hope of an answer! Let us at least try to outline a possible building-sequence.

At this stage of the work, we must assume that the axis of the passage and chamber, the centre point of the latter and the position which the roof-slit must occupy relative to it, have already been determined by the expert who had been taking the solar observations. The width and length of the passage and the layout of the chamber with its side and end cells would also have been determined. Probably at this time too, the kerb was marked out, taking into account the pre-existing turf mound of which we found evidence on the north side of the ridge. The orthostats of the inner part of the passage and of the chamber were stood in their firmly packed sockets and cairn stones were piled against them on the outside to create a broad flat working-platform, level with their tops. The outer edge of the platform was a sloping ramp of a gradient suitable for bringing up the roof-corbels. The toe of the ramp was held by a few courses of large stones forming a retaining feature. Turves were laid over the ramp of loose cairn stones to prevent it from slipping and rolling about.

Working from the platform, each layer of corbels was raised into place in the roof. All joints were broken, that is, the corbels in one course overlay the joints in the course below and this can be clearly seen when one looks up into the vault from the chamber. The slabs were laid with an outward slope and as the weight increased on their inner ends, these ends became more tightly locked together, so that in effect, each course became a horizontal arch. As slabs of very varied sizes, thicknesses and weights were being used, very careful positioning, bedding and bonding had to be achieved, and in doing this, two groups of builders were working together, one group outside, the other inside. The latter group had scaffolding to stand on and work from and it was their job to watch over the amount of inward overhang of each corbel, to insert the flat spall-infilling in the interstices and to pick-dress and thus partially round off the inner edges of the slabs. The pick–dressing sometimes goes over the arris onto the upper surface and so must have been done before the next corbel above was put in place. The interior group also saw to the propping where necessary of the inner ends of the corbels as the roof rose higher and higher. The props were vertical timbers rest-ing on opposed wedges on the floor – horsing in modern parlance. The horsing held the corbels in balance until the circuit of each course was completed. We have seen that the horizontal movement of the settlement pressures of the cairn pushed the tops of the passage and chamber orthostats inward in course of time. So much so that or-thostat C10 in the end recess broke off from its base, some roof-slabs cracked – the

plate 57

decorated roof-slab of the east recess, a corbel in the end recess and a couple of others in the western part of the roof. The fact that the roof did not collapse during this sett-lement shows how well built it was, and that it still stands today is a very great tribute to the expertise of the builders involved. We have calculated that this process caused a lowering of the whole roof of the chamber in course of time by approximately 50 cm.

Plenty of timber must have been needed in the form of planks, levers, rollers, wedges, and so on, and for lifting the slabs some form of shear-legs was probably used. There must have been plenty of multi-ply ropes available, and these could have been made of twisted slivers of furze *(Ulex)* (Lucas 1954, 96) or bog-deal (sub-fossil pine) and who knows, it may be that pulleys were employed also. Perhaps the older cattle helped in this part of the work also. Experienced stone-workers, such as quarrymen and masons, move large slabs about with apparent ease and little physical effort, as in-deed we found at Newgrange in the experiment already mentioned (p. 112) where no modern lifting gear was employed. The sophistication of the workmanship in every part of Newgrange that we have examined shows that the master-builder-cum-archi-tect, and the foremen of his various work-gangs, were intelligent and experienced and well able to direct and supervise the tasks they had set themselves.

When the interior workers had completed the inside of the chamber vault, we envi-

fig. 13

sage that they joined those on the outside in the building of a mini-cairn. This was based on the platform of cairn material from which the exterior group had been

plate 50

working. Cairn stones were laid onto the outside of the vault and, as they were put up layer by layer, the boulder-cap revetment was built, course by course, of large selected boulders. This revetment was itself of considerable weight and so that it should not bear on the passage roof where it passed over it, a 'relieving arch' in the form of a cross-lintel was devised. Two large decorated slabs, stones X and Y, were laid on the cairn-stone platform, their lengths lying roughly parallel with the passage but just beyond its sides. These two slabs supported a great cross-lintel on which the boulder-cap revetment wall was based. The space under the cross-lintel was sealed with sea sand and burnt soil putty (from which one of our C14 dates was obtained). Two small slabs (stone Z and another), with spalls in between, were pushed in outside the sealing material. These two small slabs have some doodled, lightly scratched designs. When the mini-cairn with its revetment cap was complete, its weight on the tails of the roof-corbels held them in balance and the timber horsing inside the chamber could now be dispensed with.

fig. 55

Meanwhile, work on the main cairn was going ahead. Cairn stones were being piled in and after each goodly layer had been laid, with a slight revetment of larger stones at its toe, another gang of men moved in and placed a layer of turves over the stones to keep them in place. Thus, the main cairn was increasing in size outward from the tomb structure by an addition of roughly penannular layers which came around from each side towards the passage, where the orthostats of the outer part were now being erected. An embrasure, the sloping sides of which were covered with a layer of turves, had been left there by the cairn-builders so that the above operation could go ahead without interference. When the orthostats had been set up the embrasure was filled in with cairn stones, working from the completed inner part outwards. The structural experts had meanwhile been setting up the entrance stone and the adjacent kerbstones, and when these were in place and firmed up, the rest of the embrasure was filled in up to the level of the tops of the outer-passage orthostats, thus creating a level platform once again on each side.

fig. 13

plate 49

Work now began on the roofing of the outer part of the passage and on the building of the roof-box, for which much delicate adjustment of the latter must have been necessary. The carvers, who had been following behind the structural experts, had been cutting the water-grooves under the direction of the overseer. Perhaps to while away the time while the latter was making his calculations about the likely direction the flow of rain-water would take, the carvers picked out the various decorations on the roof-slabs and on the back of the roof-box. The roof-joints were then caulked with the burnt soil putty.

fig. 18b

plate 43

Once the passage roof had been completed the structural experts returned to the kerb and continued to set the slabs in place, either in sockets or set up on built bases so as to achieve an even top-line all round the perimeter. All this time, the cairn was being extended with layers of cairn stones, followed by layers of turves to hold them in place as needed until the kerb was reached. Layers of turves were put immediately inside the kerbstones on the old turf surface and were covered by a layer of stones. When the mound had become level with the tops of the kerbstones the revetment had to be built, course by course, as the mound rose higher. When both revetment and cairn were nearing their full height, another layer of turves was added and above that again, a final layer of cairn stones. Meanwhile, the master-carvers would have been at work on the entrance stone, the lintel of the roof-box, K52 and K67, and so on.

The above is merely an attempt to set out a work pattern which will at least fit the facts as we observed them. Needless to say, we cannot know if we are correct in detail and our system of gangs to do specific things is speculative, but we have no doubt whatever that the whole undertaking was carefully thought out and planned from first to last and carried out with something like military precision.

121

12 The cult of the dead

The building of Newrange and of the two other equally imposing mounds of Knowth and Dowth, all within a few kilometres of one another, cannot be regarded as other than the expression of some kind of powerful force or motivation, brought to the extremes of aggrandizement in these three monuments, the cathedrals of the mega-lithic religion. The time-span involved in the building of the three is not known; we can guess at a few centuries and, still guessing, but with somewhat more assurance, say that Newgrange was the earliest, followed by Dowth and Knowth.

The religion itself spanned a much longer period and the building of passage-graves was the work of only one of the various sects; others erected court cairns, portal dolmens and wedge galleries, and this represented only the manifestation of the reli-gion in Ireland. It was spread throughout Britain and western Europe, each sect devel-oping its own response to the cult of the dead. We have long argued that the mega-lithic religion was disseminated, not by invasions or immigrations or any other kind of mass-movement of peoples, but by a spread of ideas which took root when the time was ripe. For Ireland, this time had arrived before 3000 bc. Farming, both pastoralism and agriculture, had been developing from about 4000 bc and by 3000 bc a well-fed settled population had evolved in Ireland which now had time and reserves of wealth in food sufficient to enable them to look beyond the questions of day-to-day survival and to adopt the spreading cult of the new religion.

We are concerned here with only one aspect of the cult – the building of passage-graves. About 150 examples are still extant in Ireland, grouped for the most part in 'cemeteries': that of the Boyne valley, that of Loughcrew in the west of Co. Meath, and the two in Co. Sligo, Carrowkeel and Carrowmore. This total must be far short of the original. Within the passage-grave framework, there are numerous variants, dif-ferences in size, in shape and structure of tomb, and also in the fact that ornament was carved on the stones of some of the monuments and not applied at all in other cases. The only unifying factor appears to be the composition of the grave-goods, of which those found at Newgrange are representative (with one exception – the absence of pottery). While in many respects, therefore, Newgrange is a typical Irish passage-grave, there are several features which set it apart and these are not solely its size and the excellence of some of its carvings.

Purpose and siting of the roof-box

Standing in front of the tomb entrance, one now sees the roof-box recessed between the flanking quartz walls, the quartz continuing around over the decorated lintel. The structural details have been described above, but what was its purpose? Needless to say, it has given rise to much speculation because it is so-far unique, nothing comparable being known from any other megalithic site. Ritual is a much abused word in the context of prehistoric tombs but there is some justification for invoking it here. The tomb would have been closed by the slab now set up beside the entrance and we have envisaged that, when it was in its closing position, the space between it and the back of the entrance stone would have been filled in with cairn stones or perhaps even with quartz. Access to the roof-box would then have been easy by climbing from this on to the first roof-slab of the passage. Was the box used as an offering place in which gifts were put on special days to be taken in by the spirits of the dead whose mortal remains were within? We have no evidence similar to that from some of the Scandinavian chambered tombs, for example, where thousands of fragments of broken pots were found on the ground in front of and on each side of the tomb entrance, representing pots containing offerings which had originally been placed as on shelves on the tops of the adjacent kerbstones and obviously renewed every so often. In fact, at Newgrange not a single sherd of pottery which could be connected with the tomb builders was found. Even though much disturbance had taken place in the entrance area in the past, some evidence should have survived if tangible offerings had originally been made.

Nevertheless, the scratch-marks on the floor of the roof-box, which show that the slit had been opened and closed by movement of the two quartz blocks, must mean that there was at least a periodic return to the front of Newgrange for some purpose or other. Was the slit a soul–hole through which the spirits of the dead could come and go when the quartz blocks were pulled back to release them? As has been shown, the name Newgrange, unlike those of Dowth and Knowth, is relatively modern. It was originally known as *An Brug*, the abode or mansion, and it belonged to the chief of all the gods, *An Dagda*, the Good God, and his son, Oengus.

Another tradition, but a much more modern one or at least one more familiar in modern times, had been mentioned to us by many visitors particularly in the early stages of the excavations when we were working almost totally in the dark as far as factual information was concerned. This was to the effect that a belief existed in the neighbourhood that the rising sun, at some unspecified time, used to light up the three-spiral stone (C 10) in the end recess. No one could be found who had witnessed this but it continued to be mentioned and we assumed that some confusion existed between Newgrange and the midsummer phenomenon at Stonehenge. Since Newgrange faces southeast it was clear that no such comparison was valid but when we began to think about it, we realized that it might be worth while to investigate the winter solstice when the sun rises in that quarter. We first did so in 1967. On 21 December 1969 we recorded the following observations on tape:

At exactly 8.54 hours GMT the top edge of the ball of the sun appeared above the local horizon and at 8.58 hours, the first pencil of direct sunlight shone through the roof-box and along the

fig. 22

plates VIII, 8

123

passage to reach across the tomb chamber floor as far as the front edge of the basin stone in the end recess. As the thin line of light widened to a 17 cm-band and swung across the chamber floor, the tomb was dramatically illuminated and various details of the side and end recesses could be clearly seen in the light reflected from the floor. At 9.09 hours, the 17 cm-band of light began to narrow again and at exactly 9.15 hours, the direct beam was cut off from the tomb. For 17 minutes, therefore, at sunrise on the shortest day of the year, direct sunlight can enter Newgrange, not through the doorway, but through the specially contrived slit which lies under the roof-box at the outer end of the passage roof.

Dr Jon Patrick, who has devoted much time to the problems of solar, lunar and stellar alignments with particular reference to ancient monuments in Ireland and Britain, was asked to make a survey so as to determine if this phenomenon could have occurred when the tomb was newly built. He reported as follows (1974, 518–19):

The passage is in the form of two curves so that for a ray of light to travel directly from the roof-box to the back wall of the rear recess it must be in the azimuth range 133°42′–138°24′. The elevation of the distant horizon (0°51′) is the minimum elevation at which the sun's direct rays can enter the slit. The floor of the chamber is about 15 cm lower than the roof-box, so at the minimum elevation sunlight will extend across the floor and into the rear recess. Light rays will not enter the chamber when the elevation exceeds about 1°40′. This range of azimuths and elevations, reliable to about 15′ and 5′ respectively, means that the sun's rays will shine directly into the chamber if its declination lies between −22°58′ and −25°53′. It therefore seems that the sun [in theory] has shone [into] the chamber ever since the date of its construction and will probably continue to do so for ever, regardless of secular changes in the obliquity of the ecliptic. It also means that the spectacle occurs for a number of days before and after the winter solstice.

Unfortunately, the vagaries of time have had their effect on the passage and some of the stones are now leaning inwards, thus trimming down the width of the beam of light. At the time of construction the beam would have been about 40 cm wide whereas now it is only 17 cm. The two principal orthostats causing the obstruction are L18 and L20. The first ten orthostats on either side of the passage have been straightened but there is no way of straightening the rest without dismantling the whole structure.

From this unambiguous evidence of direction and altitude Dr Patrick concluded that the orientation of Newgrange was deliberate. Observations made since have shown that direct sunlight penetrates to the chamber for about a week before and a week after 21 December. It might be thought that sunrise would rarely be clearly seen at this time of the year in the Irish climate, but we have seen the phenomenon at Newgrange every year for the past eleven years on one or more of the three or four days centring on 21 December.

What were the problems of the builders in setting up this orientation, and did they need to have abstruse knowledge to do so? It seems to us that no particularly specialized knowledge would have been required. It would have been necessary for an observer to be on the proposed site for a period before the solstice to watch for the point of sunrise on the local horizon and to note its southward movement until the point was reached when the sun began to move back again. If optimum weather conditions were present, perhaps one period of observation would have been sufficient, but if the observer were unlucky enough to encounter bad weather he might have had to watch for a number of solstice periods before building could begin. (In our experience, accurate observation with modern surveying equipment is needed to determine any difference in the point of sunrise as between the 20, 21 or 22 December at Newgrange.) Having determined the southernmost point of sunrise, the Newgrange observer of old must have put a line of pegs into the ground, aligned on that point, thus marking the axis of the proposed passage and chamber, the axis about which the builders were to do their work. He would next have to observe the particular point on the hillside, level with the local horizon, which the horizontal beam of light would strike at the first moment of sunrise. This point would be designated as the centre-point of the chamber.

Another point which would have to be accurately determined concerned the slit in the floor of the roof-box at the outer end of the passage; the horizontal beam should be able to strike through this. Since the tomb was being built on the natural rise of the hill, the floor at the entrance would be considerably lower than that of the chamber (there is actually a difference of almost two metres in height between them) and accordingly, roof-slabs 1 and 2, which comprise the floor of the roof-box, would have to be set at specific heights so as to enable the above process to be carried out. Roof-slab 1 *fig. 19* rests directly on the passage orthostats and its back edge forms the bottom of the slit, while roof-slab 2 forms the top of the slit and is set on corbels built on the passage orthostats. Some experimentation may have been necessary to get RS2 at the right height – the slit is 20 to 25 cm in height – but as it is small and light (0.25 tonne) as compared with RS1, adjustment would not have been difficult for men who could handle 10 to 12 tonnes with apparent ease.

The above sequence seems to us to be a practical and feasible solution to the problem of the orientation of Newgrange on the winter solstice. There may be other and better ones but we believe that there is a particular one which can be ruled out, namely, that of chance.

While the Newgrange roof-box is without parallel, it may be that other passage-graves were similarly equipped. We have suggested elsewhere that the entry-points at sites K and L (immediately west of Newgrange) may not have been fully sealed by their closing slabs. The passage of L was destroyed, but it has been suggested that it ended at the point where two well-marked stone-holes were found, indicating that the stones which stood in them were tall, substantial ones supporting a lintel, and a space may have been left between the underside of the latter and the top of the outer blocking (M. J. O'Kelly *et al.* 1978). The excavator of site L, Frances Lynch, has made the same argument in respect of the entry-point at Bryn Celli Ddu in Anglesey (1973, 158). At site K, a two-phase monument, the closing slab of the primary monument remained *in situ* and did not reach as far as the underside of the capstone above it. In phase II the passage was extended and another closing slab was put in place. It too did not reach as far as the underside of the lintel above it. Of course, in both cases the spaces could have been closed by the addition of a second stone; there is no certainty that a space or slit was left above the closing slab in either instance. We have no evidence on this matter from site Z as the orthostats had been wholly destroyed.

As regards orientation, sites K and L face south and site Z faces south-sontheast; at Loughcrew, Co. Meath, of the 11 tombs for which reliable plans are available, 6 are orientated within the southeast quadrant and these include the 2 principal ones,

Cairns L and T. A similar phenomenon has been observed in Brittany in respect of passage-graves with a long passage, e.g., Gavrinis, lle Longue, Mané-Lud, etc. The same applies to the tombs of Barnenez South and to a majority of all other Breton passage-graves (L'Helgouach 1965, 76–7).

House for the Dead

We have already seen that every effort was made by the builders to keep the inside dry – the outward slope of the chamber and passage roof-corbels, the caulking of the roof-joints with putty-like burnt soil and sea sand and the cutting of water-grooves on roof-slabs and passage corbels. Surely this must mean that the structure was thought of, not merely as a tomb, but as a House for the Dead, in which the spirits would live in dry comfort and in an even temperature, a constant 10 °C, though it is hardly likely that the builders knew of this kind of measurement! The House for the Dead had to be built of great stones so that it should last for ever; the houses of the builders themselves must have been ephemeral things of wood and thatch that have disappeared without leaving any trace above ground.

The evidence from the human remains found in the tomb during the excavation indicates that at the very least, 5 persons were represented, 2 unburnt and 3 cremated. While cremation seems to have been the normal rite in Irish passage-grave practice, there is clear evidence also that unburnt bodies were placed in such tombs as, for instance, that of Fourknocks, Co. Meath, not far from Newgrange (Hartnett 1957). That tomb produced from the 3 cells some 24 people, men, women and children. After the roof had collapsed, cutting off access to the chamber and cells, several more burials were thrust into the passage, bringing the total identifiable number of people to 67. The small passage-grave, the Mound of the Hostages at Tara, in Co. Meath, contained the cremated remains of a hundred or more. However many or few were contained in these tombs they must surely have been special in some way. The number of workers who built Newgrange, and their families, must have been considerable and yet they were not buried in or immediately around it. We have no way of knowing in what way the people who were put inside Newgrange were special; it does not necessarily follow that they were royal or priestly, they may have been special in some quite different way. The evidence from Fourknocks and Tara suggests that the people were put in at one moment of time in a single collective burial and that the tomb was then closed. If this happened at Newgrange, the one-tonne closing slab would have been raised into place and perhaps the narrow space between it and the back of the entrance stone filled with stones.

Despite the fact that the closing slab was no longer in place when the tomb was discovered in 1699, no further interments had been made nor was there any trace in the tomb of the Late Neolithic/Beaker-period people who squatted around the edge of the collapsed mound hundreds of years later. There was no Bronze Age, Iron Age, Early Christian or Anglo-Norman interference with the mound itself, as happened at Knowth, and almost certainly, at Dowth also. Was Newgrange so special that, even in decay, its renown as a House of the Dead kept it inviolate? It was celebrated in Early

Irish tradition and literature as the abode of the Irish gods. It was a place where precious offerings were made at various times down the years, as witness the objects of many periods that we and others have found. The most spectacular of these were perhaps those of fourth century AD date, the gold ornaments, coins, brooches and glass left, in our view, by visiting Romans from Britain who had been told of the powerful gods who lived there.

What of the stone carvings? There is no reason to think that any of them were taken from another monument or monuments and reused here, as has been suggested. Some of the carvings were done after the stones had been brought onto the site but before they were built into place. Others such as the entrance stone and K 52 were carved after they had been positioned. The various motifs and combinations of them must have had a meaning for those who saw them, but we are unlikely ever to know what that meaning was. It must remain part of the mystery which was the Brú or mansion of the ancient gods and which is also the Newgrange of today.

plate 78

The turf stripping

Another singular feature connected with Newgrange is the amount of turf stripping which had taken place over a large area outside the mound. We have seen that when the quartz/granite revetment wall collapsed it fell onto a subsoil surface. The subsoil was exposed in all of the excavated area on the southern side of Newgrange, whereas the old turf and humus layer was clearly present inside the kerb and it was clear also that the kerb sockets had been cut through it. In the area excavated on the north side of the mound, the old turf was present beneath the slip.

When did the turf stripping take place or was there more than one? We must assume that the oval stone-setting just east of the tomb entrance is a primary feature and that, whatever its purpose, it must have been put there by the builders of Newgrange immediately after the completion of the monument. Excavation showed that the setting was built on a subsoil surface. This suggests that one stripping at least was done at a very early stage, perhaps even during the building of the monument, and in dealing with the finds we have assumed that the paucity of objects belonging to the builders is due to their having been taken away in the turves. This first stripping may have been done to provide the material for the layers we found in the cairn itself, so that by the time Newgrange was completed the area outside the southern front was bare of turf and humus.

It is unlikely that K96 (which had fallen flat and lay on a subsoil surface) and the quartz revetment wall collapsed immediately. So vegetation – grass and weeds – would have quickly begun to grow and, unless they were constantly kept cleared, would have developed into quite a mat of turf in three to five years, as we saw happening during the excavation on areas that had been cleared to the natural boulder clay.

The turf stripping had gone out from the Newgrange kerb beyond the satellite passage-grave, site Z, and there had been some domestic activity on the stripped surface under Z – post-holes, a hearth, a burnt area, animal bones, flint debitage, a stone axe and a hollow-based arrowhead – but these had become covered again by a 10 cm-thick turf *before* Z was built. Presumably this turf covered the whole area that had been stripped. The mound of Z had been built of turves. Was the whole area outside its kerb again stripped for this purpose? We have argued elsewhere (M. J. O'Kelly *et al.* 1978, 343) that Z is later than Newgrange, though we do not know how much later except that at the time of its building, the edge of Newgrange may already have begun to decay. Was it onto this second-time-stripped surface that K96 and the quartz revetment collapsed or might there have been yet other strippings? On the basis of the radiocarbon dates the Late Neolithic/Beaker-period squatting was taking place at 2000 bc and at this time the quartz revetment and some of the cairn edge behind it had collapsed. If there had been an interval of some hundreds of years between the completion of Newgrange and the collapse of the revetment, a considerable development of turf and humus would have taken place, so one must argue either that the revetment collapsed almost immediately after completion, or that there were several strippings of the turf. We can be reasonably sure of two, but perhaps there were more.

We have seen too that the great layer of turves which we found under the north side of the cairn may be part of the covering mound of a small pre-existing passage-grave. The mounds of satellite passage-graves K, L and Z were also built of turves. Eogan has shown that there are numerous layers of turves in the mound of Knowth and several of its satellites had turf mounds. All of this means that vast areas in the neighbourhood of the various sites were stripped of turf and that it was common practice, a work readily undertaken by the people of the time. It may well be therefore, that the turf around Newgrange was stripped not just twice, as we have shown, but several times between 2500 bc when it was built and 2000 bc when squatters were living around the edge of the collapsed mound. This turf stripping for the building of burial mounds (Houses for the Dead) was a prodigal extravagance in that it destroyed the fertility of the surface soil, thus preventing tillage and at the same time destroying the grazing for the farm animals.

Date

In the past it was held that Newgrange was near the end of a line of devolution which had begun in the tholos tombs of Mycenae, but it is clear now that Newgrange is older by at least a thousand years. Likewise, it continues to be argued that passage-grave building in Ireland began in the Boyne valley, with the great monuments of Newgrange, Knowth and Dowth, and that as the invading colonist-builders moved westward across the country, first to Loughcrew (Co. Meath) and thence to Carrowkeel and Carrowmore (Co. Sligo), there was a gradual deterioration in building techniques, so that the rather simple monuments of the Carrowmore cemetery in Co. Sligo were at the end of the line. Time and much new work have shown that this is an oversimplified view. It is clear now that several of the small simple passage-graves, some of those at Knowth for instance, and perhaps sites K and L at Newgrange, are earlier than the great monuments and if an evolutionary sequence is present at all, it must be from the simple to the complex. Radiocarbon dates from securely related samples from Irish megalithic tombs in general are very few, but, such as they are, they support the

The north cutting

38 The cutting made into the cairn on the north side, behind K51-K53.

39 The bottom course still *in situ* of what must have been the original revetment wall on the north side. The kerbstones on which the wall had been built have fallen forward.

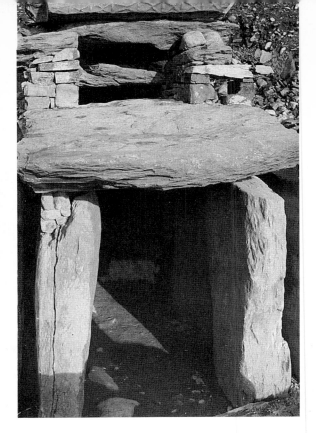

40,41 The entrance, roof-box and lintel *(right,* detail of lintel *above)* as revealed after the removal of the overlying cairn. (Length of lintel, 1.55 m.)

The roof-box

42,43 The passage roof and roof-box from the side *(below)*, after the cairn had been removed. Right to left: lintel of roof-box, back corbel (detail of ornament, *left)* RS2 (partly beneath back corbel) and the very large slab, RS3 (note water-grooves).

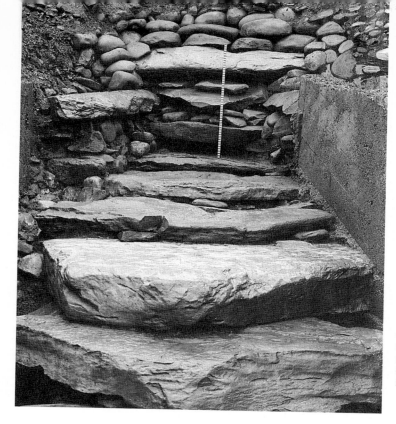

44 From RS5 onwards the passage roof resembled a flight of steps when viewed from above. At the junction with the chamber roof, two decorated slabs (stones X and Y) support a massive cross-lintel which in turn supports the bottom course of the boulder cap.

The passage roof

45,46 The final part of the passage roof *(right)*, viewed from inside the chamber. From the low lintel (RS12) onwards, the roof rises all the time until at the chamber entrance the last roof-slab, RS17 (detail *above*), is 3.6 m above the passage floor.

47–49 *(Above left)* The unrestored passage orthostats after the roof-slabs had been removed. *(Above right)* The passage orthostats after their restoration to the vertical. *(Below)* The orthostats of the front part of the passage as they must have appeared to the construction 'gangs' of 2500 bc.

50 The boulder cap slopes upward from the passage roof (here already covered by the modern protective concrete tunnel) as far as the capstone of the chamber, which it surrounds but does not cover.

51 The gap—an original one—between R3 and R4 in the passage. A sketch of 1773 shows it closed by dry-stone walling, and this was reinstated after excavation.

52 Water-grooves on RS3. The grooves averaged 6 cm in width and 1 cm in depth.

The west recess

53 Detail of the corbelled vault of the chamber. Each course oversails the one beneath, and has an infilling of flat spalls.

54,55 The west recess during excavation. The basin stone *(above right)* had been moved during earlier conservation work in order to insert a concrete plinth as the base for a supporting pillar. The plinth was removed in the course of excavation *(above left)*. Cf. pl. 13.

56 The 'fern' motif picked on C4 in the west recess.

The east recess

57 The roof-stone of the east recess, unfortunately now cracked so that part of the ornament is out of register.

58 The east recess during excavation. The modern pillar at the back had to be left in order to support the roof.

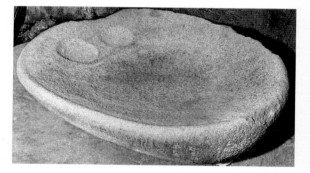

59 The upper of the two basins in the east recess. Made of granite (either Newry or Wicklow), it is chiselled all over, inside and out. Note the two circular depressions, 20 cm and 45 cm in diameter respectively. Dimensions of basin: 1 m to 1.2 m.

Restoring the façade

60–63 (*Above*) A wall of reinforced concrete was built on a foundation trench dug behind the kerb. (*Above right*) Pattern of multiple zigzags, eighteen rows deep in places, on kerbstone K93. (*Right*) Detail of scratched ornament on K91. (*Below*) The restored entrance area. Originally the white quartz wall would have extended as far as the edge of the entrance stone on both sides, before swinging in towards the roof-box, but this arrangement had to be modified in the restoration to allow enough space for access by the large number of modern visitors.

Restoring the entrance and passage

64 The lintel of the roof-box being replaced after the straightening of the passage ortho-stats.

65 The whole of the passage was enclosed within a concrete tunnel. Note the manhole which provides access for inspection of the ornament and water-grooves on the passage roof-slabs.

Ornamented kerbstones

66–69 *(Above)* Unweathered ornament on the back surface of K13. *(Below)* Part of the ornament on the back surface of K4. *(Right)* A detail of K9, showing motif low down on the front surface. *(Below right)* A detail of the ornament at the bottom of K6, now below ground level.

70–73 *(Top left)* Ornament on the under surface of K18, which was discovered only when the kerbstone was taken out to record the carvings on the back surface. *(Above left)* A pattern laid out but not finished on stone Y, the eastern support-stone for the cross-lintel. Cf. pl. 44. *(Above right* and *right)* Details of the back surface of K18.

Ornamented orthostats

74 A zigzag, lozenge and spiral pattern on L19 in the passage.

75 A four-spiral ornament at the bottom of L19, almost obliterated by pick-dressing.

76 Pick-dressing, which finishes 25 cm above ground level, almost eliminates the large spiral near the bottom of R3 in the passage.

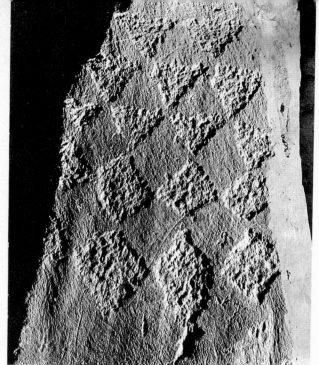

77 Ornament near the bottom of L22 in the passage.

78 Detail of ornament on C16 in the chamber.

79 Orthostat R21 (with R20 on the right) at the junction of passage and chamber. Note the five shallow grooves with rounded ridges in between, uniformly picked all over. Similar 'ripple-dressing', if such it is, is found on R12.

Ornamented corbels

80 Corbel Co.1/C2 on the south side of the west recess. The underside of the stone is cracked.

81 Corbel Co.2/C14 at the back of the east recess immediately beneath the decorated roof-stone. The ornament runs into the cairn at each side. (The modern supporting pillar had to be left in place.)

82 Corbel Co.1/C7 immediately above orthostat C7 in the end recess, discovered during the survey of the tomb in 1965.

83 The unburnt human skeletal remains from Newgrange.

a Part of frontal bone, internal aspect. The frontal crest is lying vertically. An unusual, low conical elevation projects inwards from the lower right part of the bone (arrowed).

b (Top left) part of left petrous temporal bone; (Top right) part of right petrous temporal bone; (Bottom left) part of frontal bone; (Bottom right) part of occipital bone.

c Near-complete clavicle, inferior aspect.

d View of body and inferior ramus of pubis. Note the eversion (arrowed) of the inferior ramus.

e Dorsal view of laminae, articular processes and base of spine of a thoracic vertebra. The joint surfaces on the articular processes (arrowed) show no evidence of arthritis.

f Evidence that the unburnt material is derived from more than one skeleton: View of superior surfaces of two damaged radial heads. The upper specimen comes from a larger bone than the lower.

g Evidence that the unburnt material is derived from more than one skeleton (Left) two medial left cuneiform bones; the upper comes from a larger skeleton than the lower. (Right) right fifth metatarsal bones; the complete upper bone is to a larger scale than the incomplete lower one.

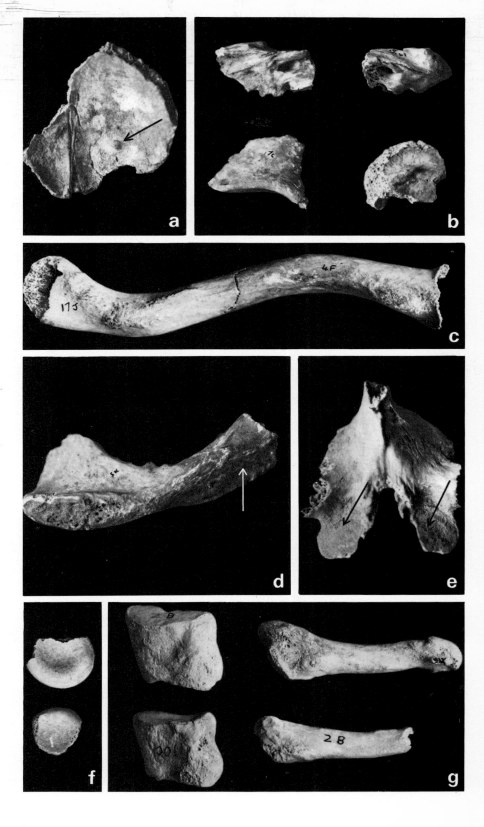

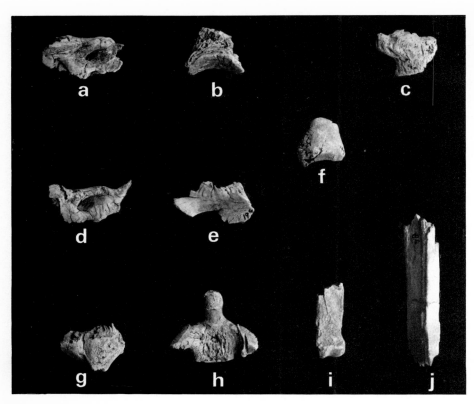

84 Fragments of burnt human skeletal remains from Newgrange: *a* left petrous temporal; *b* root of spine of scapula; *c* left mastoid process; *d* left petrous temporal; *e* body of mandible; *f* right lunate; *g* inferior part of squamous temporal; *h* axis vertebra; *i* distal part of phalanx of hand; *j* fibula.

85 Human dental remains from Newgrange.
a Mesial view of xi) 8| showing an abrasion groove at the cervical margin.   *b* Palatal view of xv)|1 showing a large erosion cavity.   *c* Mesial view of xxv) |5 showing heavy coronal deposits of calculus.   *d* Occlusal view of xviii) |5 and xix) |6 showing gross occlusal attrition and the articulation of these two teeth at the worn interproximal contact areas.   *e* Scanning Electronmicrograph of the floor of the erosion lesion on xv) |1 showing an absence of abrasion scratches. ×450.   *f* Scanning Electronmicrograph of the floor of the abrasion groove in vi) 3| showing the parallel scoring caused by the passage of fine grit across the tooth surface. ×450.   *g* Scanning Electronmicrograph of the interproximal contact area in vi) 3| showing a polished surface marked with a few fine scratches of no preferred orientation. ×450.

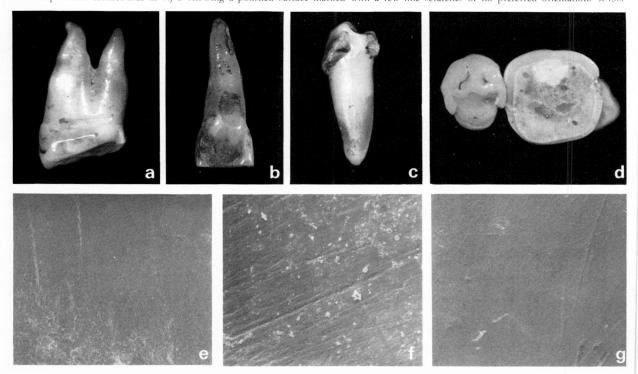

simple-to-complex sequence; recent dates range from 3200 bc to 2900 bc for two of the Carrowmore tombs. Are we then to see the zenith of passage-grave building in Ireland in the three great monuments of the Boyne valley – Newgrange, Dowth and Knowth in that order of date, according to our guess? The latest passage-grave date that we have is that of 2100 bc for the Mound of the Hostages at Tara. By 2000 bc Newgrange was in decay and squatters were living around its collapsing edge. The great megalithic tomb/House for the Dead building-era was at an end. Did this elaborate cult become the undoing of the rich Neolithic farmers? Did the enormous expenditure of effort, man-time and wealth as seen at its peak in the Boyne valley break the economy, and was there a great collapse? If this was the case, how far did the practice of turf stripping, alluded to above, contribute to it? Did the bright young people emigrate leaving the dull ones at home to eke out an existence by pastoralism – the forest was regenerating, as the pollen studies show, and fields that had grown corn were reverting to scrub?

Did the young who had gone abroad come back with new ideas? Forgotten was the House for the Dead cult which had wrecked the economy of their forefathers. Now it was a simple pit burial, easy to prepare and cheap, which some of their ancestors in Late Neolithic times had already been practising. These returning emigrants had seen the quality Beaker pottery abroad and the cult practices to which it belonged and the simplicity of the single-grave burial rite. Did they bring home a few beaker pots which were then copied here as a necessary part of the paraphernalia of the cult? Irish Neolithic pottery had deteriorated in quality and style and thus it is that at about 2000 bc at Newgrange, and elsewhere in Ireland, we find a few fairly typical beaker pots present together with rough native styles. Our studies of the pottery from the Beaker-period settlement around the edge of Newgrange are showing that *all* of the pottery, including the 'classical' Beaker ware, was locally made, the pot-building techniques being those of the indigenous Late Neolithic potters. There is no evidence that Beaker people as such ever came to Newgrange.

Amongst the finds from the Beaker-period settlement area are a flat metal axe and a number of stone objects which are probably the tools of a metal worker (O'Kelly and Shell 1978). The axe can be seen to have been cast in an open mould and to have been finished by forging, grinding and polishing. A metallographic study has shown this to be so. Spectrographic analysis has shown that the metal is a high-tin bronze (13 per cent tin, 87 per cent copper), and the fact that such a metal has come from a horizon radiocarbon-dated to 2000 bc will perhaps be found surprising, especially as the axe would be placed rather late in a typological sequence – as late as 1500 bc or near the end of the Early Bronze Age; but it has been notoriously difficult to date bronze implements since the very great majority of them are chance finds whose context is virtually unknown. The Newgrange find is one of the few discovered in a context by careful excavation. That such a high-tin bronze was being made in Ireland at 2000 bc must mean that metallurgy had begun here long before – well back in the Late Neolithic period, and before Beaker pottery had made its appearance. Evidence of this kind is accumulating in Britain also and again it suggests that metallurgy was introduced into Ireland by Late Neolithic Irish travellers returning from abroad.

fig. 7

Part V CORPUS OF NEWGRANGE ART
Claire O'Kelly

13 The ornament

The art of Newgrange has attracted attention ever since Edward Lhwyd in 1699 commented on the rude carving and 'barbarous sculpture' of some of its stones. The designs and motifs have been reproduced in drawings and photographs many times since then but, as is natural, a good deal of selectivity has been employed and the same stones have tended to be illustrated over and over again, thus giving a somewhat unbalanced and unrepresentative view of Newgrange art as a whole.

This corpus contains all the decorated surfaces known at present at Newgrange. They are all shown at the same scale (1:12.5), so the art as a whole can be evaluated without danger of undue emphasis being placed on the better-known, and better-carved examples such as the entrance stone, and the roof-box lintel. The uniform scale usefully draws attention to the great differences in size which can exist between motifs otherwise similar. For example, the three conjoined spirals in the three-spiral motif on C10 are in actual fact less than one-third of the size of somewhat similar ones on the entrance stone, something seldom made clear by photographs.

By and large, the range of motifs employed in Irish passage-grave art in general is fairly small and may conveniently be divided into ten categories though, as can be expected, there are many motifs so indeterminate as to defy categorization. I refer to ones such as quasi-oval and quasi-circular shapes, meandering lines, and so on, and there are others which are not sufficiently common or sufficiently well-defined to be placed in a group of their own, e.g., criss-cross patterns, single and multiple arrow- or anchor-shapes and cupmarks. The latter pose particular difficulties since it is often extremely hard to decide whether they are wholly natural or whether they were natural to start with and were subsequently deepened by the artificers. In some cases also they appear entirely artificial, but in these instances as a rule they are smaller and more dot-like, e.g. those on K13, and those at the ends of radial lines, e.g. K6. A good example of natural hollows which were subsequently 'treated' and incorporated into an overall design is found on K52.

Of the ten categories, five are curvilinear i.e., circles, spirals, arcs, serpentiforms and dot-in-circles and five are rectilinear i.e., zigzags or chevrons, lozenges, radials or starshapes (usually with a central dot), parallel lines and offsets or comb-devices. It will readily be appreciated that this grouping is no more than an attempt to rationalize a very wide and diverse range of abstract motifs and to make it sufficiently comprehensive to provide a framework for Irish passage-grave art as a whole. The ten groups

plate 14
fig. 47
fig. 24

figs 26, 30
plate 69
fig. 28

merely list the motifs most commonly found but no two devices in any one group are ever identical. There are infinite variations in the degree of skill employed, in the size of point used to pick out the motif, in the size of the motif itself and in the way it is or is not combined with other devices to form a panel of ornament.

A survey of Boyne art has shown that, however random the individual motifs may sometimes seem, each tomb appears to have had a repertoire and a style peculiar to itself (C. O'Kelly 1973). While all, or nearly all, motifs are held in common, it is apparent that some are preferred in one site and some in another, nor does the degree of difficulty in executing a particular device seem to have had any bearing on the selective process. For example, the lozenge would seem to be easier to carve than the concentric circle motif, yet at Dowth, where in general the standard of carving is inferior to that of Newgrange, the latter is fairly common and the lozenge does not occur at all in one of the tombs (Dowth North) and is found only on one slab in the southern tomb. It seems as if particular forms were appropriate to particular tombs, leading to the contrast in content evident between one decorated tomb and another, even those closely associated topographically, as is the case with sites K, L and Z at Newgrange. Differences in the date of building may have some bearing on this.

The lozenge and zigzag (chevron) are the commonest motifs at Newgrange, with   plate 80
the former particularly prominent in the tomb. The circle is the next most frequently used symbol, though this is somewhat misleading since it is not commonly used on any of the prominent slabs; rather it occurs on the backs of kerbstones or in various inconspicuous positions. Spirals, on the other hand, though numerically inferior, are far more prominently displayed, being found on some of the most important and well-   plate V
placed stones. The finest examples of carving have lozenge, spiral and zigzag as their main components in varying combinations. Sometimes the pattern is composed of spiral and lozenge, as in the entrance stone; sometimes of spirals only, as in C10 (the well-known three-spiral stone); and sometimes all three are used, as in the equally well-known L19 in the passage. The rarest motifs at Newgrange are radials or radiat-   plate 74, *fig. 41*
ing lines, usually with a central dot, parallel lines and offsets (comb-devices). The lat-   *fig. 30*
ter are very rare indeed at Newgrange (I know of only one, on K7, and even this is not very definite), though all three motifs are well represented at Loughcrew.

All the motifs employed at Newgrange are geometrical and non-representational, at least in an overt sense (though it must be said that there are two 'doodles', one on the   *figs 32, 52*
back corbel and the other on K50 which invariably bring to my mind a child's drawing of stick-like human figures!). Granted that, to present-day eyes at least, the ornament is abstract, to what extent was it a conscious ornamentation of a particular surface and to what extent had it a symbolic content?

When George Coffey, who displayed amazing prescience in everything to do with Newgrange, made a study of the ornament in the 1890s, he was of the opinion that 'the conditions of the inscribings at Newgrange are fully satisfied by those of ornament, that in fact, the markings simply represent the style of decoration of the period, and that their explanation is to be sought in that direction. It is possible that some of the figures were in their origin symbolical . . .' (1892, 22). It seems to me that for once, Coffey put the cart before the horse; that the symbolical meaning was the original inspiration for Irish passage-grave art, beginning with the random carving of motifs which had a meaning for those who applied them, or who caused them to be applied, and that it was only with the passage of time, as the tomb builders became more expert and sophisticated generally, that the aesthetic element in the carvings began to emerge and develop and designs and patterns began to be achieved, though perhaps this aspect never entirely overruled the symbolism, latent or otherwise. The later manifestations of passage-grave art, in which I would particularly bracket the kerb of the main monument at Knowth, are almost purely decorative, displaying large, bold, often symmetrical patterns, far removed from the naivety of the undisciplined profusion of motifs found, for example, on the backs of K13 and K18 at Newgrange, impressive as these surfaces are when taken as a whole.

fig. 27
plate 66

Nevertheless, there is no denying that conscious ornamentation of particular slabs was employed at Newgrange. The entrance stone, the lintel of the roof-box and K52 are obvious examples. A sculptural quality is evident in these which can owe nothing to chance. Not only are the designs conspicuously well-balanced, but they are adapted in a seemingly effortless way to the surfaces of the stones in question. Other stones also display elements of conscious ornament, e.g. K67, L19, C3 and some of the chamber corbels. Against these, however, must be set the fact that the bulk of the so-called art consists of disjointed, isolated and not very well-executed motifs. Some of them are readily classifiable as circles, spirals, lozenges, and so on, but many others consist of amorphous shapes to which the name of 'doodles' may be aptly applied. One finds motifs carved without apparent regard to the suitability of the surface or to their position on it; one finds a single insignificant-looking motif on a stone of perhaps three square metres in surface area; one finds motifs scratched or picked on the sides of orthostats while the main face remains unadorned, such as L13.

plate 40

fig. 52

fig. 29

plate 72

fig. 40

In order to explain the presence of these apparently random engravings, often side by side with artistic creations, one is inclined to suggest that the actual carving of the devices was the important thing, fulfilling a ceremonial or spiritual or symbolical purpose, but that as far as some of the more important stones were concerned, the carving was entrusted to experienced and artistic workers who united the motifs into designs that were pleasing as well as meaningful. The entrance stone, the roof-slab of the east recess and the roof-box lintel come to mind.

A curious feature encountered during the excavations was that decoration was discovered on a number of surfaces that in the normal course would be completely hidden. Some of these slabs were in or above the passage roof; other decorated areas were found near the bottom of orthostats, close to or even below old ground level. One profusely decorated stone was built into the roof of the chamber as a corbel and only a small part of the ornament can now be seen (Co.1/C7). In addition, at least five kerbstones are decorated on their back surfaces; in the case of two of them, K13 and K18, the ornament covers the entire area.

plate 68

fig. 49

The simplest and most direct explanation is that expediency dictated the positions of the slabs and the fact that the ornament could not be seen was of little import to the builders once it had been applied to the stones. On the other hand, one has become suspicious of postulating expediency in explanation of any feature of the Newgrange tumulus, because it is not a characteristic normally to be associated with it. Up to the present our experience has been that every feature, structural, architectural, and so on, was carefully thought out. For this reason alone, one must pay rather more attention to apparent anomalies than is generally the case. The positions of the hidden stones may indeed be fortuitous (the question is very much an open one), but for the record a few factors are worth mentioning. One of them is that radials and dot-in-circles are found chiefly on hidden stones or in hidden or obscure positions. Another factor is that the positioning of many of the hidden stones seems meaningful. For instance, one of them forms the back of the roof-box, two others are corbels to right and left of the roof-box, respectively, and two others again are at the junction of passage and chamber roof, again to left and right sides. Can it be that the policy of decorating important slabs obtained whether the ornament was to be seen or not?

plate 70

A great many, perhaps the majority of the stones were carved before being positioned and there can be little doubt but that some of them, at least, were destined for particular locations, the decorated corbels in the chamber are cases in point. The carving is on the forward-facing narrow side of the stones, showing that they were meant to be viewed edge-on. That they were carved in advance is demonstrated by the fact that in many cases, such as Co.2/C14, the ornamented surface continues into the cairn at the sides. This occurs too in the case of the roof-stone of the east recess, a very large slab, the underside of which is covered by a profusion of motifs.

fig. 50, plate 81

The entrance stone, however, was carved *in situ* before the kerbstones on either side were placed in position. The ornament and the all-over pick-dressing stop near the bottom of the stone at a horizontal line which represented ground level at that time. Also, the ornament is present in areas that could not have been carved were the neighbouring stones in place. There is therefore nothing accidental about the siting or the ornamentation of this fine slab. K52 was also carved *in situ*.

fig. 24

plate 4

Techniques

The motifs were usually picked on the natural surface of the slab by making a series of small pits or pickings, using a sharp point, perhaps one of flint or quartz. Occasionally, however, motifs were incised, cut or scratched, though this method is mainly associated with unfinished or poorly made motifs. There is evidence that it was also used to mark out guide-lines, as, for instance, when a pattern of lozenges, triangles, etc. was intended, the outlines were first scratched on the slab and later picked over.

plate 71

The picking takes many forms. There is line-picking such as can be seen in spirals, circles and serpentiforms, etc., when a line of picks traces out the motif. Where subsequent weathering has not blurred them, these pickings are often as fresh as the day they were made and enable one to see clearly the grade of point used. Sometimes the line of picking was finished off by rubbing with a pebble so as to produce a continuous grooved line. This has been done in the case of many of the finest motifs. Sometimes, too, instead of line-picking, solid or area picking was used, as when the interiors of circles or lozenges were picked all over, or when half, or even a quarter of the lozenge was solidly picked and the remainder was picked in outline only so as to create a

fig. 49

chequered effect. The most sophisticated effect of all involved picking the surface of the slab, leaving an unpicked area in relief which provided the pattern or motif. This was frequently done in the case of spirals or zigzags, the broad, smooth band between the picked lines or grooves providing the pattern rather than the picking itself. This technique is seen on some of the finest stones at Newgrange and Knowth but has not so far been recorded at Dowth, nor has it been recorded elsewhere outside the Boyne valley except on one stone, Stone B, in Fourknocks (Hartnett 1957, pl. 77).

fig. 24

The entrance stone at Newgrange is the example *par excellence*. The bands of ornament are about 4 cm wide and the channels between are about the same width and about 1 cm deep. The channels or grooves were smoothed and rubbed so as to produce an even surface. The whole decorated face, including channels and bands, was then pick-dressed all over with a fine point so as to remove all the original weathered surface. Kerbstone 52 rivals it in the excellence of its ornamentation and indeed could well have been carved by the same hand, so similar is the technique.

fig. 28

Pick-dressing

Another interesting feature of the monument is the extensive use of pick-dressing on the slabs, as distinct from the picking of the ornament. Every orthostat in the passage has some amount of dressing and the same is true in the chamber with one or two exceptions. Furthermore, almost all the inside corbels of the chamber, even the very high-up ones, are dressed. Areas of pick-dressing occur also on some of the kerbstones but they are mostly of a random nature.

As far as can be ascertained, though done with the same tools as the ornament, the pick-dressing of the slabs of passage and chamber was applied after they were positioned. Pick-dressing seems to occur only on surfaces which would have been accessible after the tomb was built. In the passage, for example, the dressing is confined to the main face of the slabs, whereas ornamental devices are often found in inaccessible positions such as the sides (L13 and R12). Some of the forward edges of the passage and chamber corbels are dressed, but never on surfaces which would have been inaccessible after the slabs were in place.

There are several curious features to be noted. Some areas of the face of a slab are dressed in what appears to be a haphazard manner to the exclusion of other parts of the surface. L2 is one of many such slabs. Was this to reduce minor protuberances? When the uneven surfaces of the undressed Dowth slabs are compared with the dressed Newgrange ones, it is realized how much labour must have been expended on the latter to bring them to such a finish. Another curious feature is the frequency with which the dressing is brought to about 20 cm or so from (present) ground level, where it ends in a definite line, often oblique. L10 is one example. This may be due to the fact that when the slabs were being dressed the floor was at a higher level than now and was perhaps a good deal more uneven.

In the case of decorated slabs, sometimes the face is dressed back on each side of the ornament so as to leave it slightly proud of the rest. L19 is one of the best examples. Often the opposite procedure is followed and the dressing obliterates for all practical purposes the previously applied ornament. The 'ghosts' of four very fine spirals can be seen near ground level on L19, all but obliterated by picking, while beneath them, well buried below floor level, are rows of chevrons still as fresh as when first applied because they were exempt both from the pick-dresser's zeal and from the effects of weathering.

plate 75

A similar instance of obliteration can be seen at the bottom of R3. The pick-dressing on this slab extends downward to about 30 cm above present floor level, obliterating the top three-quarters of a 25 cm spiral in the process, while lower down, on the undressed part, is an ornamented area of remarkable freshness. Another example is the very fine panel of divided lozenges on the upper third of R8, which has been so thoroughly picked-over that the ornament was only noticed for the first time during the excavations.

fig. 42

fig. 42

This obliteration of ornament is not confined to Newgrange (Macalister 1943, 135) and must remain a puzzle. When it occurs in the passage and chamber, bad light could be blamed, but it is also found on the kerb (K97 among others). The great kerbstones, K1 and K52, and the lintel of the roof-box were exempted from haphazard pick-dressing, in fact, the surfaces of these slabs were most expertly dressed all over so as to enhance rather than destroy the ornament, but in most other cases it seems as if it was largely a matter of luck that the ornament was spared. Let us hope no bad blood was engendered between the carvers and the dressers!

Finally, there is the curious ripple-dressing on R12 and R21. This has been wrongly compared with the maul-dressing on some of the Stonehenge slabs. In the latter case parallel grooves were worked in the surface of the slabs by pounding them with mauls so as to produce an initial reduction of the surface. This was necessitated by the extremely intractable nature of the Stonehenge sarcens, whereas the broad, shallow grooves on the Newgrange orthostats were made by picking, just as in the case of any other dressed area. But for what purpose, whether necessitated by the shape of the slab or as a form of embellishment, is not known.

fig. 43
plate 79

Irish passage-grave art

Within the relatively restricted framework of geometrical motifs it is clear that there was ample scope for Irish passage-grave builders to express individuality by characteristic groupings of motifs, to which names such as Newgrange style or Loughcrew style can be applied. Generally speaking, there is a definite similarity between all the decorated stones of a particular tomb. Where exceptions occur, as for instance, at Knowth, and in the case of the two Dowth South orthostats, C6 and C7 (C. O'Kelly 1973, fig. 4), interesting questions arise as to whether successive building phases, secondary decoration of stones, and so on, are responsible. Certainly at Knowth it is hardly to be expected that a unitary style of decoration would prevail, since, apart from any other considerations, the monument complex, consisting as it does, of at least seventeen satellite passage-graves, in addition to the two in the main mound itself, must span a considerable period of time. Enlargement of some tombs, destruction of others and reuse of their decorated stones cannot be ruled out. How much the various art styles are idiosyncratic, how much the product of particular or even personal beliefs or cults, how much due to chronological, and sometimes topographical factors, are some of the intriguing problems still to be solved.

However wide the divergence between different styles appears to be, it is minimal compared with that between Irish passage-grave art and the Iberian and Breton examples with which it has so often been linked. Heretofore, the tendency has largely been to concentrate attention on alleged anthropomorphic and representational elements in the Irish material, to the exclusion of more unequivocally abstract ones. This has led to a linking of Irish carvings with a variety of media far removed spatially as well as chronologically. Irish passage-grave art has been said to be derived from the stone idols, amulets, stone plaques and small anthropomorphic figures found in Iberian tombs, for example, as well as from the designs engraved and painted on the walls of the tombs themselves.

Gavrinis, in Brittany, has repeatedly been brought forward as an example, if not an exemplar, of Irish art, often without due regard to the fact that this tomb is an exotic in the context of both Breton and Irish art. Petit Mont (Arzon) has also been cited as an Irish parallel, mainly on the strength of its zigzag and radial lines, but non-Irish motifs such as axes and shields (*écussons*) are also present. Other putative sources are designs on pottery from Iberia and Scandinavia, but unless all or any of these proposed models can at the very least be shown to antedate the Irish examples there is little point in the comparisons, no matter how apposite. Now that Newgrange has been shown to belong at least to the mid-third millennium bc, many of the above comparisons can be ruled out straightaway. Moreover, the overtly representational nature of much of the Breton and Iberian carvings indicates a fundamental difference which is not negated by the fact that a small range of motifs such as arcs, U's, circles, radials, and zigzags is held in common.

14 Corpus of decorated stones

Method

Since only about one-third of the perimeter has been fully exposed by the excavations the total number of the decorated stones in the kerb is not yet known. Though ornament can be seen on the tops of some of the partially exposed kerbstones in the unexcavated areas these are not included in the corpus. It is also possible that there is ornament inside the tomb structure in inaccessible places and this may never be discovered. The corpus comprises 75 decorated stones (84 decorated surfaces, since some stones are ornamented on more than one surface). They are distributed as follows: 31 in the kerb, 16 in the passage, 18 in the chamber and 10 in the passage roof.

All of the ornament was traced directly from the stones onto either cellophane or clear polythene. It was then re-traced onto tracing paper and photographically reduced to one-quarter of the actual size and it was from these reductions that the finished pen-and-ink drawings were made. They were still large enough for every detail of the ornament to be faithfully reproduced, and yet of manageable size for the printer who had to effect further reduction. While the above sequence may seem cumbersome, and while it was certainly laborious and time-consuming (for example, the pen-and-ink tracing of K13 from the cellophane took 14 hours), there was little alternative. The sheer size of most of the stones, particularly the kerbstones, made the full-size tracings extremely difficult to handle. In the final printed result the scale used, 1:12.5, is the largest which is compatible with the exigencies of the printed page.

When seen against the background of the huge cairn one fails to comprehend the true size of the kerbstones, and the same applies when one enters the tomb. For example, the full-size tracing of the entrance stone (by no means the largest stone in the kerb) when laid flat would take up most of the floor-space of the average living room; the tracing of the roof-stone of the east recess was even more awkward to manage as it *fig. 51* was extremely large and almost square. In many cases the expedient of illustrating only the decorated areas has had to be adopted but 'miniatures' of these stones have been included at a scale of 1:62.5 on which the ornamented surfaces are indicated. However, in cases where the entire surface is decorated, e.g. kerbstones 1, 4, 13, 18, 52 and 67 and some of the stones in the tomb, the full outline is given at the larger scale. It has not been thought necessary to give verbal descriptions of the decorated stones as the illustrations speak for themselves, but attention may be drawn to a few matters concerning them.

As a general rule, so-called cupmarks are not illustrated save where they have been incorporated into the ornament, as in K52 in the kerb and R20 in the passage. Few if *figs 28, 44* any of the many cupmarks are manmade, at least in their initial stage, but they have been frequently deepened and rounded and sometimes outlined by picking. The main inhibiting factor as regards illustrating them, however, is that when shown on a small scale they can be mistaken for picked 'solid' circles. Areas of pick-dressing are shown as a rule only when they are integral to the ornament, as in L19, or where they partially obliterate it, as in R8. Finally, the limitations imposed by the attempt to portray on a flat surface the rounded, or angled or uneven or fissured surfaces of the various stones must be borne in mind.

Corpus of
decorated stones

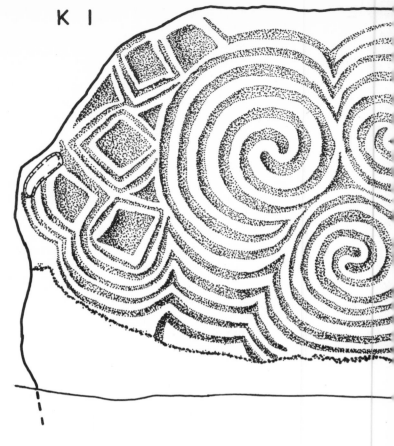

24 *The entrance stone (K1).*

25 *K4 (back of stone). The front of the stone is*
also decorated (fig. 32), and there is a scratched
criss-cross pattern on the side of the stone.

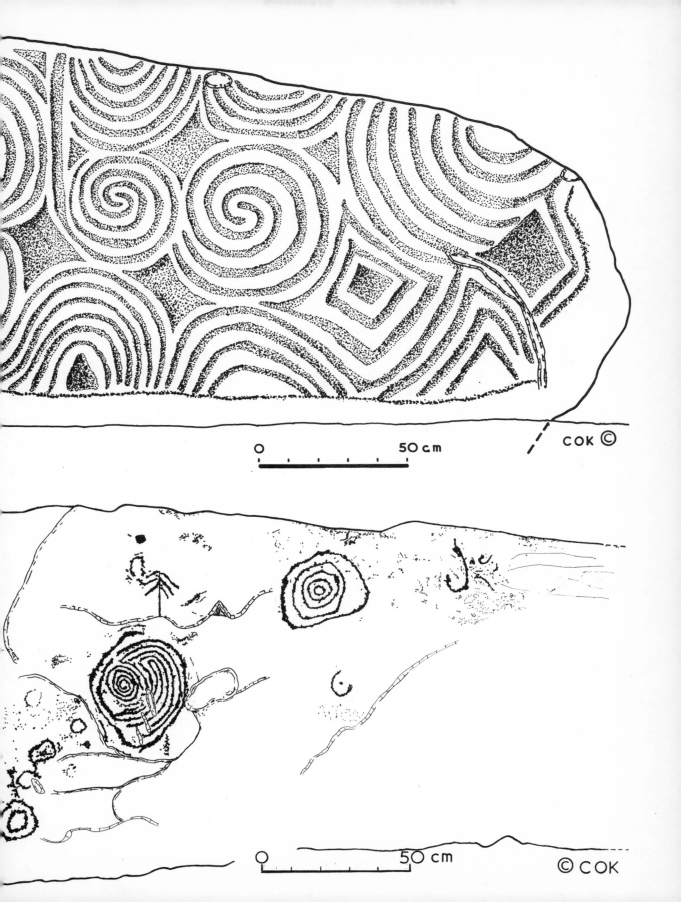

0   50 cm

COK ©

0   50 cm

© COK

K13 Back

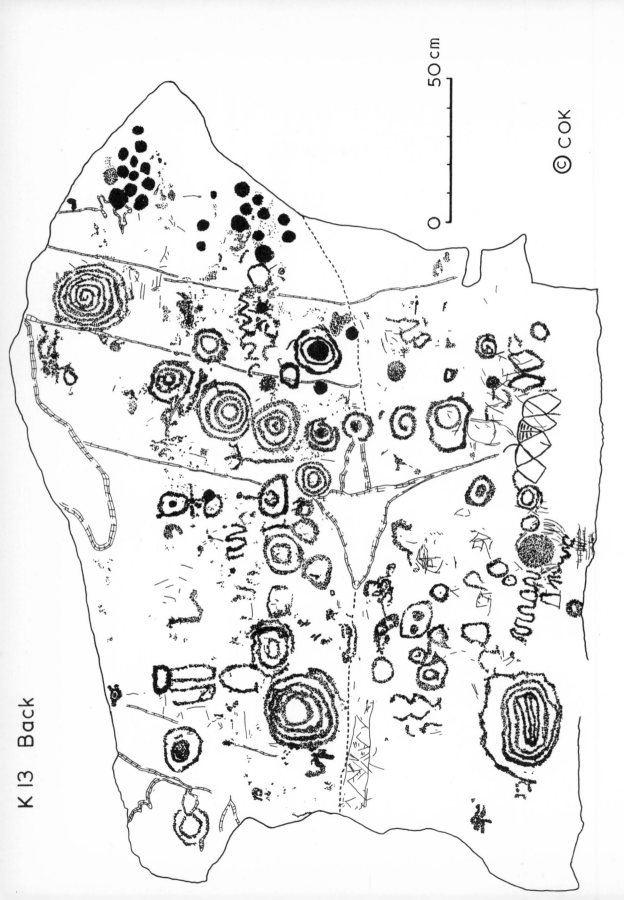

50 cm

© COK

26 *K13 (back of stone). The surface consists of two planes, inclined at an obtuse angle to each other. Almost 100 separate motifs are present. The ornament can no longer be seen as the stone has been replaced as found.*

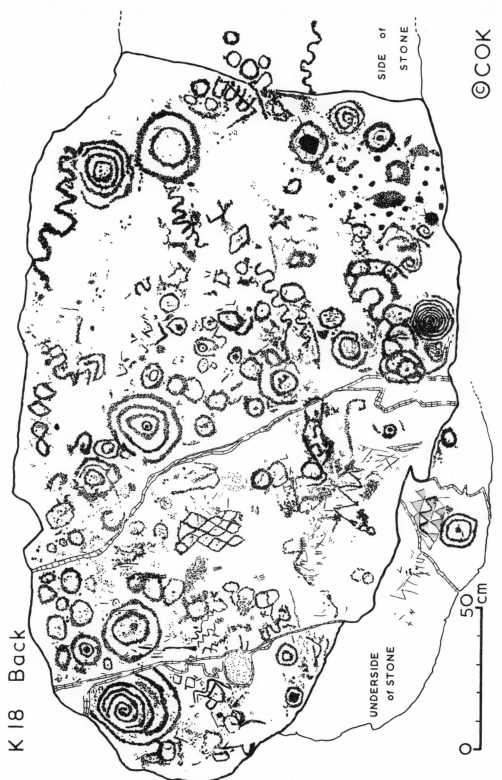

K 18 Back

SIDE of STONE

©COK

UNDERSIDE of STONE

0   50   cm

27 K18: ornament on the back, underside and west side. More than 100 separate motifs are present. The ornament cannot now be seen as the stone has been replaced as found.

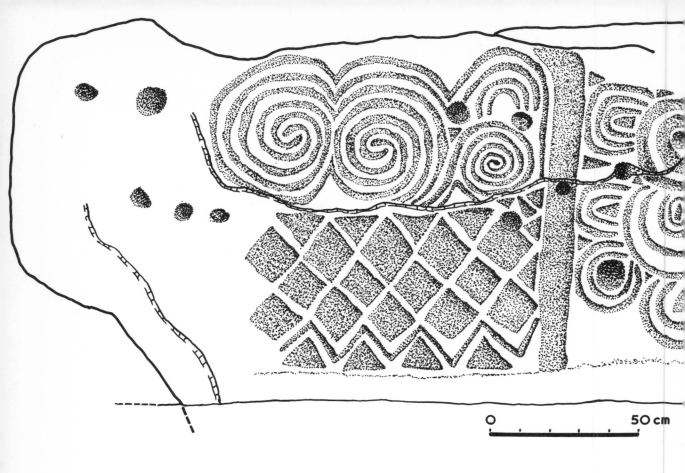

0   50 cm

28 K52: rivals the entrance stone in the quality of its design and the excellence of its technique; the same broad channels and relief-bands are present and the same overall pick-dressing which ends at a horizontal line. A vertical channel divides the face into two parts; a picked line continues upwards from this, dividing the top surface of the slab also (fig. 35). Hollows or cupmarks have been skilfully incorporated into the design.

29 K67: S-spirals (or returning spirals) are rare at Newgrange, being found otherwise only on C10 and the bottom of L19.

0   50 cm

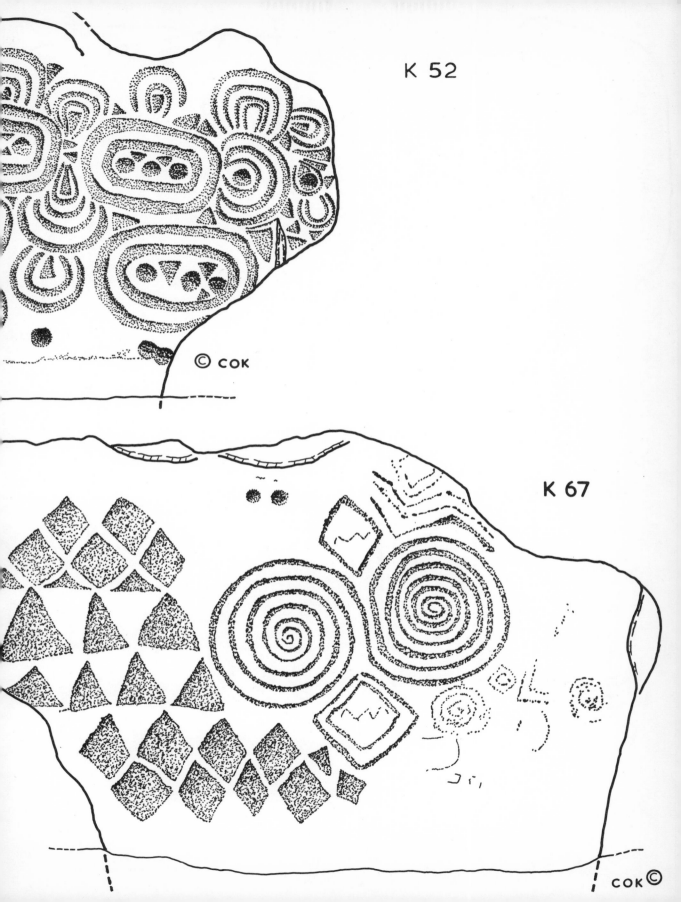

K 52

© COK

K 67

COK©

Kerb

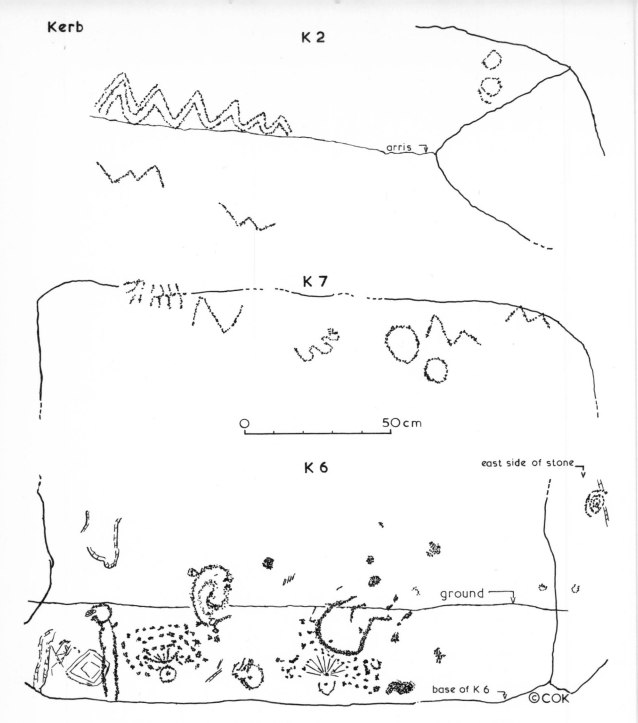

30 *K2: overall pick-dressing has almost obliterated the ornament which is just above and below the arris; K6: most of the surface is very rough and spalled; the ornament is at the bottom, below present ground level, on a smoother part of the surface; K7: note possible offset device. There is a good deal of random pick-dressing, widely spaced.*

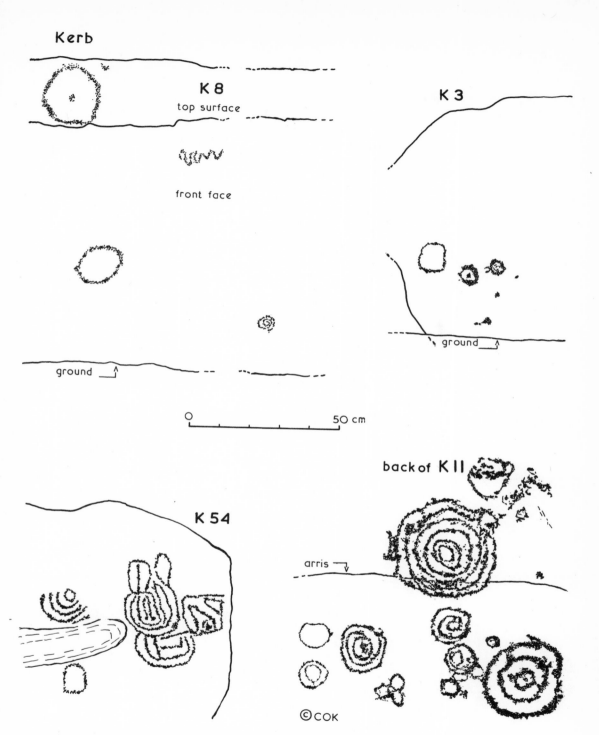

Kerb

K 8

top surface

front face

K 3

ground

ground

50 cm

back of K 11

K 54

arris

©COK

31 *K3: irregular area of pick-dressing all along top of face; K8: note dot-in-circle on top surface; K11 (ornament is on back of stone and cannot now be seen); K54.*

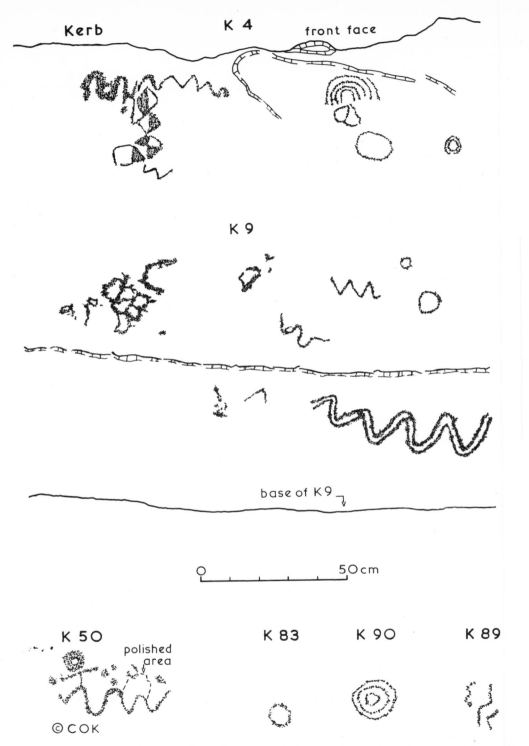

32 K4 (front of stone) ; K9; K50: device is on sloping top of stone above the arris and is one of the 'doodled' figures mentioned on p. 147; note smooth polished area; K83; K89: a good deal of random pick-dressing; K90: some random picking of surface.

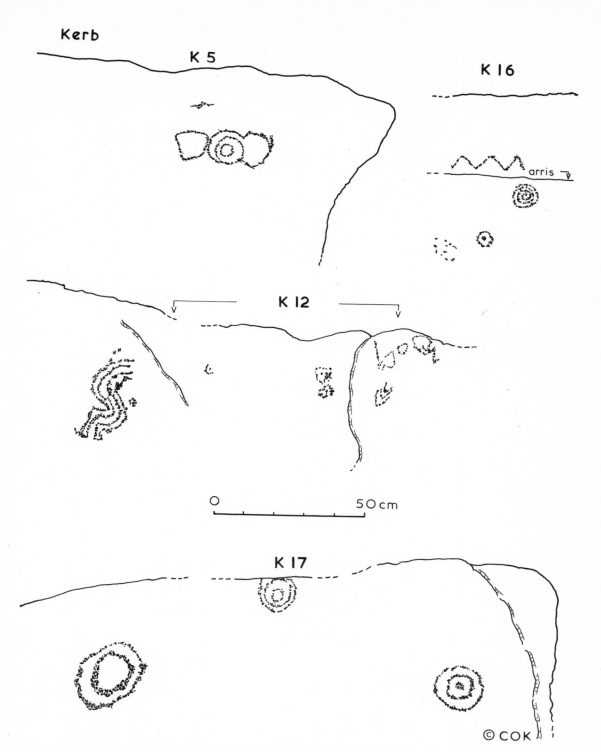

Kerb

K 5

K 16

arris

K 12

O   50 cm

K 17

© COK

33 K5: many hollows, some of which have been deepened by picking; K12: the longest stone in the kerb (4.7 m), the bottom is raised on boulders to maintain the even top-line of the kerb; K16; K17.

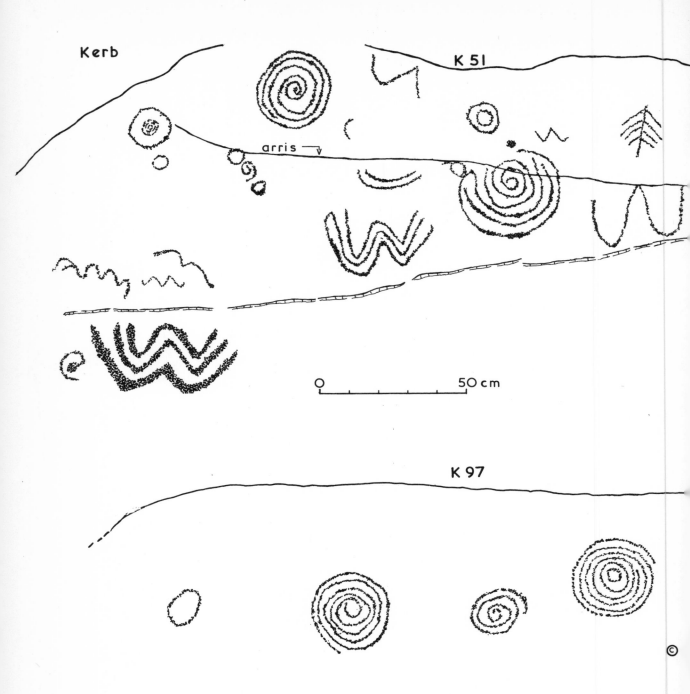

Kerb

K 51

arris →

0   50 cm

K 97

34 *K51: a fine smooth rounded boulder which one would have thought would have been preferred by the master-carver of K52, since K52 has a poor surface with many protuberances, cracks and hollows and must have presented great difficulties; K97: ornament very difficult to see as all-over pick-dressing has almost obliterated it.*

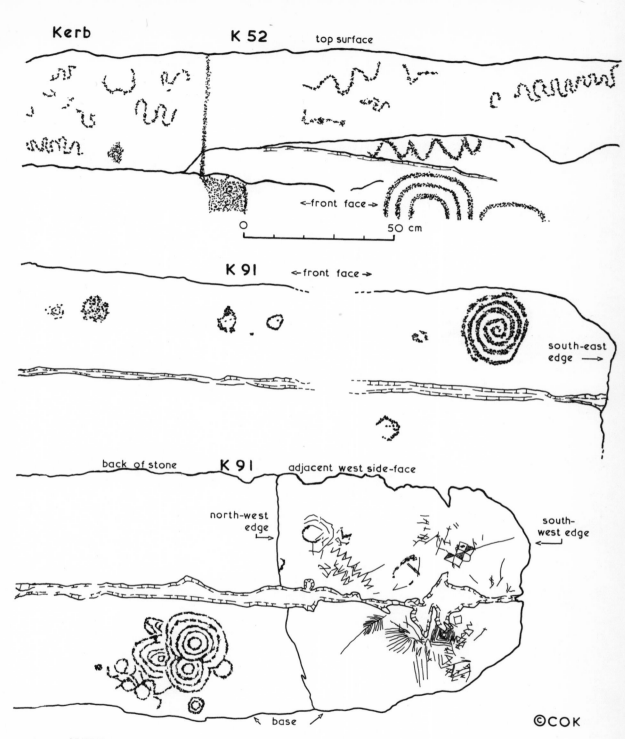

Kerb   K 52   top surface

←front face→

50 cm

K 91   ←front face→

south-east edge →

back of stone   K 91   adjacent west side-face

north-west edge →

south-west edge ←

base

©COK

35 K52 (top surface, now concealed by revetment); cf. fig. 28; K91: front, back and west side ornamented; only front can now be seen.

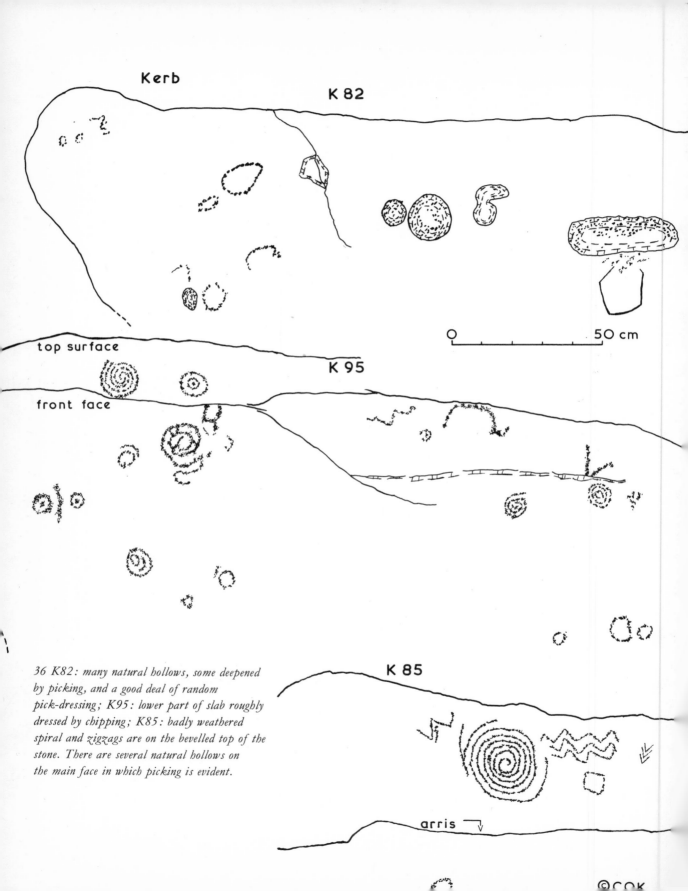

Kerb

K 82

top surface

K 95

front face

0   50 cm

K 85

*36 K82: many natural hollows, some deepened
by picking, and a good deal of random
pick-dressing; K95: lower part of slab roughly
dressed by chipping; K85: badly weathered
spiral and zigzags are on the bevelled top of the
stone. There are several natural hollows on
the main face in which picking is evident.*

arris

©CÓK

Kerb

K 88

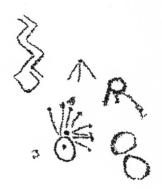

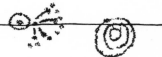

ground↓

O |—|—|—|—|—|—|—| 50 cm

K 93

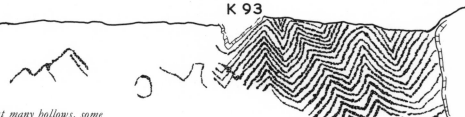

37 *K88: a great many hollows, some of them 'improved' by picking; motifs are diverse and randomly distributed; K93: poor surface yet multiple chevron pattern is very well executed; K96: as well as picked motifs, there are many scratch-marks, only a few of which could be traced with certainty. The marks are deliberate and are thought to be original, because excavation showed that the stone fell forward soon after the monument was built; it was raised again to the vertical only in 1966. Had the stone been exposed to the same degree of weathering as most of the others the marks would long ago have been obliterated.*

K 96

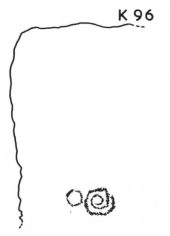

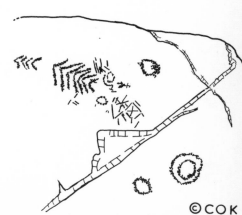

©COK

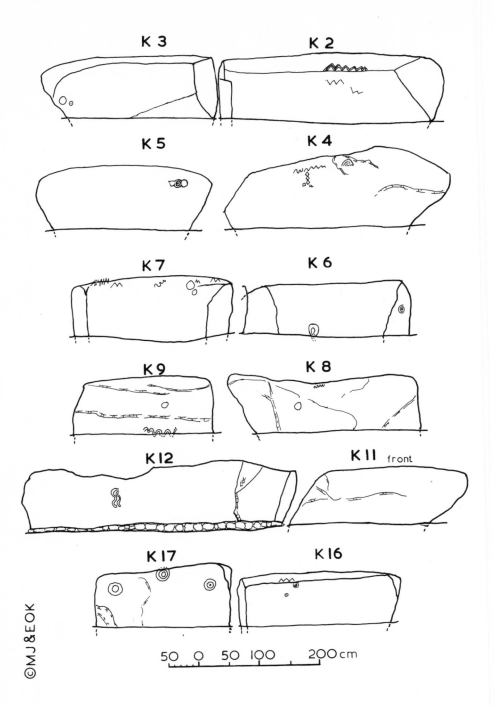

Kerb   K 2 – K 17

K 3   K 2

K 5   K 4

K 7   K 6

K 9   K 8

K 12   K 11 front

K 17   K 16

©MJ&EOK

50 0 50 100   200 cm

38 Outlines of ornamented kerbstones west of entrance.

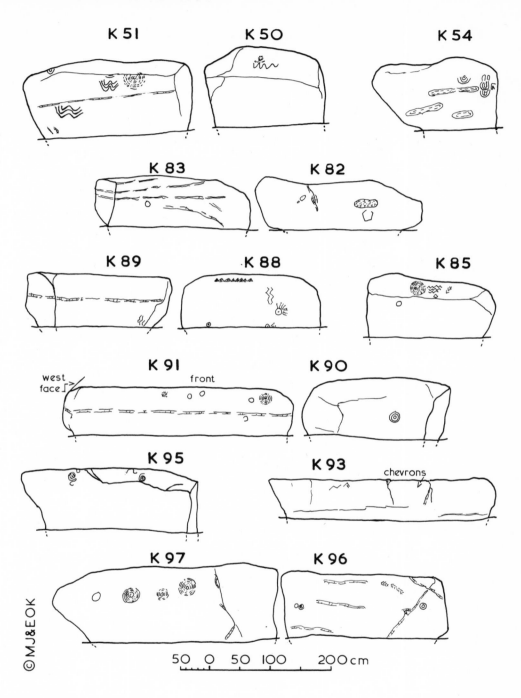

Kerb   K 50–K 97

K 51   K 50   K 54

K 83   K 82

K 89   K 88   K 85

K 91   K 90

west
face
front

K 95   K 93

chevrons

K 97   K 96

©MJ&EOK

50 0 50 100   200 cm

39 Outlines of ornamented kerbstones in north cutting and east of entrance.

169

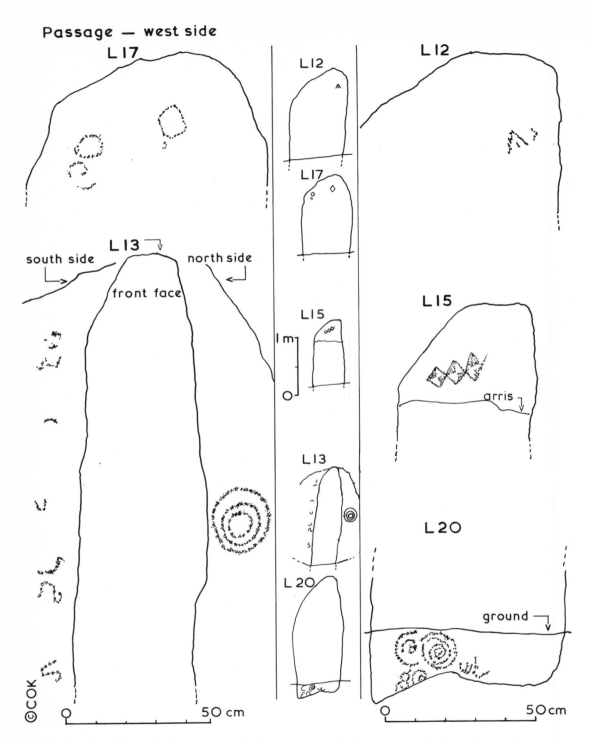

Passage — west side

L 17

L 13

south side   north side

front face

L 12

L 17

L 15

1 m

L 13

L 20

L 12

L 15

arris

L 20

ground

©COK

50 cm

50 cm

40 *L12; L13: main face undecorated; devices on both sides but only part of the surfaces can be seen;*
L15; L17; L20: ornament below present ground level but inspection pit provided.

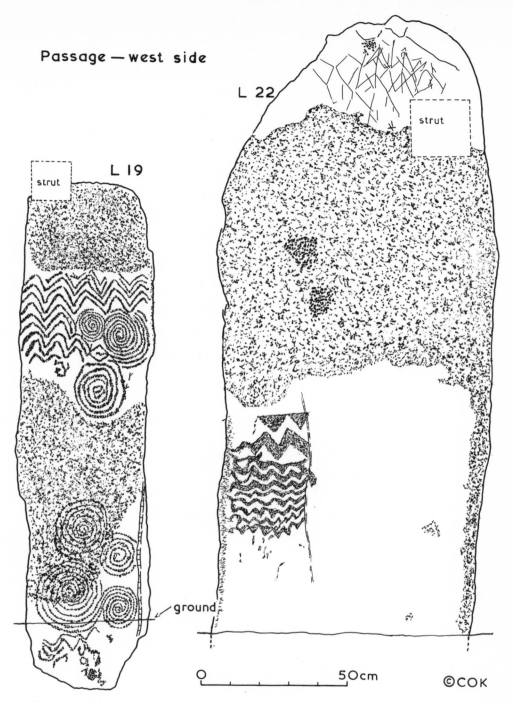

Passage — west side

L 19

strut

L 22

strut

ground

O   50cm

©COK

41 *L19: one of the best-known stones in the passage. The surface above and below the panel of ornament has been dressed so that the ornamented area is slightly proud of the remainder. Note how dressing follows the irregular edge of the ornamented area without overrunning it, in contrast to the ornament at the bottom where part of the design is all but obliterated; L22: here too the pick-dressing avoids the panel of ornament; note scratched pattern on top, undressed, part of surface.*

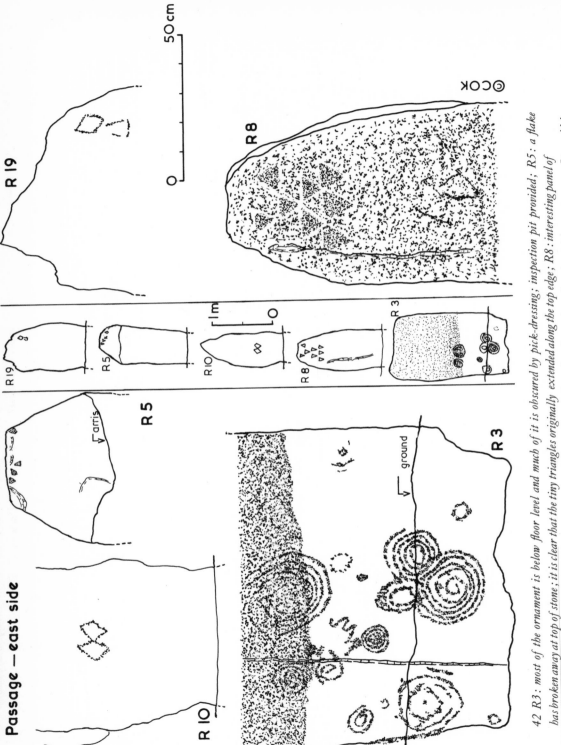

Passage — east side

R 19

R 8

R 5

R 3

R 10

50 cm

©COK

1 m

42 R3: *most of the ornament is below floor level and much of it is obscured by pick-dressing; inspection pit provided; R5: a flake has broken away at top of stone; it is clear that the tiny triangles originally extended along the top edge; R8: interesting panel of horizontally divided lozenges, both halves of lozenges are picked, one half with a fine point, the other with a coarse one. It would have been very striking had not the surface been subsequently pick-dressed; R10: the lozenges are in slight relief compared to the rest of the surface which is dressed; R19.*

Passage—east side

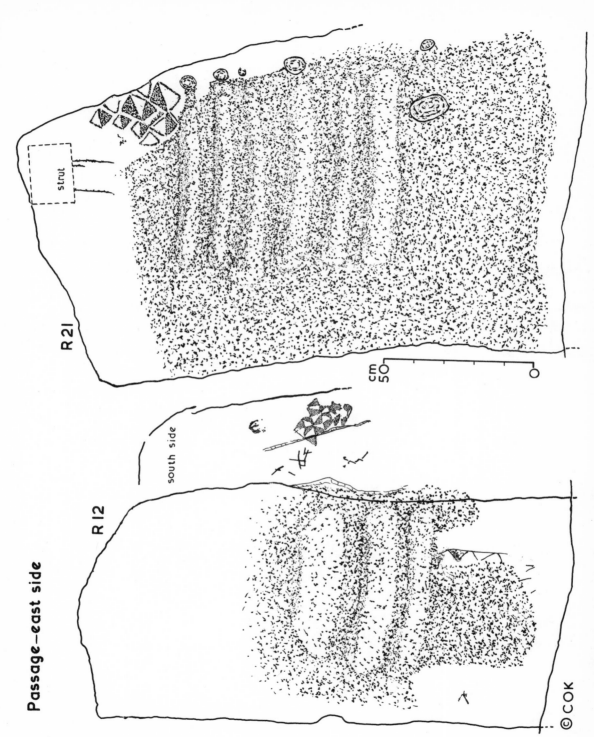

43 R12: *three broad shallow grooves were picked across the surface with well-marked rounded ridges in between, and the whole surface was then pick-dressed; panel of ornament on south side; R21: grooves are similar to those on R12; note cupmarks which have been deepened by picking.*

© COK

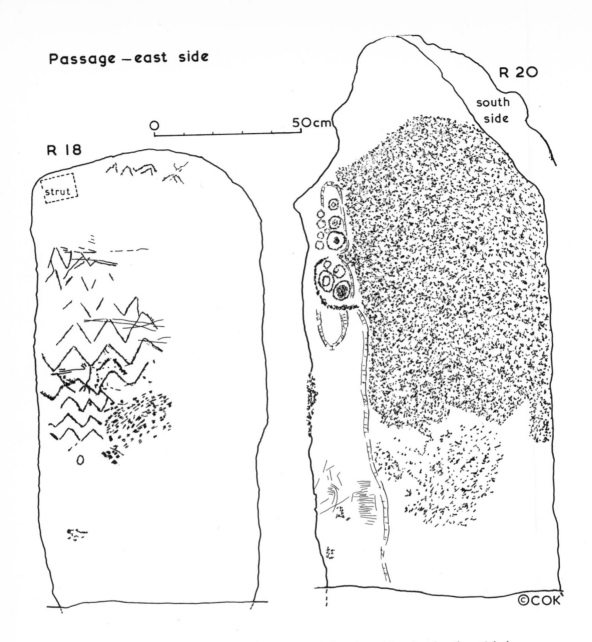

Passage — east side

R 18

R 20

south side

strut

0   50cm

©COK

44 *R18: stone is of very soft quality and motifs have been chipped rather than picked;*
R20: natural hollows utilized for purpose of ornament by deepening and outlining
with picked circles; the major part of the face is pick-dressed.

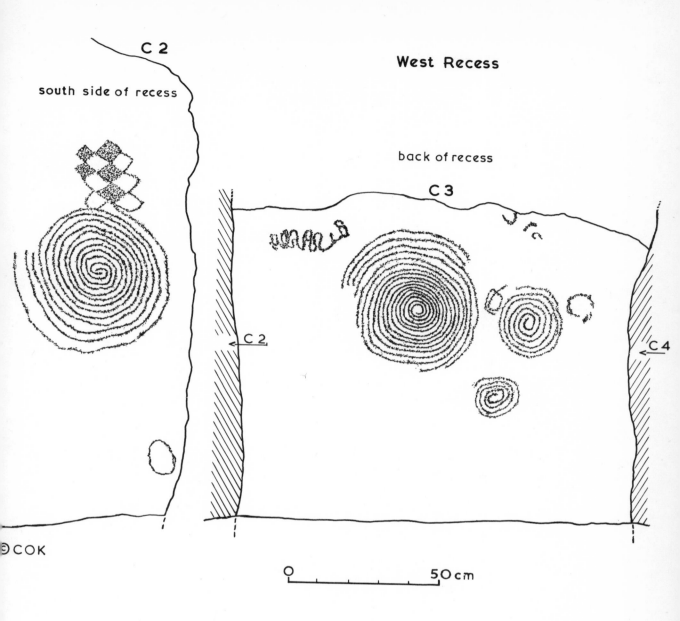

West Recess

C 2

south side of recess

back of recess

C 3

C 2

C 4

©COK

0   50 cm

45 West recess: C2 (left side); C3 (back of recess).

West Recess

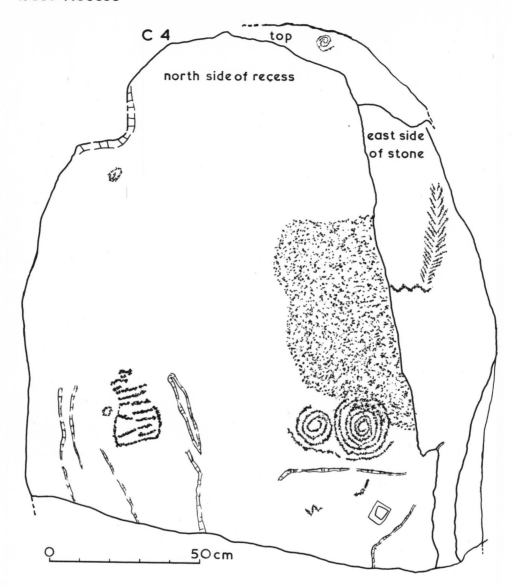

46 West recess: C4 (right side): decorated on two adjoining faces.

Chamber

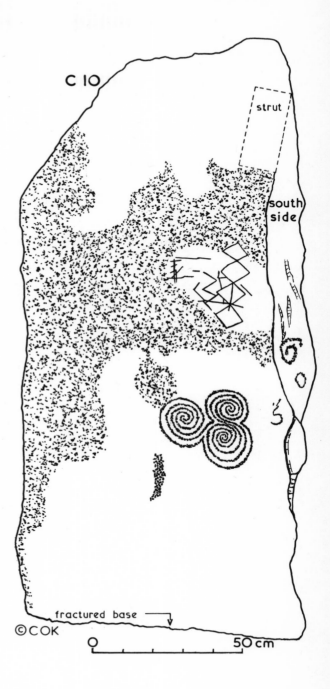

C 10

strut

south side

47 C10, the three-spiral stone (often wrongly called a triple spiral: since a double spiral, like those on the entrance stone, consists of two parallel coils, by analogy a triple spiral should consist of three; in fact, the design consists of three double spirals, the two on the right being S- or returning spirals as well). In order to integrate the left-hand spiral into the design the two free ends of its outermost double coil were separated so as to sweep concentrically around the two other spirals and to meet again having encircled the S-spirals. The whole pattern is only 30 × 28 cm. The spirals are beautifully picked in broad shallow channels so that the intervening bands stand in relief. The design is executed on the undressed surface, but an area of pick-dressing on the left partly encroaches on it.

fractured base →

©COK

0   50 cm

Chamber

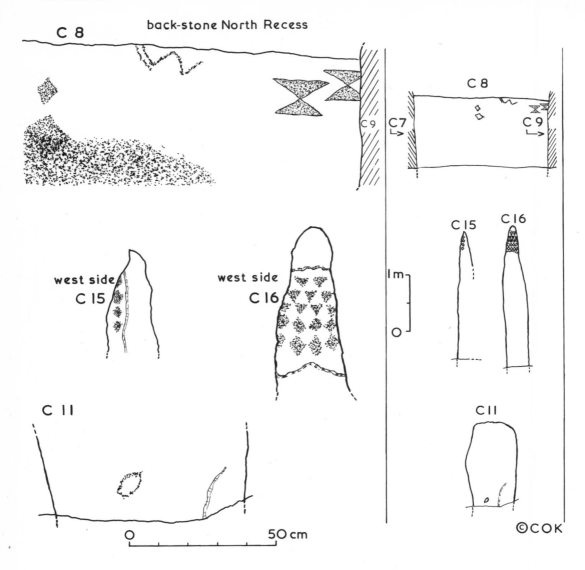

48 C8 (back stone of end recess); C11; C15; C16.

49 Co.1/C2 (above left side of west recess); Co.1/C7 (above left side of end recess). Ornament almost completely hidden and was only discovered during the survey of the tomb; Co.4/C8 (roof stone of end recess); Co.1/C10: the ornament is on the underside of a large corbel directly behind C10. When the latter broke from its base and fell forward (p. 37), all the corbels in this area became displaced. When repairs were effected at least one other corbel on which spirals and concentric arcs were carved was built into the wall behind C10 and can no longer be seen (p. 37); Co.1/C11; Co.2/C11.

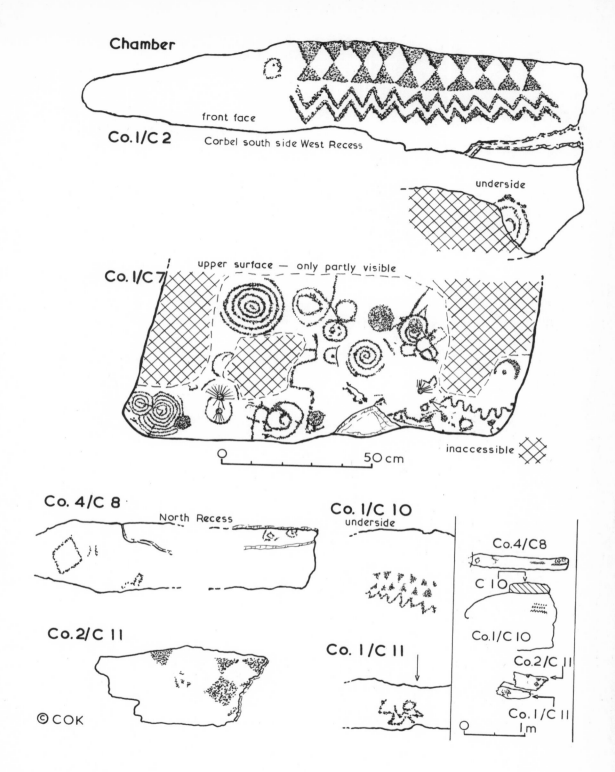

Chamber

Co.1/C2   Corbel south side West Recess

front face

underside

Co.1/C7   upper surface — only partly visible

inaccessible

50 cm

Co.4/C8   North Recess

Co.1/C10   underside

Co.4/C8

C10

Co.1/C10

Co.2/C11

Co.2/C11

Co.1/C11

© COK

Co.1/C11

1m

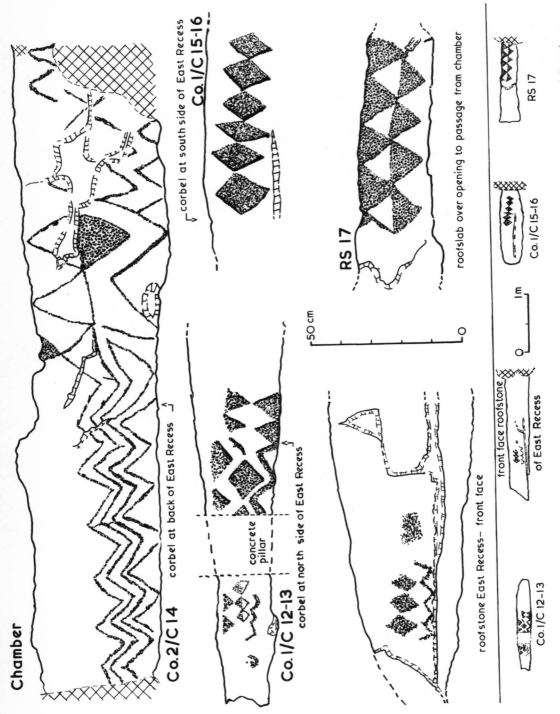

Chamber

Co.2/C14 corbel at back of East Recess

corbel at back of East Recess

corbel at south side of East Recess

Co.1/C 15-16

Co.1/C 12-13
corbel at north side of East Recess

concrete
pillar

RS 17

roofslab over opening to passage from chamber

50 cm

roofstone East Recess— front face

front face roofstone
of East Recess

Co.1/C 12-13

Co.1/C15-16

RS 17

1m

50cm
0

0

50 *Co.1/C12-13 (obscured by concrete pillar); Co.2/C14 (at back of east recess): ornament continues into the cairn at left and right sides; Co.1/C15-16; RS17: the last roof-slab of the passage, at junction of passage and chamber, ornament seen from chamber; Roof-stone of east recess-forward edge. (Cf. fig. 51.)*

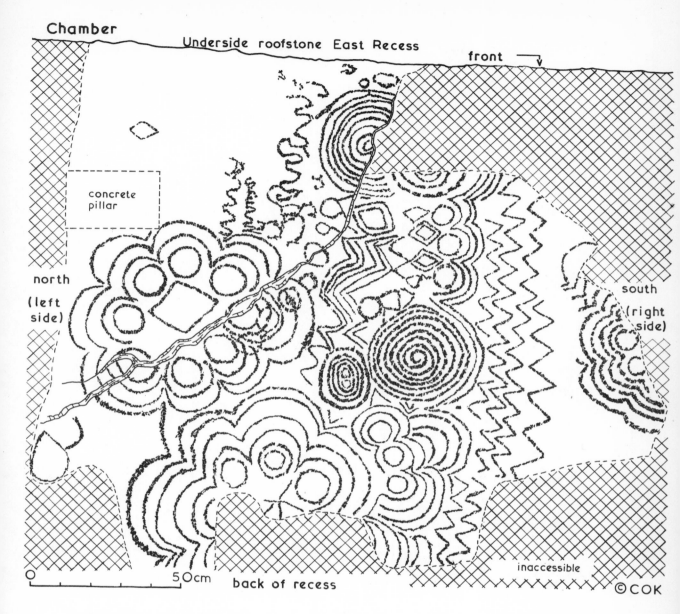

Chamber

Underside roofstone East Recess

front

concrete pillar

north (left side)

south (right side)

inaccessible

0   50cm   back of recess   ©COK

51 *Roof-stone of east recess–underside: this is one of the glories of Newgrange, the whole underside of the slab being virtually covered with motifs of great range and virtuosity. Not all can be seen in their entirety as they continue into the cairn at sides and back. Unfortunately, also, the slab is cracked and one part of the design does not now register with the other. The difficulties of tracing this slab were immense but were worth while as the design can now be seen as a whole for the first time, something which could not be achieved by photography.*

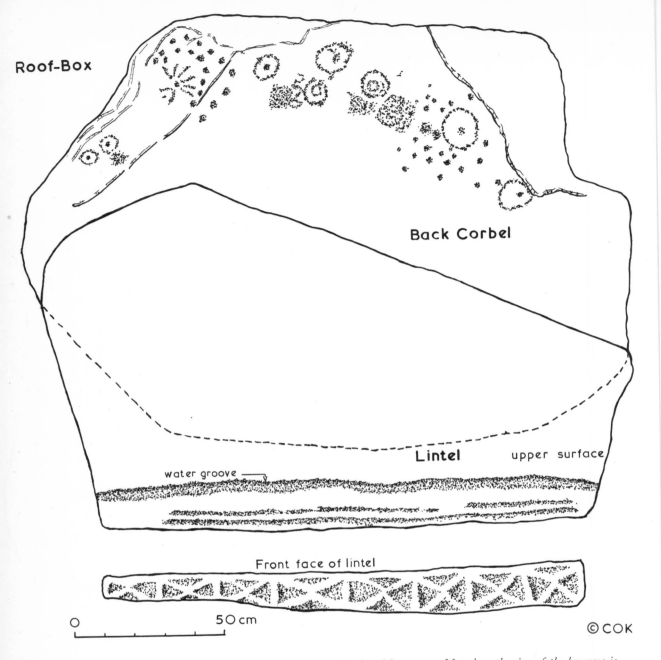

Roof-Box

Back Corbel

water groove

Lintel　　upper surface

Front face of lintel

O　　　　　50 cm

©COK

52 Roof-box. Lintel: one of the most expertly executed designs found at Newgrange. Note how the size of the lozenges is adapted to meet the variation in thickness of the slab; note also the raised band or moulding which runs along the top surface close to and parallel with the edge of the decorated surface. The slight grooves on either side of the mouldings must be distinguished from the purely functional water-groove a few centimetres farther back. The edge of the cairn when finished would have come to a point just short of the groove. The whole of the decorated surface is pick-dressed so as to give it an all-over finish, and the dressing was brought up over the part of the top surface which was free of the cairn. In the excellence of its design and technique this slab rivals the entrance stone and K52.

Back Corbel (the supporting stone for the lintel). The ornament is on the part which is free of the lintel and which curves downward to close in the back of the roof-box. Part of the surface has spalled away carrying some of the ornament with it.

Passage roof   Corbels

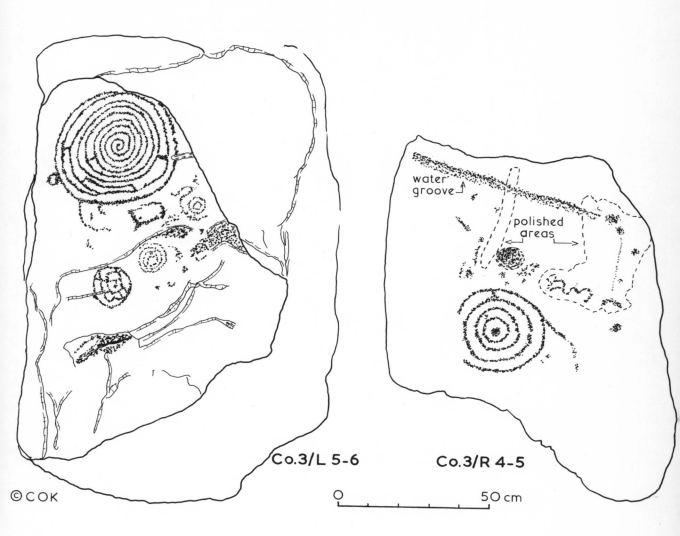

Co.3/L 5-6

water groove

polished areas

Co.3/R 4-5

©COK

50 cm

53 Co.3/L5-6 (see p. 96): the decorated surface was turned downward and the upturned face had a water-groove. Part of the surface has spalled away; Co.3/R4-5 (see p. 96): the decorated face was uppermost and partly covered by roof-slab 3 which rested on it. Note axe-sharpening groove and smooth polished areas for grinding and polishing stone axes.

Passage Roofslabs — upper surface

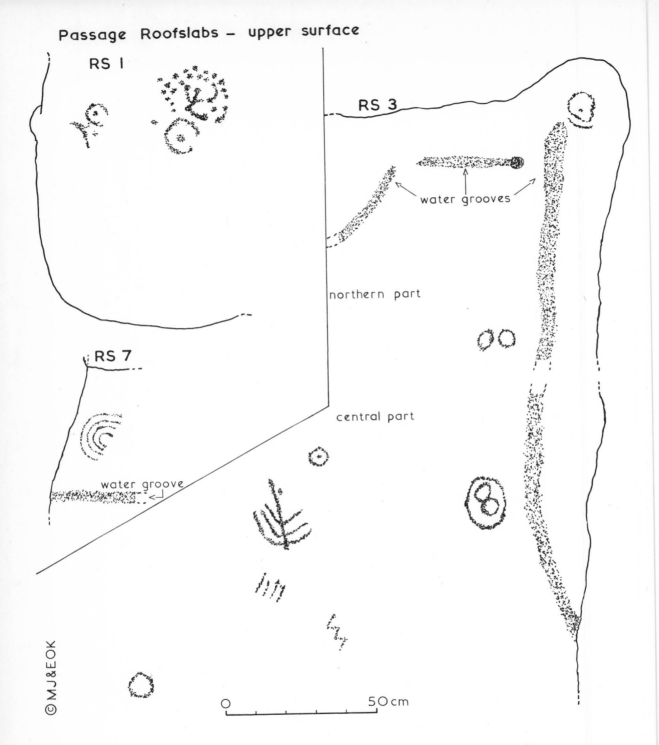

RS 1

RS 3

water grooves

northern part

RS 7

central part

water groove

©MJ&EOK

0   50 cm

54 *RS1: roof-slab covering the mouth of the passage; the roof-box rests partly on its back edge. Two water-grooves are cut near the back edge to prevent water running into the gap in the floor of the roof-box; RS3: a slab of massive proportions, 4 m in length and from 40 to 50 cm in thickness; there is an elaborate arrangement of water-grooves; cf. fig. 18b; RS7: water-groove present here also.*

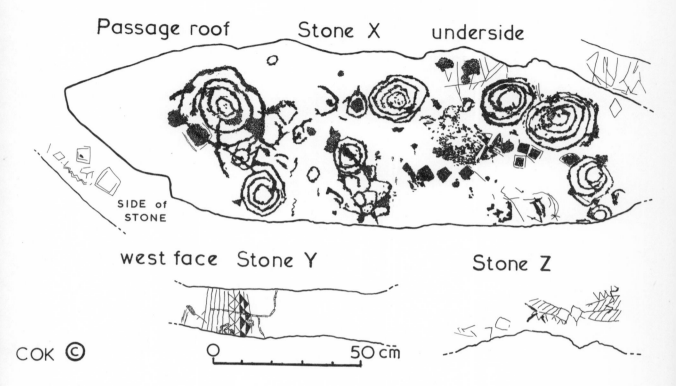

Passage roof   Stone X   underside

SIDE of
STONE

west face Stone Y

Stone Z

COK ©

O   50 cm

55 *Stone X: at west side of junction of passage and chamber roofs (p. 99), the ornament being on the underside. Owing to its protected position it was remarkably fresh and sharp, though inexpertly executed; Stone Y: same position as stone X but on the eastern side (p. 99). Pattern is scratched on the forward-facing side and is incomplete. Perhaps the artificer was not allowed time to finish it because the construction gang was hot on his heels! Stone Z: this and another stone were loosely laid near the two mentioned above. Stone Z is little more than a 'doodle'.*

APPENDIX A

The finds

M. J. O'Kelly, *Department of Archaeology, University College Cork*

The finds from the excavation have been deposited in the National Museum of Ireland, Dublin; the find numbers given below are those of the museum register. The finds are described in the following order: those from the cairn slip, those from the cairn and those from the tomb.

The cairn slip

It has been shown above that the turf and humus lying on the old ground surface outside the kerb on the south side had been stripped off and in the process artefacts dropped by the Newgrange builders must have been removed also. Nevertheless, a number of finds which may be considered to belong to the building period or immediately after, were found. A few objects were also recovered from the oval stone-setting and since features such as this are associated with other Irish passage-graves, they may be considered to be of the same date as the monument itself. A few objects were associated with the hut foundation west of the tomb entrance, another early feature which, while it may not coincide with the building of Newgrange, was certainly earlier than the collapse of the quartz/granite and the Beaker-period settlement. Consequently these finds are dealt with below.

Oval stone-setting

fig. 56   E56.1754 Stone object – a phallus? Made from a fine-grained sandstone with a highly polished surface all over except at one end which is fractured; has an oval cross-section, 7.4 × 4.5 cm, and ends in a blunt polished point; length 24 cm. It was lying as a cobble in the paved floor of the stone-setting.

fig. 57   E56.440a A trimming flake from the outside of a flint core; made in the form of a parallel-sided blade, the long edges of which are serrated from use. L (length) 6.5 cm; W (width) 2.7 cm; max. T (thickness) 1 cm. Found among the water-rolled quartz stones inside the setting.

fig. 57   E56.440b Waste flake, max. dimension 3.1 cm. Found with previous object.

fig. 57   E56.455 Flint knife belonging to the class generally called 'petit-tranchet-derivative arrowheads'. Only a small flake, L 3 cm; W 1.9 cm; max. T 7 mm, is now present. One straight edge has been finely bifacially pressure-flaked and the opposite sharp edge is gapped from rough usage. The two short edges are fractured but if these are recon-

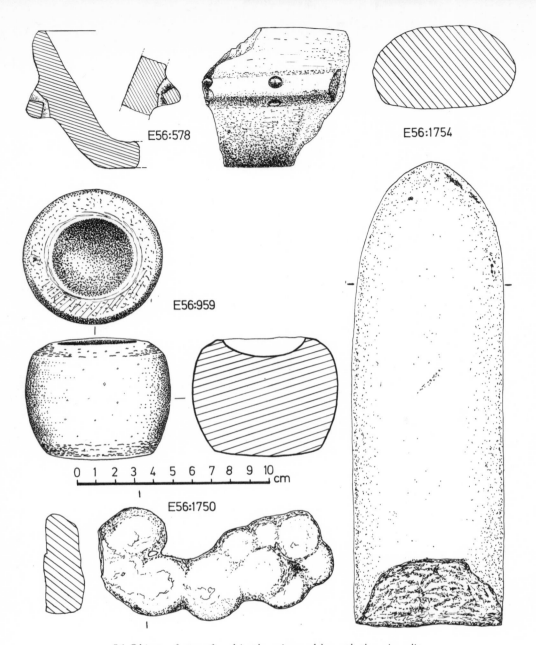

E56:578

E56:1754

E56:959

0 1 2 3 4 5 6 7 8 9 10 cm

E56:1750

56 Objects of stone found in the cairn and beneath the cairn slip.

structed in a drawing it becomes clear that it belongs to the class of object above-mentioned. Many of these have been found in a complete state in the overlying Late Neolithic/Beaker-period settlement horizon and it is the knowledge of these that has enabled this fragmentary example to be reconstructed with certainty. In its reconstructed state it would be approx. 6.2 cm in length. As the drawing shows, it had a short rounded tang formed by pressure-flaking, the flaking carried all along one edge, thus forming a backed blade. The opposite edge is the natural sharp edge of the flake – the cutting edge of the backed blade. When the tang is held between the thumb and middle finger with the index finger resting on the roughened back, the object becomes a very effective knife. Experiment with several complete examples has shown that this is indeed the case. These knives have been found at other Irish and British sites of the Late Neolithic/Beaker-period (Ó Ríordáin 1951, 50; Sweetman 1976, fig. 18). It was found on the pavement in the southeast quadrant of the stone-setting.

HUT FOUNDATION

fig. 56 E56.578 Fragment of a stone bowl. The bowl was a shallow flat-bottomed vessel very expertly made and has a smooth almost polished surface inside. The outside clearly shows the roughly horizontal striae of the final grinding process. The lip has a simple rounded profile and on the outside, 2.6 cm below it, there is a horizontal bevel-ended lug with two vertical V-bored perforations. The reconstructed diameter at the lip is approx. 14 cm; thickness of base 1.4 cm. The rock from which it was made has been identified as *andesite*, a type of igneous rock which outcrops a short distance to the west of Newgrange, therefore the bowl may have been locally made. No parallel for it is known to us in the Irish or British material (Appendix G). It was found in the foundation trench of the hut.

fig. 57 E56.677 Fragment of a polished flint axe. The axe appears to have been narrow and rather small, the surviving piece amounting to about one-third of the whole. This preserves most of the cutting edge which remains very sharp in the ungapped parts. The surfaces are very highly polished, though this finish did not remove some of the roughing-out flake-scars. Subsequent damage was caused by burning. Length of existing cutting edge 2.5 cm; max. T 2.1 cm. Found embedded in the subsoil surface immediately south of the hut foundation.

fig. 57 E56.776 Microlithic perforator made on a rather scrappy fragment of flint. The working point was achieved by means of a very fine pressure-flaking technique. Max. dimension 2.3 cm. Find-place as for previous object.

OTHER FINDS

fig. 57 E56.309 Tanged knife similar to E56.455, but though complete, is smaller and less well made. Its roughened back was produced by unifacial pressure-flaking and its tang is not as pronounced as in other examples. Cutting edge much gapped from use. L 3.6 cm; max. W 1.8 cm; max. T 5 mm. Found embedded in the turf-stripped surface between the stone-setting and K97 and pre-dates the collapse of the quartz/granite revetment wall.

fig. 57 E56.314 Hollow scraper made on a very scrappy flake from the outside of a flint nodule – the cortex is present. The working hollow edge was expertly produced by a very fine pressure-flaking technique. Slight traces of sheen which had developed in use are visible. Such objects are at home in several Neolithic contexts. Max. dimension 2.8 cm. Found in same area as previous object.

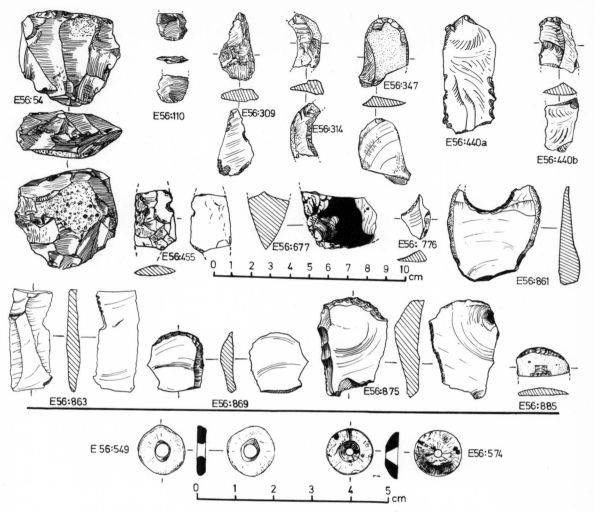

E56:54 E56:110 E56:309 E56:314 E56:347 E56:440a E56:440b

E56:455 E56:677 E56:776 E56:861

0 1 2 3 4 5 6 7 8 9 10 cm

E56:863 E56:869 E56:875 E56:885

E 56:549 E56:574

0 1 2 3 4 5 cm

57 Objects of flint and disc beads from the cairn and from beneath the cairn slip.

E56.549 Stone disc-bead made from a greenish-grey mottled stone, probably serpen-   *fig. 57*
tine, highly polished. It is a true disc, flat on both faces with an average diam. of
1.3 cm and a thickness of 2 mm. The perforation, diam. 5 mm, was drilled from both
faces. Found embedded in the subsoil surface directly in front of the entrance stone
but 12 m distant from it and 4.7 m north of the great circle; thus it lay between the
mound and the circle.

E56.549a Stone disc-bead (not illustrated) found in same area as previous object.
Made from a hard brown stone streaked on one face with grey; it is highly polished,
the edges and faces showing small facets. Plano-convex in section, 3 mm thick at the
centre and thinning to 1 mm at the edges; diam. 1.4 cm; diam. of perforation 5 mm.

The perforation is cylindrical and was drilled from the plano-face – the drill striations are clearly visible.

fig. 57 E56.574 Stone disc-bead from same area as previous two. Made from a greenish-grey mottled stone, probably serpentine, similar to no. 549, and is highly polished. Its plano-convex section is of the same dimensions as no. 549a. Diam. 1.2 cm; the perforation was drilled from the plano-face in this example also, but the drilling is conical in section; diam. 5 mm at the plano-face and 1 mm on the convex face. The drill striations are clearly visible. It is not certain whether or not the above three objects are primary.

fig. 57 E56.54 Flint core from which several trimming flakes had been struck. Max. dimension 5 cm. It was embedded in the subsoil surface under the quartz/granite layer, 2 m south of K93.

The cairn

A small number of flints were recovered from various cuttings made behind the kerb, either in the layer of transported turves or in the old turf layer beneath. They must, therefore, be of the same date as Newgrange, or earlier. A few also came from among the cairn stones which covered the passage roof; three of the cairn stones themselves were found to have some picked ornament. These latter are additional to the two loose slabs (stone Z and another) found under the 'relieving arch' over the passage. Stone Z is illustrated in fig. 55.

INSIDE THE KERB

fig. 57 E56.110 The butt end of a microlithic parallel-sided blade which has a fine pressure-flaking to thin the bulb of percussion at the butt. The forward end of the blade has broken off but the cutting edges are serrated from use. The flint itself is a translucent light brown colour. Max. L 1.5 cm; W 1.5 cm; T 2 mm. Found in the transported turves behind K 92.

E56.863 A parallel-sided blade now 5.5 cm in length but its fractured end shows that it was originally longer. There is a slight unifacial pressure-flaked retouch at one edge of the fracture. The retouch and the fracturing of the edge may have been done to convert the corner of the flake into a burin. The flint is china-white throughout. Max. W 2 cm. Found on the surface of the transported turves immediately behind K 90.

E56.869 Round scraper made on a thin flake of china-white flint. The scraping edge was achieved by a very fine pressure-flaking technique. Max. L 3 cm; max. W 2.9 cm. It was found on the surface of the transported turves behind the junction of K 15 and K 16.

E56.861 A hollow scraper made on a large flake of grey-coloured flint. The working edge, semicircular in shape, was achieved by a fine pressure-flaking technique and shows traces of sheen developed when in use. The wear-pattern suggests that it was used spokeshave-fashion on some hard substance such as bone. Max. dimension

5.7 cm; thickness at butt 9 mm. Found on the old turf layer under the transported turves.

E56.875 A rather thick flake struck from a nodule of poor quality flint of a greyish-brown opaque quality. One end has been converted into a scraping edge by using a very coarse pressure-flaking technique, while an adjacent long edge has been made into a saw by means of a very fine unifacial pressure-flaking. Max. L 5.3 cm; max. T 1 cm. Found on the old turf layer under the transported turves.

ABOVE THE PASSAGE ROOF

E56.347 A trimming flake from the outside of a nodule; the cortex is present over most of the outer surface. One end of the flake has been made into a round scraper by means of a fine pressure-flaking done unifacially on the cortex surface. Max. dimension 3.8 cm; max. T 5 mm. Found when the cairn material was being removed to expose the passage roof. It was 1 m deep in the cairn stones above the outer end of the passage and behind the roof-box.   *fig. 57*

E56.885 A round scraper made on a cortex-covered external flake from a nodule and, as in the previous find, the minute pressure-flaking was done only on the cortex face. Max. dimension 2.8 cm; max. T 5 mm. Found in the burnt soil 'putty' packed in under the 'relieving arch' structure above the passage roof. The 'putty' was made from burnt turves and presumably the flint was in one of them as it is also burnt. The small-twig-charcoal extracted from the 'putty' has given one of the C14 dates for the tomb structure (Appendix H).   *fig. 57*

E56.1751 Decorated cairn stone. A flattish water-rolled stone of thin oval cross-section; of sandstone – probably greywacke – grey on the weathered surfaces but showing green where the chiselling has been done. A pointed chisel had been used to create four parallel grooves which run from one face over the edge and on to the opposite face. The grooves average 1.5 cm in width and about 5 mm in depth. A zigzag of seven points has been chiselled with the same point on one face and beside this there are other chiselled grooves. Max. dimension 24.5 cm; max. T 5.5 cm. Found among the material removed from above the passage roof.   *fig. 58*

E56.1752 Decorated cairn stone. A large boulder which has several roughly picked areas and a few picked U-shapes and groups of dots inexpertly done. The stone is carboniferous sandstone. L 38 cm; W 24 cm; T 16 cm. Found in same area as previous object.   *fig. 58*

E56.1753 Decorated cairn stone, also of carboniferous sandstone. Whole of one surface occupied by a spiral-cum-concentric-circle device, picked with a broad pointed chisel, the whole carelessly done. Max. L 28 cm; W 21 cm; T 11.5 cm. Found in same area as two previous objects.   *fig. 58*

E56.1750 Sandstone concretion, curiously shaped but of natural formation. Max. dimension 11.8 cm; max. T 2 cm. Found in the shallow basin-like depression on the upper surface of the back corbel of the roof-box where, in all probability, it was deli-   *fig. 56*

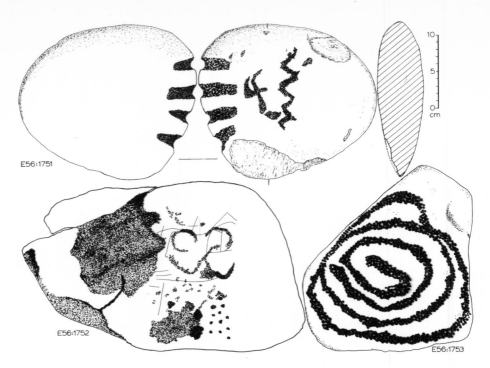

E56:1751

E56:1752

E56:1753

58 Decorated cairn-stones.

berately placed, having attracted attention in the first instance by its unusual shape. Naturally-formed but strangely-shaped stones have been found in significant positions at site K, Newgrange, and at site 1, Knowth. At site K a 'flying-saucer'-shaped concoid was centrally placed on the ground at the outer end of the passage (M. J. O'Kelly *et al.* 1978, 282). At site 1 Knowth (the main mound), a semicircle of strangely shaped concoids stands outside the entrance to the western tomb. It seems clear, therefore, that the Boyne passage-grave builders were as intrigued by these stones as anyone would be today.

The tomb

The marbles, pendants, beads and bone objects found in the tomb during the excavation in 1967 are similar to finds recovered from the three Newgrange satellites and are also typical of those recovered from Irish passage-graves in general. When one considers the amount of disturbance caused by well-meaning 'restoration' and also the number of times the floor must have been 'tidied-up' by equally well-meaning land-owners and others, including the OPW, one is slow to believe that the whole of the original deposit is represented by the grave-goods catalogued below. The specialists who examined the human remains mentioned the possibility that much of the unburnt material at least had been removed. Coffey (1892) records a clearing away of 'the loose stones [on the floor] mentioned by Lhwyd' and there were many other such operations both before and after Coffey's time.

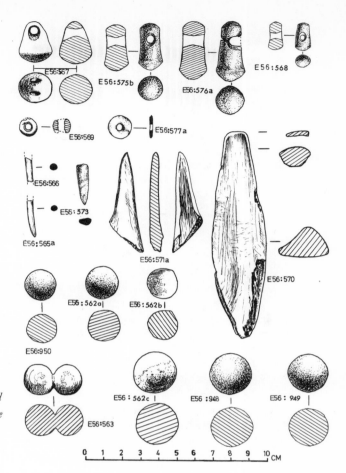

59 *Pendants, beads, bone objects and marbles found in the tomb during the excavation.*

Two old finds are included below, one from 1699 of which there is now no trace and the other from the present century.

PENDANTS AND BEADS

fig. 59

E56.567 Baetyl-shaped pendant; the broad end hemispherical and narrowing sharply to the perforated end. It is of a brick-red colour and seems to have been made of pottery. It had a thin greyish-white slip, now somewhat discoloured and partially flaked off. It is difficult to say with certainty what material was used in any of the four pendants found – it may be pottery or some kind of soft stone – and to find out, some samples of all of them would have to be sacrificed. Max. length of above object 2.25 cm; max. diam. of horizontal section 1.7 cm; diam. of perforation 4 mm. Found at a depth of 35 cm in the central chamber in front of the basin in the west recess. It was in the sandy soil below the layer of roof-spalls and in a small spread of burnt human bone fragments.

E56.568 'Hammer' pendant. It is best described as this because of its almost cylindrical shape. It is slightly greater in cross-sectional diameter at one end than at the other and the perforation is near the thicker end. It may be made of pottery but it has a highly polished surface on part of which there is an accretion of a chalky substance – a whitish slip like that in the previous example. The general colour is a dull brown. L 1.5 cm; max. sectional diam. 7.5 mm; min. sectional diam. 6.5 mm; diam. of perforation 4 mm. Found amongst burnt bone fragments in front of the lower basin in the east recess.

E56.575b Hammer pendant which appears also to be made of pottery. Colour is light brown but there are traces of a whitish slip. Perforation is of hour-glass form. L 2.6 cm; max. sectional diam. 1.22 cm; min. sectional diam. 1.06 cm; max. diam. of perforation 8 mm; min. diam. of perforation 4 mm. Found at a depth of 25 cm in the sandy soil below the layer of roof-spalls at the side of the central pit and in an area disturbed by an animal burrow.

E56.576a Hammer pendant, light brown in colour; upper end has broken off and one side of the perforation has gone. Appears to have been made of pottery. L 3.35 cm; max. cross-sectional diam. 1.53 cm; min. cross-sectional diam. 1.07 cm; diam. of perforation 4.5 mm. Found 7 cm below the then surface in the centre of the passage floor at the junction of passage and chamber in a disturbed area.

E56.569 Barrel-shaped bead made of pottery and reddish in colour. The core of the bead has been given a slip of finer, harder clay, this in turn, covered by a whitish slip, only traces of which survive. Max. diam. 9 mm; diam. of perforation 3 mm. Found 5 cm below the then (1967) surface of the floor of the east recess in a disturbed area containing many burnt human bone fragments.

fig. 59   MARBLES

E56.562a, b, c. Three marbles which are whitish in colour and have been made from chalk, probably from that of Antrim. The surfaces have deteriorated a little so that they are now irregularly spherical. Diameters: 1.7 cm; 1.85 cm; and 2.25 cm respectively. Found in the top of the socket of C16, 10 cm below the modern floor surface, very near a limestone plinth which had been put in as a base for a metal bar-support for the decorated roof-slab of the east recess, thus the find-place was a disturbed one.

E56.563 Dumb-bell-shaped object consisting of two marbles joined together and cut out of a single piece of white chalk. The surfaces of the marbles are finely finished and have a light polish. Perhaps it was the intention of the maker to sever them at the junction but this was not done. L 3.2 cm; max. diam. 1.7 cm; sectional diam. of the neck 8 mm. Found, as the previous three objects, in the upper part of the socket of C16, 13 cm below the then floor level, beneath the OPW plinth and partly under the edge of a packing stone supporting the front edge of the lower basin stone in the east recess.

E56.948 Marble of polished stone, dark green in colour over most of the surface, but of a light greenish creamy colour on one side. The stone may be serpentine. It is irregularly spherical. Average diam. 2.23 cm. Found at a depth of 15 cm in southwestern part of central chamber under the layer of spalls fallen from the roof and on the light-coloured sandy soil below.

E56.949 Marble similar to previous one except that its colour is black throughout and its surface is highly polished all over. Polishing striations clearly visible. It is more exactly spherical than previous example. Diam. 2.19 cm. Found in the southeast of the central chamber at a depth of 30 cm in the loose fill of an animal burrow.

E56.950 Marble made of chalk of a brownish-white colour. Diam. 1.68 cm. Found at a depth of 10 cm in the loose fill (recently disturbed) on top of the socket of R20 in the passage.

BONE OBJECTS

fig. 59

E56.577a Bone disc-bead. Diam. 1.3 cm; T 1.7 mm; diam. of perforation 3 mm. Found near entrance to the chamber in the layer of roof-spalls but the area was much disturbed by animal burrows.

E56.565a Point of a polished pin which had been burnt. L 2 cm; diam. of section 3 mm. Found in west recess in the layer of roof-spalls, mixed with burnt human bone fragments.

E56.566 Part of the shank of a polished pin similar to above object; burnt. L 1.2 cm; diam. of section 4 mm. Found, as previous object, with burnt bones in the west recess.

E56.566b Fragment of the spatulate head of a bone pin; burnt (not illustrated). It had been polished on the surfaces and the top shows a facet which also had been polished. L 12 mm. Found with burnt human bone under the northeast edge of the basin in the west recess.

E56.573 Fragment of the point of an unburnt pin made from a small long-bone. Plano-convex in section. L 2.3 cm; max. W 7 mm; max. T 4.5 mm. Found in west recess in disturbed soil under basin.

E56.573b Bone point with traces of a polished surface; unburnt. L 3.8 cm; max. T 1.1 cm. Found with previous object (not illustrated).

E56.571a Bone point, polished but unburnt. Broken at end opposite to point. L 5.6 cm; max. W 1.5 cm; T 3.5 mm. Found in the eastern part of the central chamber in an area very disturbed by animal burrows in the angle between C16 and C17.

E56.570 A 'chisel' similar to others that have been found in Britain in various Neolithic contexts (Piggott 1954, 85 & fig. 22) and to one found in the chamber of site L, Newgrange (M. J. O'Kelly *et al.* 1978, 271). The bone has been rubbed smooth on all surfaces and is highly polished at the chisel end. The striae of shaping and polishing are clearly visible on all surfaces. L 11.5 cm; max. W 2.95 cm; max. T 1.8 cm. Found under the back edge of the lower basin in the east recess; animal bones found here also.

E56.572 and 574a (not illustrated). Two fragments of flat bone, perhaps from a scapula, which have been rubbed and polished and have faceted edges. The striae of smoothing and polishing are clearly visible. They look as if they had been used as burnishers or polishers. No. 574a may be a fragment of a disc, and if so, the diameter would have been approximately 4 cm; Max. dimension of no. 572 is 7.2 cm; average T 3 mm. Both found in the west recess below the basin.

Flint

E56.880 Eleven fragments of flint, all waste pieces, found in a disturbed area in the central chamber in front of the west recess (not illustrated).

E56.880a Flake of waste flint found in a disturbed area in front of the base of C6 (not illustrated). Animal bones were found here.

E56.881 A gun-flint. Working edge chipped from use. L 19 mm; W 17 mm; T 5 mm. Presumably an intrusion of post-1699 date. Found in main chamber in layer of spalls (not illustrated).

Other objects

E56.951 Small cowrie shell. Max. L 9.3 mm. Found in the northern quadrant of the central chamber (not illustrated).

E56.946 Blob of brass, modern (not illustrated). When molten it fell on to a flat surface and solidified. It probably comes from a brazing operation on one of the iron struts or supports put in by the OPW in the past. Found south of the edge of the basin in the west recess.

Old finds

'A stone wrought in the form of a cone, half a yard long and about 20 inches in the girth and having a small hole at ye big end. This I mett with in ye right hand cistern under ye bason above mentioned.' This annotation to a plan made in 1699/1700 has already been discussed (p. 26). The whereabouts of this object is not known.

plate 19

Nat. Mus. Reg. no. 1959.10 A ball-like object of granite, slightly flattened on two opposite sides, in one of which there is a shallow depression. The object is presumed to be a stone lamp (*JRSAI* 91, 1961, 71-2). Max. diam. 11.8 cm; height 8.9 cm; diam. of depression 5.8 cm; depth of depression 1 cm.

According to the report in *JRSAI*, the object was found in the centre of the main chamber under the basin stone which had formerly been in the east recess but had been moved to the central position some time in the 1890s. The discovery was made when the basin was being restored to its rightful position in the recess.

fig. 56

A very similar lamp of granite, E56.959, better made and highly polished on all surfaces, was found 9 m south of K92 at the base of the Late Neolithic/Beaker-period horizon. Another very similar example was found in the surface soil due south of Newgrange near the bank of the Boyne while ploughing was in progress. Nat. Mus. Register no. 1962:265 (*JRSAI* 94, 1964, 96-7). Yet another was found in the northern tomb at Dowth in the 1840s. Nat. Mus. Register no. W.30 (Wilde 1857, 146).

1 The human skeletal remains

T. P. Fraher, *Department of Anatomy, University College Cork*

The human skeletal material consisted of both unburnt and burnt material.

Unburnt material

The samples containing unburnt human material also included large numbers of animal bones as well as about 750 unidentifiable fragments. Apart from some complete hand and foot bones, all human specimens consisted of small fragments.

The unburnt material identifiable as human consisted of:

1. SKULL   plate 83

a) Approximately one-third of the frontal bone, mostly from the right side but extending across the midline. On the inner aspect the frontal crest is clearly marked. The inferior edge of the specimen shows smooth excavations for one of the frontal air sinuses which extended across the midline and would have been within the normal size range. The temporal lines are well marked. The upper right margin of the specimen includes the posterior free edge of the frontal bone at its suture with the right parietal. This shows partial fusion between the two bones, beginning internally and extending about half way between the inner and outer surfaces of the bone. This degree of fusion suggests an age of between 30 and 40 years. However, this must be a rough approximation because fusion is not an accurate indicator of age. Markings associated with the underlying cerebral hemispheres are clearly visible. There is an unusual, low, conical elevation, projecting 5 mm into the cranial cavity from the right part of the bone.

b) Petrous part of left temporal bone (length 41 mm), showing the posteromedial wall   plate 83b
of the middle ear cavity and of the tympanic antrum. The specimen also includes excavations for the mastoid air cells.

c) Middle three-fifths (approx.) of the petrous part of right temporal bone (length 37 mm).

The two specimens of petrous temporal bone closely resemble each other in their dimensions, shape and the prominence of their markings.

d) Fragment of the mastoid part of a right temporal bone, showing a well-marked sigmoid sulcus. This part of the bone has not been invaded by air cells. It includes the mastoid emissary foramen.

e) Fragment of right temporal bone including mandibular fossa, the lower part of the squamous portion and the root of the zygomatic process.

f) Lower left part of frontal bone, including part of the orbital plate where excavations for the frontal air sinus are present. The lower end of the temporal line is sharp. A supraorbital foramen is present.

g) Part of the alveolar process of a mandible.

2. AXIAL SKELETON

(i) Vertebrae
a) A lower cervical vertebra, transverse processes slightly damaged.
b) A few small fragments of cervical vertebrae.
plate 83e   c) 4 vertebral arches from the middle thoracic region.
d) 11th thoracic vertebra, body slightly damaged.
e) Left half of the arch of a lumbar vertebra.

(ii) Sacrum
a) 2 fragments from the left side of one sacrum.
b) Fragment from the right side of a sacrum.

(iii) Ribs and sternum
a) Neck and proximal part of shaft of a small right first rib.
b) Proximal ends of 3 ribs from the middle of the series, 2 of which were considerably larger than the third.
c) 13 fragments of rib shafts.
d) Upper part of the body of a small sternum.

(iv) Pelvis
plate 83d   Part of the right hip bone, consisting of the body and inferior ramus of pubis. The specimen is heavily built and possesses a well developed pubic tubercle. The lower margin of the ramus is markedly everted, suggesting that this specimen originated from a male skeleton.

3. UPPER LIMB GIRDLE
plate 83c   a) Right clavicle in two pieces, medial end missing. The fragments could be joined together.
b) Lateral end of a smaller and more delicate right clavicle.
c) 3 fragments of scapula, one more delicate than the other two.

4. LARGE LIMB BONES
plate 83f   a) Trochlea and capitulum of a small humerus.
b) Head and part of neck (damaged) of a small radius (head diameter: 20 mm approx). Articulation of this with the capitulum of (a) above shows excellent congruity between them.
plate 83f   c) Part of the head of a larger, heavier radius (head diameter: 23 mm).
d) Mid-portion (136 mm long) of the shaft of a radius of average proportions.
e) Greater trochanter of a left femur.
f) Fragment of the head of a smaller femur.

g) 2 fragments of the lateral condyle of a small femur.

h) Fragment of the shaft of a fibula.

5. WRIST AND HAND BONES

a) Wrist: *Left side:* scaphoid (1), lunate (1), triquetrum (1), hamate (1).

        Right side: trapezium (1), trapezoid (2), capitate (1), hamate (1).

b) Hand:

Table I

	METACARPALS					PHALANGES*		
	1	2	3	4	5	PROXIMAL	INTERMEDIATE	DISTAL
LEFT		1			1	10	10	3**
RIGHT			1		1			

* two further phalanges could not be identified as proximal or intermediate due to damage.
** all from thumb.

The majority of these bones were complete or nearly so.

6. FOOT BONES

Right side: Talus (1), cuboid (1), intermediate (1) and lateral (1) cuneiform.

Left side: Medial cuneiform (2).

plate 83g

Table II

	METATARSALS*					PHALANGES		
	1	2	3	4	5	PROXIMAL	INTERMEDIATE	DISTAL
LEFT	1	1	2	2	1**	8***	2	2****
RIGHT	1	2		2	2			

* one metatarsal could not be identified due to damage.
** this consisted of only the base of the bone.
*** includes one from great toe.
**** both from great toe.

In addition there were many small fragments of skull vault whose general appearance, thickness, curvature and marking were consistent with an origin from the human skull.

The majority of unidentifiable fragments were from long bones and were very comminuted; many consisted of trabecular bone only and lacked a cortex of compact bone.

All of the unburnt material which could be identified as human was in good condition and was not fragile or crumbling. The extent to which this material had been broken was remarkable. With the exception of most of the hand and foot bones found, and one vertebra and one clavicle, both of which were substantially intact, all the remaining material consisted of small pieces. Very few fragments of skull base were found, despite the ease with which even quite small fragments from this region can be confidently identified. Apart from one small piece of the alveolar process, no fragments of mandible were found. Of the large limb bones the only substantial fragment was one consisting of approximately the middle third of the shaft of a radius. The remainder were small. They measured at most only a few centimetres in length and were generally considerably smaller. The ribs had been less comminuted than the limb bones; many fragments were 10 cm or so in length. Most of the vertebral bodies had disappeared. These findings, together with the scarcity of skull fragments raise the possibility that much of the unburnt material had been removed. Ten fragments of human skull vault have been found in front of the tomb entrance (van Wijngaarden-Bakker 1974). These, however, have a different appearance from those found within the tomb, described above; compared with the latter, they were much paler and more chalky. Accordingly, it seems unlikely that they had a common origin with the bones found in the tomb.

Only the hand and foot bones were sufficiently complete to enable measurement of overall dimensions (Tables III and IV).

Apart from the small conical ingrowth on the internal aspect of the frontal bone, there was no evidence of pathology in the unburnt specimens. The joint surfaces on the fragments of vertebrae and limb bones showed no evidence of arthritis which has been commonly found in Neolithic skeletons (Wells 1962).

plate 83e

Measurement and observation shows that the unburnt material falls into two classes: in one the bones are moderately heavily marked, in the other they are slight and delicate. It was only from the hand and foot regions that substantial numbers of complete bones were obtained. Identification of these as well as the side of the body from which they arose shows that they could well have originated from two skeletons. Thus, the unburnt material is likely to have been derived from a pair of skeletons, one of which is male and considerably larger and more heavily built than the other. It is not possible to give any accurate estimate of body size due to the lack of suitable material on which to base predictions.

plate 83f, g

The distribution of the material in the passage, chamber and recesses shows that the fragments have been widely scattered and intermingled with one another. There was no evidence of any epiphyses being unfused. This, together with the evidence from the fragment of frontal bone suggests that at least one and probably both of the individuals were adults.

Burnt material

Approximately 2,200 fragments of burnt bone were found, weighing in all 1051 g. The majority were from long bones; only 10% to 15% originated from the skull.

Most skull fragments were rectangular or oval. Though the longest dimension of a few reached 30 mm, in the majority of cases it was under 15 mm; most pieces were considerably smaller than this. Of the fragments of long bone, two measured over 50 mm in length (65 mm, 54 mm). The great majority were less than 20 mm long and did not include the whole circumference of the bone. Most of the long bone fragments were so comminuted or so distorted and cracked that it was not possible to identify their site of origin. Colours ranged from ivory through various shades of grey and blue-grey to black. Approximately one-third of the specimens were blackened in whole or in part. Most fragments were small and could not be identified. The precise location of the origin of 76 fragments derived from the human skeleton could be determined. These were as follows:

1. SKULL

a) Temporal bone
(i) Middle part of left petrous temporal bone (length: 32 mm) showing the internal auditory meatus and the wall of the carotid canal, the middle ear cavity and the impression for the jugular bulb.   plate 84a

(ii) Middle part of left petrous temporal bone (length: 32 mm), similar to (i) above.   plate 84d

(iii) Medial part of petrous temporal bone, including the medial end of the bony part of the auditory tube.

(iv) 2 lower parts of petrous temporal bone, both showing the wall of the carotid canal.

(v) Inferior part of right petrous temporal bone showing part of the impression for the jugular bulb.

(vi) Outer table of left mastoid process; the process was honeycombed with air cells.   plate 84c

(vii) Outer table of upper part of mastoid process near junction with squamous part.

(viii) Inferior part of the bone including the medial part of the articular eminence and the root of the zygomatic process.   plate 84g

(ix) Proximal part of the root of a left zygomatic arch.

(x) Fragment from left side at junction of mastoid and squamous parts.

b) Frontal bone
(i) Small fragment of the orbital plate, excavated for the frontal air sinus.
(ii) 2 small fragments of the orbital plate.

c) Sphenoid
(i) Fragment of left medial pterygoid plate.

d) Parietal bone
(i) Fragment showing a short length of one of the temporal lines, lower part showing bevelled articular surface for temporal bone.
(ii) Fragment of lower part of a parietal bone.
(iii) Other fragment.
(iv) 3 probable fragments.

201

SEGMENT	BONE	SIDE	MAXIMUM LENGTH	WIDTH	
				PROXIMAL	DISTAL
HAND	MC3	R	65	14	13.5
	MC5	R	55	14	11
	MC?	R	–	–	–
	MC2	L	71	18	13.5
	MC5	L	55	14	11
	PP1	–	30	–	12
	PP	–	40	16	11
	PP	–	41	14	10
	PP	–	40	14	10
	PP	–	28	13	9
	PP	–	31	14.5	8.5
	PP	–	40	16	10
	PP	–		–	11
	PP	–		–	11
	PP	–		–	–
	? PP or 1P	–	–	–	8
	1P	–	27	13	10
	1P	–	17	10	6.5
	1P	–	24	12	9
	1P	–	22	13	9
	1P	–	24	12	9
	1P	–	27	6.5	9
	1P	–	23	13	9
	1P	–	19.5	10	–
	1P	–	–	13	–
	1P	–	–	–	9.5
	1P	–	–	–	10
	DP1	–	23	15	9
	DP1	–	22	13.5	8.5
	DP1	–	22.5	13.5	9

Table III

SEGMENT	BONE	SIDE	MAXIMUM LENGTH	WIDTH	
				Proximal	Distal
FOOT	MT1	R	55	–	18
	MT2	R	–	12	–
	MT2	R	–	14	–
	MT4	R	–	12	–
	MT4	R	–	12	–
	MT5	R	69	22	12
	MT5	R	–	16	–
	MT1	L	–	–	19
	MT3	L	69	12	10
	MT4	L	67	12.5	10
	MT4	L	72	14	9
	MT4	L	65	11	11
	PP1	–	35	21	–
	PP	–	30	13	9.5
	PP	–	28	11	6
	PP	–	26.5	13	8.5
	PP	–	24	11.5	8
	PP	–	27.5	10	8
	PP	–	26	10.5	8
	PP	–	21	11	9
	1P	–	13	11	9.5
	1P	–	14	11	10
	1P	–	26	19	11
	DP	–	25	20	10.5

Table IV

Table III Overall dimensions of hand bones (mm): MC, Metacarpal; PP, Proximal phalanx; IP, Intermediate phalanx; DP, Distal phalanx; R, right; L, left. The number of the metacarpal or phalanx follows the code for the bone, e.g. MC3 = third metacarpal.

Table IV Overall dimensions of foot bones (mm): MT, Metatarsal; PP, Proximal phalanx; IP, Intermediate phalanx; DP, Distal phalanx; R, right; L, left. The number of the metatarsal or phalanx follows the code for the bone, e.g. MT1 = first metatarsal.

e) Occipital bone

(i) Fragment of squamous part, showing internal occipital crest.

(ii) Possible fragment bounding hypoglossal canal.

f) Maxilla

(i) Upper part of body showing the anterior surface, a small part of the orbital surface and a small part of the surface forming the wall of the maxillary air sinus.

(ii) Fragment of palatal side of alveolar plate in the region of the left incisor and canine teeth.

(iii) Fragment of maxilla possibly from the level of the right molar teeth. There is evidence of alveolar bone resorption due to periodontal disease.

g) Mandible

(i) Upper part of left coronoid process.

(ii) Upper part of right coronoid process.

plate 84e   (iii) Fragment of lingual side of right alveolar plate with parts of the sockets for the second premolar and first molar teeth. Some periodontal disease was present with resorption of the crest of the interdental septum between the sockets. Part of the mylohyoid line is present.

Many further fragments of skull vault whose origin could not be determined exactly possessed serrated edges and had a curvature and appearance consistent with an origin from the human skull. The sutures which these bounded in life had begun to fuse internally in many cases, indicating that much of the material originated from young adults. In a smaller number of fragments the sutures were fused over almost their entire thickness indicating greater age than the former. In many cases the outer and inner tables had split apart from one another in the plane of the diplöe.

2. AXIAL SKELETON

a) Vertebral column

plate 84h   (i) Body and odontoid process of axis vertebra.

(ii) Fragment of the left lateral mass of an atlas vertebra.

(iii) Fragments of bodies of 5 cervical vertebrae together with part of the transverse process.

(iv) Body of a cervical vertebra.

(v) 3 Fragments of vertebral arch.

b) Ribs

6 fragments of rib shafts.

3. UPPER LIMB GIRDLE

plate 84b   Root of spine of scapula (2 specimens).

4. UPPER LIMB BONES

a) Arm

(i) Fragment of capitulum of humerus.

(ii) Fragment of trochlea and capitulum of humerus.

b) Forearm

Fragment of mid-part of shaft of radius.

c) Hand

(i) Right lunate bone.

(ii) Distal ends of 2 metacarpal bones.　　　　　　　　　　plate 84f

(iii) Distal part of proximal or middle phalanx (7 specimens).　　plate 84i

(iv) Part of head of proximal phalanx.

(v) Distal phalanx of finger (2 specimens).

5. LOWER LIMB BONES

a) One fragment from upper part of shaft of femur.

b) 10 fragments of fibula. Two of these could be put together (overall length: 58 mm).　plate 84j

c) Foot

(i) Base of 5th metatarsal bone.

(ii) Distal part of a metatarsal bone.

The remaining burnt material included large numbers of comminuted fragments of the cortex of long bones. A number of specimens included joint surfaces. Though it is likely that several skeletons were involved, on the basis of the identified fragments it can be stated with certainty that the burnt material included remains from three or more human skeletons, how many more it is impossible to tell.

References

Van Wijngaarden-Bakker, L. H. 1974 The animal remains from the beaker settlement at Newgrange, *PRIA* 74C, 313-83.

Wells, L. H. 1962 Report on the inhumation burials from the West Kennet Barrow, *The West Kennet Long Barrow*, London.

2 The human dental remains

V. R. O'Sullivan, *Department of Anatomy, University College Cork*

The dental remains consisted of thirty-two teeth. Two of the teeth had been cremated and damaged, but the remainder were in good condition. The individual teeth were examined in detail with a hand lens. What follows is a brief description of each one.

Unburnt material

i) 6⌋　Occlusal attrition has exposed a small area of dentine in each of the two buccal cusps and a larger confluent area in the palatal cusps. The distal contact area is worn.

There are two facets on the mesial surface of the crown, a vertical comma-shaped area on the mesiobuccal angle and a small oval-shaped area near the middle of the cervical margin. A shallow abrasion groove lies near them, below the cervical margin on the mesiobuccal root. There is a small enamel pearl 1 mm below a small interradicular extension of the cervical margin on the buccal surface of the root trunk. The mesiobuccal root tends to overlap the distobuccal root at their common origin and is fused to the palatal root for most of its course.

ii) |6 Occlusal attrition has exposed a small area of dentine in the mesiobuccal cusp and a large confluent area in the palatal cusps. The distal contact area is worn and beneath it is an abrasion groove which is confined to the enamel and which becomes less obvious towards the palatal side. Some calculus has been deposited on the middle of this cavity. The mesial contact area is also worn and is associated with an abrasion groove which involves a large portion of the crown beneath the contact area and part of the root trunk. The mesiobuccal and palatal roots are fused for approximately half of their course. The mesiobuccal root then bends towards the distobuccal, and its tip deviates buccally.

iii) ? 1̄   Attrition has markedly affected the incisal edge and labial surface, exposing an area of secondary dentine which has filled the pulp chamber and prevented exposure of the pulp itself. The mesial and distal contact areas are worn. The root is straight.

iv) ? 5| Gross occlusal attrition has involved the pulp cornu of the palatal cusp. This is completely filled with secondary dentine and the pulp chamber is not exposed. What remains of the crown shows it to have been unusually bulbous in shape and it probably had very prominent mesial and distal marginal ridges. The mesial and distal contact areas are worn, and most of the enamel on the palatal half of the crown has broken away. The root is single and shows a distal curvature near the tip. There is a periapical deposit of secondary cement.

v) |1 A large area of attrition extends over the palatal surface, incisal edge, and a small part of the labial surface as a single curved facet. This shows that while the incisor relationship was basically class I or II, some forward posturing of the mandible occurred. There is a very small abrasion cavity on the distal aspect of the root just beneath the cervical margin. The root is straight with some secondary cement deposited along the mesiobuccal angle and the apical half of the buccal surface.

vi) 3̄   An area of attrition involves the mesial slope of the cusp and the mesial part of the buccal surface, broken into several facets. Several smaller areas of attrition are present on the distal slope of the cusp and the mesial marginal ridge. The mesial and distal contact areas are worn. An abrasion groove is present on the distal aspect of the root which involves the cervical margin, and is continued over a large deposit of calculus towards the lingual side. The root is straight with shallow vertical mesial and distal grooves.

vii) |8 Occlusal attrition has exposed a small area of dentine in the mesiolingual cusp and a large confluent area in the buccal cusps. The mesial contact area is worn, situated high on the mesial surface and angled, suggesting that this tooth was tilted mesially during life. There is a comma-shaped pit on the distal surface of the crown which penetrates the full thickness of the enamel. This may be developmental in origin. The roots are fused with vertical buccal and lingual grooves. The root mass is straight and tapering with a small amount of periapical secondary cement.

viii) ? $\overline{2}$ There is marked attrition of the incisal edge. The mesial and distal contact areas are worn, and a large shallow abrasion cavity is present beneath the distal contact area. Some calculus is present as a thin layer on the rootward portion of the cavity. The root has an apical curvature and has a vertical groove on the distal aspect.

ix) ? This tooth has gross occlusal attrition and is too worn for positive identification. The pulp chamber is filled with secondary dentine which prevented exposure of the pulp. Parts of the mesial and distal contact area facets remain and there is a narrow abrasion groove beneath each facet. The root is straight, grooved along either the mesial or distal side, and elliptical in cross section. There is a small periapical deposit of secondary cement.

x) $\underline{6}$ Occlusal attrition has exposed a small area of dentine in each of the two buccal cusps and a larger confluent area in the palatal cusps. The mesial and distal contact areas are worn. The mesiobuccal root tends to overlap the distobuccal root at their common origin and is fused to the palatal root for most of their course. A large piece of normal bone is present between the roots, completely filling the trifurcation area.

xi) $\underline{8}$| Occlusal attrition has exposed a large confluent area of dentine on the crown of the tooth. Some of the remaining enamel has broken away from the palatal surface. The distal surface is rather bulbous, but interproximal wear has reduced this feature on the mesial side. A large mesial contact area is present, and beneath it an abrasion groove. The two buccal roots commence to separate after leaving the common root trunk, but the mesiobuccal then bends towards the distobuccal and fuses with it. Their fused apex deviates buccally. The mesiobuccal root is also fused with the palatal for approximately half their course.

plate 85a

xii) $\underline{6}$| Gross occlusal attrition has exposed a large confluent area of dentine on the crown. The distal surface of the crown is bulbous but occlusal attrition has reduced the mesial surface to the approximate level of the cervical margin. The distal contact area is worn, with a shallow abrasion cavity confined to the enamel beneath it. The remains of a large abrasion groove are present on the mesial surface. Three roots are present.

The mesiobuccal root is the first to leave the common root trunk and has an enamel pearl situated on its buccal aspect, 5 mm below the cervical margin. The palatal and distobuccal roots remain fused a little longer. The two buccal roots initially diverge but bend and converge slightly towards their apices. There is a small piece of normal bone present in the bifurcation area between them.

xiii) $\underline{2}$| Attrition has affected the incisal edge and distal marginal ridge, producing a single curved facet. The mesial and distal contact areas are worn. There is a shallow abrasion cavity beneath the mesial contact area, confined to the enamel. The root apex is curved distally and has a small deposit of secondary cement.

xiv) 1̲ There is gross attrition of the incisal edge and palatal surface. The enamel has broken away from the mesial surface and the mesial incisal angle. There is a very shallow abrasion cavity on the distal surface, just beneath the cervical margin. The root is straight, with a deposit of secondary cement on the mesiobuccal angle and the apical half of the buccal surface.

xv) |1̲ There is attrition of the incisal edge. The mesial and distal contact areas are worn. The palatal surface shows a saucer-shaped erosion cavity, 3 mm wide and extending 1.5 mm onto the crown and 3.25 mm onto the root. There is a thin layer of

plate 85b calculus on the rootward part of this cavity. The root itself is straight, with a thin deposit of secondary cement around the apical third.

xvi) |2̲ There is a gross attrition of the palatal surface and incisal edge producing a single curved facet which also involves part of the labial surface, showing that some forward posturing of the mandible occurred. An area of secondary dentine fills the part of the pulp chamber involved by the area of attrition so that the pulp was not exposed. The remaining enamel has broken off the mesial and distal surfaces. The root apex is curved distally, and there is a deposit of secondary cement around the apical third of the root.

xvii) ? |2̲ There is gross attrition of the labial surface and incisal edge. There is secondary dentine in the part of the pulp chamber involved by the attrition and the pulp was not exposed. The mesial contact area is worn. The root has shallow vertical grooves on the mesial and distal surfaces, and the root apex is curved distally.

plate 85d xviii) |5̲ There is marked attrition of the buccal cusp, and the enamel has broken away from the remaining buccal surface of the crown. The mesial and distal contact areas are worn. The root shows a slight distal curvature and there is a small periapical deposit of secondary cement.

plate 85d xix) |6̲ Gross occlusal attrition has exposed a large confluent area of dentine on the crown. The mesial contact area is worn. The two roots curve distally and the apical half of each is covered with a thin layer of secondary cement. A piece of normal bone is present in the bifurcation area between the two roots.

xx) ? This tooth has gross occlusal attrition and is too worn for positive identification. The pulp chamber is filled with secondary dentine which prevented exposure of the pulp. Parts of the mesial and distal contact areas remain and these are worn. Beneath one is a wide abrasion groove. The root is straight, vertically grooved along the same side as the abrasion groove, and elliptical in cross-section. There is a deposit of secondary cement on the apical third of the root.

xxi) 7̲ Occlusal attrition has exposed a confluent area of dentine under the palatal cusps. The mesial and distal contact areas are worn. The enamel has broken off what remains of the palatal surface. The mesiobuccal root tends to overlap the distobuccal root at their common origin and these two roots are fully fused over their entire course, with a vertical buccal groove between them. The mesiobuccal and palatal roots are also fused for most of their course.

xxii) $\underline{8|}$ Occlusal attrition has exposed a large confluent area of dentine on the crown of the tooth. The two buccal cusps are virtually unaffected. Some of the remaining enamel has broken away from the palatal surface of the tooth. The mesial contact area is worn, and beneath it is a shallow abrasion cavity. The mesiobuccal root tends to overlap the distobuccal root at their common origin and remains fused with it, and with the palatal root, for most of their course.

xxiii) $\underline{5|}$ Occlusal attrition has exposed a small area of dentine in each of the two cusps. The mesial and distal contact areas are worn. The root apex shows a slight distal curvature and a thin deposit of secondary cement.

xxiv) $\overline{8|}$ A large confluent area of dentine has been exposed in the buccal cusps, and the enamel over the mesiobuccal angle of the crown has broken away. The mesial contact area is worn. The two roots are fused, with deep vertical buccal and lingual grooves. The root apices are separate and curve distobucally. There is a thin periapical deposit of secondary cement.

xxv) $\overline{5|}$ There is attrition of the distal slope of the buccal cusp. The mesial and distal contact areas are worn. The mesial contact area is situated high on the mesial marginal ridge, suggesting local crowding of the teeth in that region, with a minor degree of impaction of $\overline{5|}$. The root is straight. plate 85c

xxvi) $\overline{4|}$ There is attrition of the mesial slope of the buccal cusp. The mesial and distal contact areas are worn. The distal contact area is situated closer to the cervical margin than usual, and displaced buccally, suggesting local crowding of the teeth in that region with a minor degree of impaction of $\overline{5|}$ and mesiobuccal rotation of $\overline{4|}$. The root is straight.

xxvii) ?$\overline{3|}$ There is marked attrition of the incisal edge and labial surface. The mesial and distal contact areas are worn. The root shows a slight distal curvature with vertical mesial and distal grooves.

xxviii) ?$\overline{2|}$ There is marked attrition of the incisal edge. The mesial and distal contact areas are worn. The root shows a slight distal curvature.

xxix) ? This tooth has gross occlusal attrition and is too worn for positive identification. The pulp chamber is filled with secondary dentine. There was no pulp exposure. Part of an abrasion groove remains on one side, which may be the distal as the root curves very slightly to that side. The root is elliptical in cross section and shows a thin periapical deposit of secondary cement.

xxx) ? This tooth has gross occlusal attrition and is too worn for positive identification. The pulp chamber is filled with secondary dentine and the pulp was not exposed. The mesial and distal contact areas are worn. Beneath the mesial is an abrasion groove. The root is elliptical in cross section with vertical mesial and distal grooves. The mesial groove is deeper than the distal. The root shows a slight distal curvature and the apical half has a thin deposit of secondary cement.

Burnt material

i) Cremated fragment of the root of what was probably a human tooth.

ii) Cremated molar, probably 6̱| or 7̱| , extensively damaged.

Tooth size

The original dimensions of the crowns could be measured on three teeth (Table V). The height of the crown was determined by laying a piece of fine wire along the buccal surface of the tooth, moulding it to the contour of the crown between the cervical margin and the tip of the cusp, and marking these two points on the wire. The wire was straightened and the distance between the marks measured with a Vernier callipers. The maximum mesio-distal and bucco-lingual widths of the crown were measured directly from the tooth using the Vernier callipers. All the measurements were made correct to the nearest 0.1 mm. The crowns of the other 27 teeth were so worn by occlusal and interproximal attrition that such measurements on these teeth would have little relevance.

The roots of all the teeth which had not been cremated were measured (Tables VI, VII and VIII). The length of each root was determined by laying a piece of fine wire along its buccal surface, or in the case of the palatal roots of upper molars, its palatal surface, moulding it to the contour of the root between the cervical margin and the root apex, and marking these two points on the wire. The wire was straightened and the distance between the marks measured with a Vernier callipers. The maximum mesio-distal and bucco-lingual widths at the cervical margin and halfway down the root were measured directly from the root using the Vernier callipers, the midpoint of the root being judged visually. The distances between the cervical margin and the root bifurcations were measured with a compass, the distance transcribed on a sheet of paper and measured with the Vernier callipers (Kovacs 1971).

Table V The dimensions of the crowns of three teeth shown in millimetres. The remainder were too worn for accurate measurement.

Table VI The lengths of the roots of the upper molar teeth, and the distances between the cervical margin and their bifurcations, shown in millimetres.

Table VII The lengths of the roots of the lower first molar, xix) 6̄, and the distances between the cervical margin and their bifurcations, shown in millimetres.

Table VIII The dimensions of the roots of the single-rooted teeth shown in millimetres.

Tooth	Height of crown (mm)	Maximum mesiodistal width of crown (mm)	Maximum bucco-lingual width of crown (mm)
vi) 3̄|	10.5	7.0	8:3
xxv) 5̄|	7.6	7.1	8.3
xxvi) 4̄|	7.4	6.5	7.2

Table V

Tooth	Length of mesio-buccal root (mm)	Length of disto-buccal root (mm)	Length of palatal root (mm)	Distance between bifurcation and cervical margin on mesial aspect (mm)	Distance between bifurcation and cervical margin on buccal aspect (mm)	Distance between bifurcation and cervical margin on distal aspect (mm)
i) 6⌋	14.0	13.3	14.6	12.5	3.9	6.3
ii) ⌊6	16.4	16.1	18.0	9.0	5.5	5.0
x) ⌊6	13.8	13.0	14.1	11.3	5.2	4.8
xi) 8⌋	16.3	15.9	14.1	9.0	5.1	4.0
xii) 6⌋	16.0	14.9	15.9	4.2	3.7	4.5
xxi) 7⌋	14.9	14.3	13.8	12.8	buccal roots fused	2.7
xxii) 8⌋	12.1	11.5	13.0	10.8	8.0	4.8

Table VI

Tooth	Length of mesial root (mm)	Length of distal root (mm)	Distance between bifurcation and cervical margin on buccal aspect (mm)	Distance between bifurcation and cervical margin on lingual aspect (mm)
xix) ⌊6	15.5	14.0	4.3	4.8

Table VII

Tooth	Length of root (mm)	Maximum mesio-distal width at the cervical margin (mm)	Maximum bucco-lingual width at the cervical margin (mm)	Maximum mesio-distal width halfway down the root (mm)	Maximum bucco-lingual width halfway down the root (mm)
iii) ? 1̅	14.1	3.8	6.1	2.8	4.6
iv) ? 5⌋	16.0	4.7	7.1	3.8	5.0
v) ⌊1	14.2	6.7	6.4	5.0	5.9
vi) 3̅⌋	18.1	5.8	8.1	4.3	6.3
vii) ⌊8	16.0	9.1	9.0	6.9	7.2
viii) ? 2̅	14.3	4.1	6.2	3.5	5.5
ix) ?	17.0	4.8	8.3	3.5	6.2
xiii) 2⌋	18.3	5.2	6.0	4.3	4.9
xiv) 1⌋	14.6	6.9	6.5	5.1	6.0
xv) ⌊1	14.5	5.6	6.5	4.6	5.2
xvi) ⌊2	16.9	5.0	6.1	2.9	5.3
xvii) ? 2̅	16.0	4.1	5.9	3.0	4.5
xviii) ⌊5	16.8	4.9	7.7	4.1	5.0
xx) ?	18.4	5.1	7.8	3.8	6.4
xxiii) 5⌋	13.3	5.0	7.8	4.0	6.3
xxiv) 8⌋	12.9	8.3	10.1	7.5	8.0
xxv) 5̅⌋	16.4	5.2	6.9	4.1	5.8
xxvi) 4̅⌋	16.0	4.8	6.9	3.8	5.6
xxvii) ? 3̅⌋	16.2	4.3	7.0	3.3	6.9
xxviii) ? 2⌋	14.3	3.3	6.2	3.1	5.9
xxix) ?	15.8	4.2	7.6	3.2	6.4
xxx) ?	18.3	5.0	7.4	4.1	6.0

Table VIII

Pathology

PERIODONTAL DISEASE

All the teeth had deposits of calculus, which is associated with gingival inflammation leading to chronic periodontitis, and there was clear evidence of local crowding from some of the interproximal contact areas which may have exacerbated the periodontal condition (Manson 1975). However, the calculus was confined to the crowns and, at most, the upper fifth of the roots. The presence of healthy bone in the bifurcation and trifurcation areas of some of the molar teeth is very significant and indicates that bone loss around these teeth at least was not seriously advanced. The interradicular extension of enamel noted on one molar tooth is a Grade I extension (Masters and Hoskins 1964) and this type of minor variation is not usually associated with a locally serious periodontal lesion in modern man (Leib, Berdon and Sabes 1967). It is very probable that these individuals were relatively resistant to chronic periodontal disease.

CARIES

No initial or established lesions were seen on any of the teeth. Since the incidence of decay reported from other European Neolithic populations is of the order of 2–10% (Brabant 1967) the absence of dental caries is not a wholly unexpected finding in this relatively small sample.

ATTRITION

Attrition can be defined as the loss of tooth substance resulting from the wear that occurs in tooth-to-tooth contact during mastication.

When a diet, like that of modern Europe, is low in abrasive factors, contacting teeth tend to form small polished wear facets on the enamel. All of the Newgrange teeth show a greater degree of occlusal, incisal, and proximal attrition than is found in most plate 85 modern Europeans, suggesting the presence of fine abrasive grit in the food consumed.

A deposit of secondary cement partly compensates for the loss in vertical height that occurs with advanced attrition (Sicher 1953). This process had occurred to a minimal extent, and only in the most worn specimens.

Rapid attrition with inadequate formation of secondary dentine can lead to pulp exposure and dental abscesses (Leigh 1935), but no pulp exposures were seen in the Newgrange teeth.

ABRASION

Abrasion can be defined as the loss of tooth substance resulting from mechanical wear by foreign substances.

A number of the teeth showed a horizontal grooving which was found in the region of the cervical margin on one or both of the proximal surfaces. Some were confined to the enamel and had a rounded floor, but others involved root dentine and usually in these cases the inferior, rootward wall tended to form a right angle with the pulpal wall or floor.

Such grooves are only seen in relatively primitive societies and are due to the movement of abrasives such as small particles of sand or earth in the saliva or drinking

water, or vegetable fibres, through the interproximal space beneath the contact area   plate 85f
between the teeth (Wallace 1974).

Erosion

Erosion can be defined as the loss of tooth substance caused by chemical but not bacterial action.

Erosion is produced by a variety of aetiological agents including acids found in fruits and vegetables. It has been implicated as a possible accessory factor in severe attrition (Lewis and Smith 1973).

One incisor tooth [xv] 1] showed an isolated erosion lesion on the palatal surface,   plate 85 involving parts of the crown and root.

Number of subjects

The teeth were examined and compared to determine the number of individuals they represent. Compatibility in all of the following features was considered in assessing the probability that a group of selected teeth came from one subject:

1) size;
2) crown and root morphology;
3) degree of occlusal attrition;
4) articulation between opposing teeth at occlusal wear facets;
5) articulation between adjacent teeth at interproximal contact areas;
6) amount and pattern of secondary cement deposition;
7) pattern of translucency in root dentine;
8) radiological appearance.

A complete study of the abrasion grooves and other features on the teeth using scanning electron microscopy is in progress. It is intended to section some of the teeth for light microscopy afterwards which will enable the developmental patterns of incremental growth in the dental hard tissues to be compared. This will greatly help in determining the number of subjects involved (Biggerstaff 1977).

Two groups of teeth were selected on the basis of the criteria listed above.

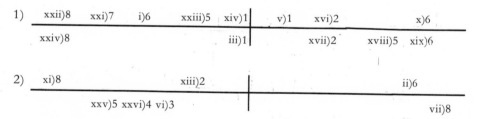

Pending the results of light microscopy, the teeth would appear to come from a minimum of two subjects. The first was aged approximately 25–35 years at death, and the second about 30–40 years. These ages are estimated from the relative amounts of occlusal attrition (Miles 1963). It is not possible at present to state whether or not the remaining teeth came from these subjects.

References

BIGGERSTAFF, R. H. 1977 Craniofacial characteristics as determinants of age, sex and race in forensic dentistry, *Dental Clinics of N. America*, 21:1, 85–97.

BRABANT, H. 1967 *Diseases in Antiquity*, ed. D. R. Brothwell and A. T. Sandison, Illinois, 546–47.

KOVACS, I. 1971 A systematic description of dental roots, in *Dental Morphology and Evolution*, ed. A. A. Dahlberg, London, 211–55.

LEIB, A. M., BERDON, J. K. and SABES, W. R. 1967 Furcation involvements correlated with enamel projections from the cementoenamel junction, *J. Periodont.* 38, 330–34.

LEIGH, R. W. 1935 Notes on the stomatology and pathology of Ancient Egypt, *J. Amer. Dent. Ass.* 22, 199–222.

LEWIS, K. J. and SMITH, B. G. M. 1973 The relationship of erosion and attrition in extensive tooth tissue loss, Case reports *Brit. Dent. J.* 135 (9), 400–404.

MANSON, J. D. 1975 *Periodontics,* London, 31–9.

MASTERS, D. H. and HOSKINS, S. W. 1964 Projection of cervical enamel into molar furcation, *J. Periodont.* 35, 49–53.

MILES, A. E. W. 1963 The dentition in the assessment of individual age in skeletal material, in *Dental Anthropology*, ed. D. R. Brothwell, London, 191–209.

SICHER, H. 1953 The biology of attrition, *Oral Surg. Oral Med. Oral Path.* 6, 406–12.

WALLACE, J. A. 1974 Approximal grooving of teeth, *Amer. J. Phys. Anthropology*, 40, 385–90.

APPENDIX C

The faunal remains

Louise H. van Wijngaarden-Bakker, *Albert Egges van Giffen Instituut voor Prae- en Protohistorie (IPP), University of Amsterdam*

During the excavation in 1967 of the passage and chambers of Newgrange a mixture of human and animal bones was recovered from the floor levels. The human remains have been dealt with by Fraher and O'Sullivan (see report in this volume) while the animal remains form the subject of the present study. The animal bone assemblage is composed partly of extremely well-preserved remains and partly of severely fragmented and corroded unidentifiable bone fragments. The well-preserved portion consists mainly of unfragmented bones with yellowish, smooth and sometimes even greasy surfaces with a distinctly white fracture. Their sizes range from medium large to very small (some of them have a diaphysal width of c. 1 mm). The size of the unidentifiable fragments does not generally exceed 1–1.5 cm. The exceptions to this are some larger flat bone pieces (with diameters up to c. 10 cm) which may have been used as polishing tools. The following identifications have been made:

		fragments
Mammalia	– *Canis familiaris* (dog)	116
	Lepus cf. timidus (mountain hare)	186
	Oryctolagus cuniculus (rabbit)	113
	Ovis aries/Capra hircus (sheep/goat)	6
	Bos taurus (cattle)	2
	Lagomorpha (lagomorphs)	201
	Chiroptera (bats)	9
Aves	– *Turdus philomelos* (song thrush)	5
Amphibia	*Rana cf. temporaria* (frog)	1
Mollusca	– *Acanthocardia echinata*	3
	Pecten maximus	1
	Donax vittatus	1
	Ostrea edulis (oyster)	1
	Aporrhais pespelicani	1
	total	646

The frequency of the different skeletal elements of the mammal species can be found in Table IX. A short description of the species is given below.

Mammalia

The 116 bones that have been identified as dog belong to a minimum of three individuals. This number has been established by the find of one complete left humerus and two left distal humerus fragments.

The bone assemblage seems to consist of three partial skeletons, one from the east chamber (27 fragments), one from just outside the end chamber (44 fragments) and one from the west chamber (45 fragments). The individual from outside the end chamber (lot 1) could be studied in some detail. This was a large dog with a shoulder-height of c. 64 cm. The spinous processes of its thoracic vertebrae have rather irregular surfaces and three vertebral bodies exhibit signs of incipient *spondylosis*, a pathological condition that is generally brought about by old age (van Wijngaarden-Bakker and Krauwer 1979). The bones from the two other partial skeletons are similar in size to the one just described. The shoulder–height of Neolithic dogs, often described as the *palustris*-type, usually does not exceed c. 50 cm as is indicated by the dogs from the Beaker settlement at Newgrange and by those from the Neolithic levels at Lough Gur (van Wijngaarden-Bakker 1974 and 1980). The large size of the present skeletons and above all their preservation condition with yellowish surfaces but white fractures strongly suggests a recent origin for the bones. Whether these skeletons belong to stray dogs that were unable to get out of the tomb or to dogs that were deliberately buried there remains speculative. The bones of the adult lagomorphs could easily be distinguished as hare and rabbit on the basis of their well-marked difference in size. Some minor anatomical differences were also observed. As the mountain hare, *Lepus timidus*, is the only hare species that is indigenous to Ireland, the Newgrange bones have been referred to this species. The brown hare, *Lepus capensis,* was introduced into

	Canis	Lepus	Oryctol.	Ovis/Capra	Bos	Lagom.	Chiropt.
cranium		5	6			8	
mandibula	1	6	4			18	
dentes	8			1	2	25	
atlas			1			1	
axis	1						
vertebrae	26	18	32			2	
sacrum	1	2	1				
costae	15					67	
scapula	2	8	1			4	
humerus	6	16	1			13	4
radius	3	15	1	1		4	
ulna	1	13	1			2	
carpalia	3	1					
metacarpus	7						5
pelvis	2	4	4			8	
femur	5	13				18	
tibia	2	9	1	3		17	
fibula	2						
astragalus	2	5	1				
calcaneum	1	12	4				
other tarsals	2	1					
metatarsus	7			1			
metapodia		39	42			10	
phalanx I	9	19	13			1	
phalanx II	7						
phalanx III	3						
total	116	186	113	6	2	198	9

Table IX

The mammal remains from the tomb chamber and passage. Frequency of skeletal elements.

Ireland in the nineteenth century, but its range is confined to counties Tyrone, Donegal, Derry and Carlow (Herity, n.d.). Apart from the adult bones, over a hundred bones from young individuals, mostly in a foetal or neonatal state of development have been recognized. As these bones could not be identified as either hare or rabbit they have been assembled under the category Lagomorpha. Into this category have also been placed the ribs and loose teeth of adult lagomorphs.

The presence of rabbit bones in the tomb certainly suggests a recent origin as this species was only introduced into Ireland in the thirteenth century AD. In each case the rabbit bones were found mixed with those of hares, but differences between them in state of preservation have not been observed. The conclusion must then be that both the hare and the rabbit bones are recent intrusions. This is supported by the presence of burrows and nests lined with moss, grass and even bits of paper in the chamber of the tomb (O'Kelly, personal communication). Such nests are characteristic of rabbits and they can be found either in the main warren or in separate small burrows (or stops). Mountain hares dig short simple burrows or take over a rabbit burrow, but their young are born above ground (Corbet and Southern 1977). The above considerations suggest that the foetal and neonatal bones found in the tomb chamber are those of young rabbits. This species has a high proportion of pregnant females in January (Corbet and Southern 1977). It seems likely that occasional severe winters have caused the death of the adult and young rabbits and hares that had sought refuge in the tomb chamber.

Most of the ovicaprid bones are recent in appearance with a smooth, uncorroded surface but a distal radius fragment and a distal tibia fragment both exhibit signs of heavy weathering. It was however not possible to decide whether these two bones or the two bovid teeth that were found are of prehistoric origin.

Due to the lack of a comparative collection the bat bones could not be identified to species level. The bones may belong to either of the six species that are indigenous in Ireland.

Aves

Five bones of the song thrush, *Turdus philomelos*, have been identified by C. H. Maliepaard to whom thanks are due. The uncorroded surfaces of the bones indicate that they are also of recent origin. Song thrushes are common in the immediate vicinity of Newgrange and their presence has already been noted in a disturbed area of the Beaker settlement (van Wijngaarden-Bakker 1974).

Amphibia

With the aid of the herpetological reference collection at the IPP, Dr R. Glastra was able to identify one tibio-fibula as *Rana cf. temporaria*, the common frog. Hibernating frogs were noted by the excavators in the outer part of the cairn itself and in the cairn slip and an assemblage of c. 50 bones was found in front of kerbstone 97 (van Wijngaarden-Bakker 1974). The present bone is also considered to be a recent intrusion.

Mollusca

Among the faunal remains nine small fragments of marine molluscs were found, eight bivalves and one gastropod. They have been identified by Dr P. Vos-Kelk to whom thanks are due. The species are listed on p. 215. The fragments all present corroded surfaces and do not seem of recent origin. They have presumably been brought into the tomb with the sea sand that was used to pack the roof-joints to prevent the ingress of water to the tomb (O'Kelly 1973).

Unidentifiable fragments

A number of flat bone pieces exhibit a smooth surface and at one side an obliquely faceted rim. They are of a whitish colour, very brittle and 1–2 cm thick. It is possible that these pieces have been used in some polishing action. There is no evidence that the ornamented slabs of the tomb were ever polished (C. O'Kelly 1978).

The remaining unidentifiable fragments are of small size and it could not be established whether they are of animal or human origin. Their small size and corroded nature may well have been brought about by extensive trampling.

Discussion

The detailed study of the faunal remains from the tomb chamber and passage gives evidence that the bone assemblage is not of prehistoric origin but instead consists of the remnants of the local *thanatocoenosis*. The study presents some interesting ecological aspects, such as the use of the tomb as a warren by rabbits, as a refuge by mountain hares, as a habitation site for bats and as a hibernating place for frogs. Presumably these animals all got into the tomb in the past three hundred years, i.e. between 1699 when the passage was first reopened and 1967 when the tomb was excavated. There are some early references from 1699 that stags' or elks' 'horns' were to be seen inside the tomb chamber but as the present material revealed no trace of them it would seem that these antlers were not only seen but also removed from the tomb. On the other hand the bodies of three dogs may have been brought into the tomb. There is thus evidence for considerable interference inside the tomb both from the human and from the animal side. Other megalithic graves that are more easily accessible than Newgrange are possibly even more disturbed.

The value of the present study lies in the fact that it clearly demonstrates that no conclusions should be drawn without the utmost caution from animal bone assemblages found within megalithic graves.

References

CORBET, G. B. and H. N. SOUTHERN (eds) 1977 *The handbook of British Mammals,* Oxford.

HERITY, P. (ed.) no date. *Provisional distribution maps of Amphibians, Reptiles and Mammals of Ireland*, Dublin.

O'KELLY, C. 1978 *Illustrated guide to Newgrange and the other Boyne monuments,* Cork.

O'KELLY, M. J. 1973 Current excavations at Newgrange. *Megalithic graves and ritual,* (See general bibliography).

VAN WIJNGAARDEN-BAKKER, L. H. 1974 The animal remains from the Beaker settlement at Newgrange, Co. Meath: first report. *Proc. Roy. Ir. Acad.* 74 C, 313–83.

VAN WIJNGAARDEN-BAKKER, L. H. 1980 An archaeozoological study of the Beaker settlement at Newgrange, Ireland. Thesis, Amsterdam.

VAN WIJNGAARDEN-BAKKER, L. H. and M. KRAUWER 1979 Animal palaeopathology. Some examples from the Netherlands. *Helinium* 19, 37–53.

APPENDIX D

Pollen and seed analysis

W. Groenman–van Waateringe & J. P. Pals, *Albert Egges van Giffen Instituut voor Prae- en Protohistorie (IPP), University of Amsterdam*

The positions of samples 1, 2 and 4 are shown in fig. 8 and those of nos 6 and 7 in fig. 15.

During the excavation campaign at Newgrange soil samples for pollen and seed analysis were taken either by M. J. O'Kelly or by the first author whenever the material seemed promising with regard to preservation conditions. The samples which gave a reasonable amount of pollen will be described here. Owing to the corrosion of the botanical material only seven of the many taken were suitable.

From a palynological point of view, the drawback of analysing pollen samples from the old ground layer or from turves in barrows is that one gets a pollen spectrum with a markedly local character. This, however, is precisely what gives the prehistorian the maximum information with regard to the culture or phase involved, its agricultural practices, its stock rearing, the extent of the open area or the type of woodland surrounding the barrow and presumably also, the nearby settlement. From this kind of research one does not obtain an impression of the vegetational succession, however, because the spectra represent only a moment in time, i.e., the pollen rain of the couple of years previous to the construction of the barrow.

If possible, we must try to fit these single spectra into a pollen diagram which will reflect the development of the regional vegetation. As this is quite well known for Ireland we shall try to place our spectra into the sequence, thus getting a rough date for them.

The pollen samples which gave more or less reliable results were as follows:

1 P1978–52. Sample taken by M. J. O'K. from lower part of turf mound in north cutting behind K53 (fig. 8).
2 P1978–50. As above (fig. 8).
3 U1968–78. Sample taken by M. J. O'K. from lower layer of turves in profile behind K94 (not illustrated).
4 R1967–84. Sample taken by M. J. O'K. from lowest layer of turf mound under the base of K53 (fig. 8).
5 R1967–85. Sample taken by M. J. O'K. from the old turf line behind K18 (not illustrated).
6 L1965–64. Sample taken by the first author from the old turf line under west side of the embrasure cutting (fig. 15).

	P1978–52	P1978–50	U1968–78	R1967–84	R1967–85	L1965–64	L1965–68
	1	2	3	4	5	6	7
	%	%	%			%	
Acer	–	–	–	–	–	4.0	2
Alnus	16.5	18.9	33.3	31	14	25.7	5
Betula	0.9	3.1	1.2	–	–	3.0	–
Corylus	50.4	32.4	25.0	9	8	24.8	6
Fraxinus	0.9	0.8	1.2	–	–	–	–
Hedera	–	0.4	–	–	–	–	–
Pinus	9.6	1.9	17.9	11	3	13.9	14
Quercus	16.5	27.0	13.7	11	5	18.8	10
Salix	1.7	0.4	0.6	–	–	–	–
Tilia	–	0.4	1.2	–	–	–	–
Ulmus	3.5	13.1	–	–	–	9.9	1
ΣAP	115	259	168	62	30	101	38
Apiaceae	0.9	0.8	3.4	–	–	35.6	3
Artemisia	0.9	–	–	–	–	–	–
Asteraceae liguliflorae	25.2	8.5	14.3	39	14	11.9	2
Asteraceae tubuliflorae	8.7	2.0	–	–	–	2.0	1
Brassicaceae	0.9	0.8	–	–	–	–	1
Caryophyllaceae	13.0	6.6	9.5	3	2	12.9	3
Cerealia Triticum type	–	–	0.6	–	–	–	–
Cerealia indet.	0.9	2.7	4.2	–	1	–	1
Chenopodiaceae	3.5	1.2	–	2	–	–	–
Cyperaceae	5.2	3.9	–	6	–	16.8	12
Dryopteris	4.4	0.8	11.9	14	–	7.9	6
Equisetum	–	–	–	–	–	2.0	1
Ericaceae	0.9	2.3	0.6	–	–	–	3
Fabaceae	0.9	2.3	–	1	–	1.0	1
Filipendula	1.7	1.2	–	–	–	1.0	–
Galium type	0.9	2.7	0.6	–	–	1.0	–
Gentianaceae	–	–	0.6	–	–	–	–
Geranium spec.	–	–	–	–	–	–	1
cf. Hypericum	2.6	–	–	–	–	–	–
Lamiaceae	2.6	1.9	–	2	–	–	–
Lotus type	0.9	0.4	–	–	–	–	–
Lycopodium	–	0.4	–	–	–	–	–
Plantago lanceolata	21.0	25.5	2.4	3	–	1.0	5
Plantago maior/media	5.2	4.3	–	–	–	–	–

Table X

Poaceae	126.1	267.6	109.5	54	33	190.1	47
Polygonum aviculare type	–	–	2.4	–	–	–	–
Polypodium	12.2	3.5	11.9	12	5	3.0	2
cf. Primulaceae	–	–	1.8	–	–	–	–
Pteridium	5.2	1.5	0.6	2	–	1.0	–
Ranunculaceae	8.7	8.1	0.6	–	–	11.9·	1
Rosaceae	0.9	0.4	2.4	–	–	–	–
Rumex–a type	8.7	3.9	–	–	–	5.0	–
Scrophulariaceae	0.9	–	–	–	–	–	–
Sphagnum	–	–	1.8	–	–	–	–
Urtica	–	2.3	–	–	–	–	–
Valeriana spec.	–	0.4	–	–	–	–	1
Varia	0.9	1.6	1.2	16	11	15.8	8
Botrychium	–	–	–	1	–	–	–
Selaginella	–	–	–	1	–	–	–

Table X *Newgrange pollen analysis*

NB   1 and 2 identified by the first author, 1979; 3 identified by A. Voorips, IPP, 1969 and the first author; 4 and 5 identified by A. Voorips, 1967; 6 and 7 identified by Mrs C. Niessen–Boomgaard, then IPP, 1967. Acer in the last two samples a recent intrusion?

SAMPLE Z1978–50 (1 = bottom, 2 = middle of turf layer)

Pastures	1	2	*Pioneer vegetations on wet soil*		
Agrostis sp.	14	12	Montia fontana ssp. fontana var.		
Carex vulpina/otrubae	–	6	chondrosperma	25	15
Juncus effusus/inflexus	1	–			
Potentilla anserina	6	1			
Prunella vulgaris	8	1	*Heaths, moors*		
Ranunculus repens	67	65	Potentilla erecta	37	20
Rumex sp.	2	9			
Stellaria graminea	–	6			
Taraxacum sect. Vulgaria	25	15	*Varia*		
			Brassicaceae sp.	2	3
Ruderals			Carex sp.	2	1
Cirsium arvense	1	–	Poa sp.	2	2
Stellaria media	14	25	Rubus sp.	3	3
Urtica dioica	4	2	Indet.	4	3

Table XI *Newgrange seed analysis*

7 L1965–68. Sample taken by the first author from transported turf lying upside down under west side of embrasure cutting (fig. 15).

The pollen samples were treated with HF, followed by the acetolysis method of Erdtman (Faegri and Iversen 1964, 69–71); the samples for seed analysis were wet-sieved through four sieves with meshes of 2.0, 1.0, 0.6 and 0.2 mm in diameter. The seeds were collected from the residue with the aid of a stereomicroscope and then identified.

Preservation conditions were rather good in samples 1 and 2; in 3–7 they were bad and the high amount of *Alnus* pollen in comparison to *Corylus* in these latter samples is certainly caused by differential preservation, *Alnus* being more easily recognized, even when badly corroded. Because of the small arboreal pollen sum in the samples 4, 5 and 7 percentages have not been calculated.

Conclusions

The conclusions from the pollen analyses, mainly based on the two most reliable spectra, 1 and 2, are:

1 The presence of *Fraxinus* and *Pinus* suggests a date in the Sub-boreal, somewhere after the middle of the third millennium BC.

2 The ratio arboreal to non-arboreal pollen, about 1:3, points to an open landscape, strongly influenced by man's herding activities, because of the presence in great quantities of pollen types such as *Asteraceae liguliflorae*, *Plantago lanceolata*, *Poaceae*, *Ranunculaceae* and *Rumex*-a type.

3 The presence of *Cerealis* pollen grains with rather high values indicates that not only stock rearing was practised but that the builders of the Newgrange tumulus also worked their crop-fields in the vicinity, probably on the higher flanks of the Boyne valley. As the cereals present in the Neolithic, i.e., *Triticum* and *Hordeum* species, are self-pollinating and so disperse few pollen, the fields must have been close to the place where the turves were cut.

4 Vegetation types of the river border (*Alnus* and *Salix* with *Dryopteris* as undergrowth) and of damp pastures in the river valley, are reflected in the pollen spectra.

The only seed sample that gave a reliable result was Z1978–50, taken by M. J. O'K. from the lower part of the turf mound in the north cutting behind K53 (not illustrated). See also pollen samples P1978–50 and 52. The results of the seed analysis partly confirm our conclusions from the pollen analysis: *Urtica dioica*, *Cirsium arvense* and *Stellaria media* are ruderal plants, once more indicating (human?) disturbance of the vegetation. Most of the plants encountered in this sample are to be found in damp pastures; some of the species mentioned may occur on cultivated land (*Ranunculus repens, Stellaria media*), but typical cropweeds are absent. This is not surprising in view of the moist environment reflected by the other plants. *Montia fontana* var. *chondrosperma* and *Potentilla erecta* are indicative of acid soils. *Montia* is a representative of pioneer vegetations on open, wet soil (e.g. animal watering places or banks of ponds and small rivers in which the water level drops temporarily). A number of records of this species from the British Isles suggest some response to clearance and settlement (Godwin 1975, 155). In view of these results there seems to be little doubt that the turves used as building material were cut in the river valley. It is perhaps this wet habitat that is responsible for the better preservation in these turf samples. Being soaked with water no air could penetrate to oxidize the plant remains.

In conclusion we can say that in Neolithic times the landscape around the Boyne must have been opened up by man to a considerable extent because of the large variety and high number of herbs. Real forest vegetation was probably only found on the river banks, composed on the higher parts by pine, oak and elm, flanked by hazel and birch, with alder and willow in the lowest parts of the river valley.

References

FAEGRI, K. & IVERSEN, J. 1964 *Textbook of Pollen Analysis,* Copenhagen.
GODWIN, H. 1975 *The History of the British Flora,* Cambridge.

APPENDIX E

Macroscopic plant remains

M. A. Monk, *Department of Archaeology, University College Cork*

Introduction

During the course of the excavation of the passage-grave mound, soil samples were taken by Professor M. J. O'Kelly and Dr W. Groenman-van Waateringe for pollen analysis. In addition, several samples were taken from turf layers in the mound for the extraction and analysis of macroscopic plant remains. Dr Groenman analysed the pollen samples while J. P. Pals, also from the Albert Egges van Giffen Instituut voor Prae- en Protohistorie (IPP), University of Amsterdam, dealt with the macroscopic plant remains from several of the larger samples (see Appendix D). However, one sample from the turf in the north cutting, made up almost entirely of mosses, was passed on to the author by Professor O'Kelly. Contained in this sample were a number of seeds which are the main subject of this appendix but also included was a considerable quantity of moss. Mosses from a similar sample from this site have been examined previously by Dickson (1973) but this material was kindly dealt with for the author by Mr Dorian Williams.

SEED TAXA LISTS	NUMBERS OF INDIVIDUALS IDENTIFIED
Ranunculus of acris/repens-group (Buttercups)	148
Stellaria media L. (Chickweed)	9
Stellaria graminea L. (Lesser Stitchwort)	3
Rubus fruticosus agg. (Bramble / Blackberry)	2
Malus sylvestris Mill. (Crab apple)	1
Montia cf fontana L. (Blinks)	92
Polygonum aviculare agg. (Knotgrass)	10
Urtica dioica L. (Stinging nettle)	6
Taraxacum officinale Weber, sensu lato. (Common Dandelion)	26
Carex sp. (the Sedges)	7
Total	304

Table XII *Moss sample from turves in north cutting.*

Methods and results

This sample was received dry and sub-sampled into smaller units for sorting and iden-tification using a low-powered stereoscopic microscope. The identifiable plant taxa are listed in Table XII.

THE MOSSES (D. Williams)
'A small sample of moss, labelled from turves in north cutting under cairn, was exam-ined; species identified were:

Brachythecium rutabulum (Hedw.) B., S. and G.   95%+
Mnium undulatum Hedw.   <5%

This composition is identical to that found by Dickson (1973, 188) for his study of mosses from "sods forming a wall, a part of the construction of the vast Neolithic bur-ial mound".

One can thus only reiterate his conclusions that they are probably derived from a damp weedy turf.'

THE SEEDS

Most of the seeds extracted from this sample were of the Buttercup group *Ranunculus acris/repens* which have a general preference for dampish meadows. There were additionally a range of other species that are commonly found in ruderal habitats including *Stellaria media*, *Polygonum aviculare*, *Urtica dioica* and *Taraxacum officinale*.

Other species present included seven individual seeds of the *Carex* sp. group (the sedges), *Rubus fruticosus* (Bramble/Blackberry) drubes, *Malus sylvestris* (Crab apple pip) and *Montia* cf *fontana* (Blinks).

Blackberry and apple are characteristic species of scrub in woodland margins and are also edible, but little significance can be attached to this evidence given the very low incidence of these remains in the sample. Both *Carex* sp. (the Sedges group – indeterminate to species) and *Montia* cf *fontana* are species characteristic of damp areas. *M. fontana*, better known as Blinks, although a colonizer of wet places, flushes and streams and often occurring in damp pastures, also occurs in southern Britain at least as a weed of arable land (Clapham, Tutin and Warburg 1962, 267).

Conclusion

The smallness of this sample both in the range of species represented and their numbers makes anything more than tentative suggestions about the overall plant ecology of the area from which the turf derived impossible. The indication, however, is of a recently moist meadow with weedy turf close to a stream-side in the general area of the site. This interpretation is broadly similar to that arrived at from the pollen and seed evidence examined by W. Groenman and J. P. Pals.

References

CLAPHAM A. R., TUTIN T. G. and WARBURG E. F. 1962 *Flora of the British Isles*, Cambridge.

DICKSON J. H. 1973 *Bryophytes of the Pleistocene*, Cambridge.

Land molluscs (1)

S. van der Spoel, *Instituut voor Taxonomische Zoölogie der Universiteit van Amsterdam*

Positions of samples shown in fig. 8.

Ten species were determined, as follows:
1 *Cepaea nemoralis* (Linné)
2 *Oxychilus draparnaldi* (Beck)
3 *Zonitoides nitidus* (Müller)
4 *Oxychilus cellarius* (Müller)
5 *Discus rotundatus* (Müller)
6 *Laciniaria biplicata* (Montagu)
7 *Cochlicopa lubrica* (Müller)
8 *Lauria cylindracea* (da Costa) + *Pupilla muscorum* (Linné)
9 *?juveniel* (da Costa)
10 *Ena obscura* (Müller)

Ecological data

1 Forest edge, gardens, park landscape, often in the vicinity of man.
2 Gardens, rubbish heaps, underneath stones, moderately humid.
3 Often very humid.
4 As 2.
5 Underneath stones, moderately humid, often in humus.
6 Forest, rich in lime, humid to dry, high grasses, nettles, bushes.
7 Shady, humid to very humid.
8 Between humus, underneath wood, stones, grasses, bushes, rather humid, often sandy.
9 ?
10 In forest edge, alongside walls, underneath bushes, rather humid.

Tentative conclusions

A Moderately humid milieu, samples 2 and 3 perhaps a little more humid than 1 and 4.
B Park landscape, with probably some higher bushes and trees.
C Probably moderately large human influences.
D According to the sound condition of the individuals, there cannot have been much transport.

NB   See note on p. 228 with regard to species nos 2, 3 and 6 above.

Land molluscs (2)

Carol Mason and J. G. Evans, *Department of Archaeology, University College Cardiff*

For positions of samples see figs 7 and 8.

Results

The method used for analysis was that described by Evans (1972). The faunas of all four samples analysed were almost identical. The major elements of the fauna were *Oxychilus cellarius*, *Discus rotundatus* and *Vitrea contracta*. Other species present included *Trichia hispida*, *Aegopinella nitidula*, *Lauria cylindracea* and *Acicula fusca*. Catholic species (*Cochlicopa* spp. and *Cepaea* spp.) were very low in abundance.

Interpretation

The high abundance of *Oxychilus*, *Discus* and *Vitrea* is typical of a rock-rubble fauna (Evans and Jones 1973). These species are carnivores and this is the key to their abundance in habitats devoid of vegetation. All three are recorded constantly from sub-fossil faunas in caves. The low abundance of other species, particularly the catholic species, adds weight to this.

The other elements of the fauna are not particularly diagnostic of any general environment, though as individual species they mostly have a preference for the moist, shaded type of habitats found in woodland. The presence of species such as *Aegopinella*, *Lauria* and *Acicula* cannot be used in this instance, however, since the habitat provided by the loose stones of the cairn provided, for a snail, all the elements of shelter, shade, moisture, etc. to be found in a wood. If a cover of vegetation was also present food would be available for the herbivores. Quite simply the cairn could have been in the middle of a grassy plain but have a woodland fauna because of the extremely good local conditions.

The presence of the earthy horizons between the loose stone layers of the cairn provided levels which trapped the shells of the dead snails as they were moved through the cairn forming death assemblages. If the earthy horizons represent stadia in the construction of the cairn then it is likely that some of the fauna is contemporary with the ground surface but there is no way of knowing which elements. Certainly the majority of snail shells were deposited after the next layer of loose stones had been placed in position.

Conclusions

The fauna is representative of a rock-rubble habitat and is later than the deposit in which it occurs. The 'woodland' element of the fauna cannot be used for environmental conclusions because of the configuration of the cairn. No indication of the general environment can be given.

References

EVANS, J. G. 1972 *Land Snails in Archaeology*, London.

EVANS, J. G. and JONES, HILARY 1973 Sub-Fossil and Modern Land-Snail Faunas from Rock-Rubble Habitats. *Journal of Conchology* 28, 103–129.

NOTE ON LAND MOLLUSCS (1)

2 *Oxychilus draparnaldi* More likely to be *Oxychilus cellarius*. The examples of *cellarius* were unusually large and could readily be mistaken for its congener. However, this is based on the two half samples we have in common, which contained no *draparnaldi* on my reckoning. Dr Evans is inclined to agree that this is correct.

3 *Zonitoides nitidus* None were found in the samples done in Cardiff.

6 *Laciniaria biplicata* This may well be a case of mistaken identity since this species is extremely rare in the British Isles, and completely absent from Ireland. The species name should therefore be *Clausilia bidentata*.

SPECIES	SAMPLE 1	SAMPLE 2	E. CUTTING 1	E. CUTTING 2
Acicula fusca (Montagu)	1			7
Succineidae spp.	2			
Cochlicopa lubricella (Porro)	6	3	3	1
Cochlicopa spp.	1		1	5
Pyramidula rupestris (Draparnaud)		2		
Lauria cylindracea (da Costa)	22	56	3	16
Vallonia excentrica (Sterki)			4	2
Discus rotundatus (Müller)	233	139	120	332
Vitrina pellucida (Müller)			1	
Vitrea contracta (Westerlund)	25	29	44	177
Nesovitrea hammonis (Ström)			1	1
Aegopinella pura (Alder)				6
A. nitidula (Draparnaud)	12	8	5	40
Oxychilus cellarius (Müller)	373	89	335	583
Clausilia bidentata (Ström)	22	8	5	9
Trichia hispida (Linné)	63	26	83	67
Cepaea nemoralis (Linné)			2	
C. hortensis (Müller)	4	1	1	1
Cepaea spp.	1		13	6
Total	765	361	621	1253

Table XIII *Newgrange land molluscs.*

APPENDIX G

A portion of a bowl

P. M. Brück, *Department of Geology, University College Cork*

The bowl has been carved out of a fragment of *andesite*, typical of the Ordovician andesites within the southern part of the Longford-Down massif and also occurring in the Balbriggan-Duleek area.

The following are the principal constituents visible:

Plagioclase (An 30)	40%
Quartz	8%
K-feldspar	5%
Sericite	45%
pyrite	2%

The rock has been much hydrothermally altered with the formation of abundant sericite. Nevertheless, some of the plagioclase (An 30 – determined optically by measuring maximum extinction angles of albite twins cut perpendicular to (010)) shows good crystal shapes with little corrosion.

The rock from which the bowl has been carved is typical of the district immediately north of Newgrange, i.e., the area, Navan–Slane–Collon–Dunleer. The same rocks also occur in the Balbriggan-Duleek district. In both areas the andesites which are of Ordovician age, occur together with greywackes, slates and tuffs.

The rock of the bowl may have been taken from an outcrop, in which case the nearest exposures to Newgrange occur a short distance to the west between Navan and Slane. Alternatively, the rock may be a piece of a boulder found in the glacial drift.

If the bowl was made elsewhere, and only subsequently brought to Newgrange, the above-mentioned sources are still the most likely, although its derivation from similar andesites occurring in other places in Ireland, Britain and elsewhere cannot be ruled out.

APPENDIX H

Radiocarbon dates

M. J. O'Kelly, *Department of Archaeology, University College Cork*

Eleven samples from Newgrange have been radiocarbon dated as this volume is going to press. Samples 1 to 6 have been measured at the Laboratorium voor Algemene Natuurkunde of the Rijksuniversiteit at Groningen in the Netherlands and samples 7 to 11 at the Radiocarbon Dating Unit of the Palaeoecology Laboratory of Queen's University, Belfast. The positions of all except samples 9, 10 and 11 are illustrated.

Radiocarbon samples

1 GrN-5462-C. Charcoal from the burnt soil 'putty' used by the tomb builders to caulk the interstices between the roof-slabs of the passage (fig. 13). 2475 $\pm$45 bc.

2 GrN-5463. Similar to no. 1 (fig. 13). 2465 $\pm$40 bc.

3 GrN-6342. Charcoal from a small pit which also contained sherds of clearly identifiable beaker ware (fig. 7). 1935 $\pm$35 bc.

4 GrN-6343. Charcoal from another pit also containing potsherds, some of which may be beaker ware but there was no ornament to help to make identification certain (fig. 7). 2040 $\pm$40 bc.

5 GrN-6344. Charcoal from a third pit containing sherds of various wares but again there was no certain beaker ornament (fig. 7). 2100 $\pm$40 bc.

6 GrN-9057. Vegetation (mainly moss) taken from the transported turves under the north side of the cairn (fig. 8). These turves were part of the covering mound of what may have been a pre-existing small passage tomb. 2530 $\pm$60 bc.

7 UB-361. From humic acid taken from transported turves in the south side of the cairn (figs 6A and 12). 2585 $\pm$105 bc.

8 UB-360. Similar to above (figs 6A and 12). 300 $\pm$45 ad.

9 UB-2392. Charcoal from one of the pits in the multiple arc of pits shown in fig. 5. 2035 $\pm$55 bc.

10 UB-2393. Charcoal from another pit in multiple arc. 2035 $\pm$45 bc.

11 UB-2394. Charcoal from a third pit in multiple arc. 1925 $\pm$90 bc.

Comments

Nos 1 and 2 provide a building date for the Newgrange tomb structure at 2475 ±45 bc and 2465 ±40 bc respectively. Nos 3, 4 and 5 are from the Late Neolithic/Beaker–period horizon which developed when the periphery of the mound was in decay and all three are pottery-associated. No. 5 came from the already consolidated turf mound which underlay the cairn of the main mound on the north side and its date of 2530 ±60 bc signals that on face-value it is earlier than the Newgrange tomb structure.

No. 7 compares well with No. 6 but no. 8 at 300 ±45 ad from the upper layer of turves appears to be anomalous. These two samples were taken by Mr Quentin Dresser who had them processed at the Belfast laboratory. His comment (*Radiocarbon* 13, 1971, 452) was that 'the loose stone structure of the mound was probably ineffectual in preventing penetration by younger materials. The upper sample (UB-360) may thus be too young, but the lower (UB-361) agrees with GrN-5462-C and GrN-5463...'.

Nos 9, 10 and 11 correspond well with nos 3, 4 and 5 and show that the pits in the multiple arc must belong to the Late Neolithic/Beaker–period occupation of the site.

Bibliography

ABBREVIATIONS

JCHAS: Journal of the Cork Historical and Archaeological Society
JRSAI: Journal of the Royal Society of Antiquaries of Ireland
PRIA: Proceedings of the Royal Irish Academy
TRIA: Transactions of the Royal Irish Academy

ARMSTRONG, E. C. R. 1933 *Catalogue of Irish gold ornaments in the collection of the Royal Irish Academy*, Dublin.

BEAUFORT, L. C. 1828 An essay upon the state of architecture and antiquities, previous to the landing of the Anglo-Normans in Ireland. *TRIA* 15, 101–242.

BECKER, C. J. 1973 Problems of the megalithic 'mortuary houses' in Denmark. *Megalithic Graves and Ritual,* 3rd Atlantic Colloquium, Moesgård 1969, edited G. Daniel and P. Kjaerum, Copenhagen, and references therein, 75–9.

BERANGER, G. 1775 Beranger Sketch Book. Royal Irish Academy MS 3C 30 f4.

BERGIN, O. and BEST, R. I. 1938 *Tochmarc Etaíne,* Dublin.

BURCHETT, R. 1874 Newgrange. Unpublished MS in the Proceedings of the Society of Antiquaries, London, 6, 112.

CARSON, R. A. G. and O'KELLY, C. 1977 A catalogue of the Roman coins from Newgrange, Co. Meath. *PRIA* 77C, 35–55.

COFFEY, G. 1892–6 On the tumuli and inscribed stones at New Grange, Dowth and Knowth. *TRIA* 30, 1–95.

1912 *New Grange and other incised tumuli in Ireland*, Dublin (Reissued Poole 1977).

CONYNGHAM, A. 1844 Description of some gold ornaments recently found in Ireland. *Archaeologia* 30, 137.

D'ALTON, J. 1844 *History of Drogheda*, Dublin.

DE LATOCNAYE, E. 1797 *Promenade d'un Français dans l'Irlande*, Dublin.

DILLON, M. and CHADWICK, N. K. 1967 *The Celtic Realms*, London.

EOGAN, G. 1963 A neolithic habitation-site and megalithic tomb in Townleyhall townland, Co. Louth. *JRSAI* 93, 37–79.

1969 Excavations at Knowth, Co. Meath, 1968. *Antiquity* 43, 8–14.

1974 Report on the excavations of some passage-graves, unprotected inhumation burials and a settlement site at Knowth, Co. Meath. *PRIA* 74C, 11–112.

1978 The Entrance Stones at Knowth, Ireland. *Antiquity* 52, 134–5.

FERGUSSON, J. 1872 *Rude stone monuments in all countries*, London.

GARDINER, M. J. and WALSH, T. 1966 Comparison of soil material buried since neolithic times with those of the present day. *PRIA* 65C, 29–35.

GARFITT, J. E. 1979 Moving the stones to Stonehenge. *Antiquity* 53, 190–4.

GIOT, P. R. 1960 *Brittany*, London and New York.

GRAVES, J. 1879 Letter in Proceedings. *JRSAI* 15, 13.

HARTNETT, P. J. 1954 Newgrange passage grave. *JRSAI* 84, 181–2.

1957   Excavation of a passage grave at Fourknocks, Co. Meath. *PRIA* 58C, 197–277.

HERITY, M. 1967 From Lhuyd to Coffey. *Studia Hibernica* 7, Dublin, 127–45.

HOARE, R. C. 1807 *A Journal of a tour in Ireland in AD 1806*, London.

LEDWICH, E. 1804 *Antiquities of Ireland* (second edition), London.

L'HELGOUACH, J. 1965 *Les sépultures mégalithiques en Armorique*. Rennes.

LEFROY, G. 1865 Proceedings. *Archaeological Journal* 22, 87–8.

LHWYD, E. 1700 Two letters to Dr T. Molyneux (unpublished). Library of Trinity College Dublin.

1709   Letter to Dr Tancred Robinson. *Transactions of the Royal Society* Abridged Series V, 1703–12, 694.

1723   Letter to Rev. Henry Rowlands. In *Mona Restaurata* by Rev. H. Rowlands, London.

LYNCH, F. 1973 The use of the passage in certain passage graves as a means of communication rather than access. In *Megalithic graves and ritual*, 3rd Atlantic Colloquium, Moesgård 1969, edited G. Daniel & P. Kjaerum, Copenhagen, 147–61.

LUCAS, A. T. 1954 Bog Wood. *Béaloideas* 23, Dublin, 71–134.

1971–3   Souterrains: the literary evidence. *Béaloideas* 39–41, 165–91.

MACALISTER, R. A. S. 1935 *Ancient Ireland*, London.

1939   *Newgrange, Co. Meath*, Dublin.

1943   A preliminary report on the excavation of Knowth. *PRIA* 49C, 131–66.

1949   *The archaeology of Ireland* (second edition), London.

MACKIE, E. 1977 *The megalith builders*, Oxford and New York.

MITCHELL, F. 1976 *The Irish landscape*, London.

MOLYNEUX, T. 1726 A discourse concerning the Danish mounts, forts and towers in Ireland. In *A natural history of Ireland, 3*, by Boate, London.

NATIONAL MUSEUM OF IRELAND 1961 Archaeological acquisitions in the year 1959. *JRSAI* 91, 71–2.

1964   Archaeological acquisitions in the year 1962. *JRSAI* 94, 96–7.

NÍ SHEAGHDHA, N. 1967 *Tóruigheacht Dhiarmada agus Ghráinne*, Dublin.

O'CONNOR, D. 1723 *A history of Ireland from the earliest times to the Anglo-Norman invasion*, Dublin.

O'CURRY, E. 1861 *Manuscript materials of ancient Irish history*, Dublin.

O'DONOVAN, J. 1836 Ordnance survey name books and letters (unpublished), Ordnance Survey Office, Dublin.

1851   *Annals of the kingdom of Ireland by the Four Masters*, Dublin.

O'GRADY, S. H. 1892 *Silva Gadelica,* London.

O'KELLY, C. 1973 Passage-grave art in the Boyne valley. *Proceedings of the Prehistoric Society* 39, 354–82.

1978   *Illustrated guide to Newgrange and the other Boyne monuments*, Cork.

O'KELLY, M. J. 1951 Some soil problems in archaeological excavation. *JCHAS* 56, 29–44.

1969   Radiocarbon dates for the Newgrange passage grave. *Antiquity* 43, 140.

1972   Further radiocarbon dates from Newgrange. *Antiquity* 46, 226–7.

1973   Current excavations at Newgrange. In *Megalithic graves and ritual*, 3rd Atlantic Colloquium, Moesgård 1969, edited G. Daniel and P. Kjaerum, Copenhagen, 137–46.

O'KELLY, M. J., LYNCH, F. and O'KELLY, C. 1978 Three passage-graves at Newgrange, Co. Meath. *PRIA* 78C, 249–352.

O'KELLY, M. J. and SHELL, C. A. 1978 Stone objects and a bronze axe from Newgrange, Co. Meath. In *The origins of metallurgy in Atlantic Europe,* 5th Atlantic Colloquium, Dublin 1978, edited M. Ryan, Dublin, 127–44.

O'RAHILLY, T. F. 1946 *Early Irish history and mythology*, Dublin.

Ó RíORDÁIN, S. P. 1951 Lough Gur excavations: the Great Stone Circle (B) in Grange townland. *PRIA* 54C, 37–74.

Ó RíORDÁIN, S. P. and DANIEL, G. 1964 *New Grange*, London.

Ó RíORDÁIN, S. P. and Ó hEOCHAIDHE, M. 1956 Trial excavation at Newgrange. *JRSAI* 86, 52–61.

PATRICK, J. 1974 Midwinter sunrise at Newgrange. *Nature* 249, 517–19.

PETRIE, G. 1833 New Grange. *Dublin Penny Journal* 39, 305–6.

1845   *The ecclesiastical architecture of Ireland*, Dublin.

PIGGOTT, S. 1954 *The neolithic cultures of the British Isles,* Cambridge (reissued 1970).

POWNALL, T. 1773 A description of the sepulchral monuments at Newgrange. *Archaeologia* 2, 236–75.

RENFREW, C. 1979 *Investigations in Orkney*, London.

ROYAL IRISH ACADEMY 1975 *Dictionary of the Irish language*, general editor E. G. Quin, Dublin.

SHEE, E. and EVANS, D. M. 1965 A standing stone in the townland of Newgrange. *JCHAS* 70, 124–30.

SWEETMAN, P. D. 1976 An earthen enclosure at Monknewtown, Slane. *PRIA* 76C, 25–72.

VALLANCEY, C. 1786 A vindication of the ancient history of Ireland. *Collectanea de Rebus Hibernicis,* 4, Dublin.

WAKEMAN, W. F. 1848 *Archaeologia Hibernica,* (third edition 1891), Dublin.

WESTROPP, T. J. 1893 Miscellanea. *JRSAI* 23, 213.

VAN WIJNGAARDEN-BAKKER, L. H. 1974 The animal remains from the beaker settlement at Newgrange, Co. Meath. *PRIA* 74C, 313–83.

WILDE, W. R. 1847 Irish rivers. *Dublin University Magazine* 5, 732–43.

1849   *The beauties of the Boyne and its tributary, the Blackwater* (third edition 1949), Dublin.

1857   *Catalogue of the antiquities of stone, earthen and vegetable materials in the Museum of the Royal Irish Academy*, Dublin.

1862–3   Proceedings. *PRIA* 8C, 292–3.

WILKINSON, G. 1845 *Practical geology and ancient architecture of Ireland*, London.

WRIGHT, T. 1748 *Louthiana*, London.

List of illustrations

Unless otherwise acknowledged the photographs and drawings are by M. J. and C. O'Kelly. Other photographs are courtesy of: the National Parks and Monuments Branch of the Office of Public Works, Ireland (OPW); the Trustees of the British Museum (BM); T. P. Fraher (TPF); the Green Studio Ltd (GS); Pehr Hasselrot (PH); Land Surveys Ireland Ltd (LSI); Jean McMann (JM); the National Museum of Ireland (NMI); V. R. O'Sullivan (VRO'S); the Librarian, Trinity College Dublin (TCD); and Yorkshire Television (YT).

Figures

Index

Bold-face numerals refer to text figures; *italic* numerals indicate plates

237